Also *by* Brad Dukes

Reflections: An Oral History of Twin Peaks

CHINA BEACH

BRAD DUKES

CHINA BEACH

A BOOK ABOUT A TV SHOW ABOUT A WAR

SHORT/TALL PRESS
NASHVILLE

 Published in the United States by short/Tall Press, Nashville.

Publisher contact:
info@shorttallpress.com

FIRST EDITION

Edited by Paisley Prophet

Book design by Ross Dudle

All interviews emboldened herein were conducted, recorded, transcribed, and edited by the author between December, 2014, and July, 2018.

LIBRARY OF CONGRESS CATALOGING-IN-PUBLICATION DATA

Dukes, Brad
China beach : a book about a tv show about a war /

Brad Dukes

ISBN 978-0-9968208-1-3 (pbk)
ISBN 978-0-9968208-2-0 (kindle)
LCCN: 2018909978

To Ms. Phượng,
wherever you are.

TRACKLIST

EVERYWHERE AND NOWHERE

TUNNEL VISION

FOREWORD

Long before Netflix was even a word, when Amazon was a distant piece of geography and not an everything company, back before there were even dreams of things called streaming services or a multiplicity of premium cable networks, back when there were only three networks and an upstart fourth called Fox, and you watched TV on the network's schedule not yours — way back then — there was a very special show on ABC that was the very definition of what all these services (once they came into existence) would desperately want to show: a quality, weighty, inspired and inspiring drama that was about something. That show, almost thirty years ahead of its time, was *China Beach.*

China Beach is one of the great underappreciated gems in the history of television. And it is underappreciated because it is really hard to see it. Even today it is not on any streaming service due to complicated rights issues involving the licensing of the incredible period music that filled the show.

We live in an era in which many of the greatest shows in the history of television (think *The Wire*) were discovered and revered in the afterlife of their original airing. Or other shows (think *Breaking Bad*) were discovered on places like Netflix in time for people to wildly embrace them deep into their original runs. *China Beach* had no such luck. It aired episodes on ABC in some cases one time ever. And after that then they disappeared forever into the ether.

Until recently, when some of the music was changed, and rights issues were resolved, and finally the show came out on DVD. Just in time for people to quit watching DVDs.

I hope by the time you read these words you will be able to immediately go somewhere and stream the show.

Ostensibly about nurses at a field hospital in Vietnam, *China Beach* is actually about ***everything***. Through the prism of this tiny hospital on a tiny beach in a remote country on the far side of the world from America, the show tackles nothing less than the deep complexities of how to live a life and find your place and purchase in a skewed, confusing and damaged world. The story is framed against the backdrop of Vietnam: a crazy, alternative universe and surreal war. And the show is, most importantly, about the triumph of humanity against the pull of dark circumstances.

It is also very significantly a show about women. They are the leads in this show, the heroes, the focus, the drive. They are not portrayed as somebody's wife or girlfriend. The show offers deep intimate and complex portrayals of women. And that is something else that just wasn't a part of the television landscape at the time.

Brad Dukes has written a deeply researched, intelligent and thoughtful history of one of the great shows of television, but even more, it is an insightful portrayal of the creative process of making television at the highest order.

I still marvel that this show ever got made. I think ABC perhaps imagined something quite different. The pitch was "a woman's steam bath in the middle of a vast men's locker room." They might have thought that was exactly what they were going to get. I'm pretty sure they had no idea how wildly metaphorical that would be. But they must be applauded for making and sticking with a show this ambitious that was very different from the shows that ruled TV at the time, like *Cheers*, *The Cosby Show*, and *Murder, She Wrote*. It was a time when the goal of network television was to reach as wide an audience as possible, when the target was to be everybody's favorite show. *China Beach* would, I have no doubt, totally flourish in this current era where the goal now is to be somebody's favorite show. As a writer and producer who has fought my own battles with obstreperous programmers, I can only imagine some of the conversations John Sacret Young, the co-creator and showrunner, faced, trying to keep to his singular and uncompromising vision in the face of programmers chasing a broad audience. (I particularly love the anecdote in the book about a script that Young turned in that was sent back from Standards and Practices not with the usual notes, but just marked "unacceptable".)

I first met John Sacret Young a few years before *China Beach*, in the mid-80s, when I was working as an assistant to a film producer at Universal. He was developing a movie with the producer. He cut a striking figure in his wool blazer, jeans, scarf and cowboy boots. I soon learned he went to Princeton. And he wore the scarfs in LA, winter and summer, which were kind of the same anyway. He was the erudite literary figure I aspired to be.

John and I struck up a friendship and a couple of years later we started a working relationship. We both had offices on the Warner Bros. lot and we started developing a movie for television, for NBC, that I was writing and we were going to produce together. The development process took a long time, and it was during that time that John began work on *China Beach*.

I would hang out in his offices as we worked on our project, amidst the swirl of activity of writing and production for *China Beach*. It was kind of like 7-Eleven — the offices were always open — day and night. I watched the comings and goings while John was doing the work of writing and making the show.

I also met Bill Broyles, the show's other co-creator, who was tall, intense, charming and thoughtful. Over the years I have learned that alchemy is the mysterious secret ingredient that is the key to the success of every TV show, and while Bill and John were very different people, the combination of their talents and experiences was a moment of magic that allowed the show to come into existence. I also got to know Rod Holcomb, who directed the pilot. Rod was the third key collaborator who's deep well of experience as a director and incredible cinematic chops helped define the look and feel of the pilot and launched the show.

Once the show was ordered, John guided the ship for four seasons, with an unrelenting commitment to creative excellence.

Being around the show turned out to be my graduate school training in TV show running. *China Beach* deeply influenced my approach to my own creative work. Shortly after *China Beach* came to an end I created my first network series, for Fox, called, *The Adventures of Brisco Country, Jr.*, many of the practical lessons I'd picked up came into play as I was thrown in the deep end of running a TV show on my own for the first time. Further downstream, as showrunner of *LOST*, I thought a lot about some of the things I'd first seen on *China Beach* —

the way rules were broken about what was possible on network TV — and I tried to do the same. Subvert expectations. Find the unexpected moments. Defy conventions. I would hear John in my brain and remember scenes he wrote with almost no words, or soliloquies with pages of words, and those memories and experiences led me to always question the way you were supposed to make television or write a scene — and do it better.

I still hear those "reflections" in my brain today, and I hope I always will. *China Beach* was a guiding light in my career. I hope Brad Dukes's beautifully told history will be informative and inspiring for you too.

Carlton Cuse
New York City
November 01, 2018

OVERTURE

The summer sun was almost boiling the concrete of the National Mall in Washington, DC. White noise of rustling trees and shuffling foot traffic hummed as I stood staring at the Vietnam Veterans Memorial. I had been there before, twenty-three years earlier. This time was different; I wasn't a distracted kid on a field trip. This time, I saw myself looking back between the names on the Wall. This time, the women veterans had their own memorial three-hundred feet away. I felt powerless, incapable of understanding why and how this loss of life happened. I only knew one name etched in the granite. I was determined to find it, press my hand to it, and say a prayer of thanks.

I knew that name because of *China Beach*.

I was born six years after the last US helicopter took off from Saigon in 1975, and watched the shadow of the Vietnam War engulf veterans among my friends and family. When I was fifteen, my great uncle Alvin lost his life to Lou Gehrig's disease. A couple of years later, my friend Amanda lost her father in a matter of months after a lung cancer diagnosis. To this day, a lifelong friend's father has refused to utter a word about his tour of duty. I have blamed the Vietnam War in my words and thoughts for these tragedies and done little else.

Growing up, I heard Vietnam referenced in movies and TV shows, piquing my curiosity at the age of six, when Robin Williams howled, "Gooooood morning, Vietnam!" in a movie trailer. I remember asking my parents and my teacher about the war and sensing their hesitation to discuss it with me. I was a child playing with *GI Joe* action figures, singing the chorus of Bruce Springsteen's "Born in the USA," and watching Hulk Hogan leg drop the Iron Sheik on TV.

America not winning a war was unthinkable.

As the eighties turned to the nineties, television was my gateway to pop culture, and a collective of shows on the American Broadcasting Company (ABC) network kept me tethered to the TV set. *Twin Peaks, The Wonder Years, Life Goes On*, and *Doogie Howser, M.D.* all had me hooked as I filled up blank tapes with recordings on the family VCR. The small screen norms of the eighties were being obliterated as my viewing tastes were coming of age. *The Simpsons* was revolutionizing animated entertainment and *America's Funniest Home Videos* was foretelling the YouTube phenomenon by almost twenty years. It was all very exciting to witness.

One of these nights, I stumbled upon an episode of *China Beach,* and the sight of a woman stripping off her clothes with languor and walking naked into a moonlit ocean was seared into my prepubescent memory. By the time my parents could kick me out of the room, the scene was over.

I reconnected with *China Beach* twenty-five years later while authoring an oral history of *Twin Peaks*. Every ABC executive I talked to during that project recalled *China Beach* with reverence. I thought of that woman skinny-dipping on the beach, and a voice told me I needed to seek out the show. Each episode was a threshold to empathy. The characters, their stories, and the production made for an immaculate TV experience, and I yearned to know more about the show and the people who made it happen. And then there was the music. Always the music.

I began tracking down the people who worked on *China Beach*. From the generals to the rear-echelon motherfuckers to the MIA. I thought I wanted to write a book about a cool TV series from my halcyon suburban youth but ended up re-evaluating a chapter of my country's history that is blanketed with denial. Many people asked me, "Why are you writing this book?" Some of their tones implied that a book about *China Beach* wasn't expected or even necessary. I wish I could take back all my rambling justifications and just say, "Because more people need to know about it."

Each question about *China Beach* gashes open a portal into a living and breathing dimension of the Vietnam War that holds more untold mystery. Every book or documentary about the war I have scoured takes me right back to the Wall in Washington, wondering *why*. Why did we go? Why did we stay? Was it just dumb pride that made us double down on the war time and again? Did Agent Orange kill Uncle Alvin and Amanda's dad? *China Beach* still has me asking.

China Beach premiered on ABC in April of 1988, focusing on the women and their respective roles at a rest-and-recreation center and evacuation hospital during the Vietnam War. The shore of the South China Sea near Danang plays host for American soldiers seeking spiritual and physical healing as a war rages on within earshot. Beers and barbecue, sutures and surgery. The main event: Round-eyed women. A great, big war surrounding a band of souls serving their country, and one another.

History and art are at unnerving odds throughout four seasons of *China Beach,* with stories from actual vets adapted into plot lines in the show. Creative liberties were taken by the writers and directors to sustain a serialized story, generating profound moments when life and its refraction on the TV screen become inseparable. A kaleidoscope of life and death, spinning to the beat of Motown Records. The only constant over four seasons of the show is change. The war, the characters, and the world around them swirl into uncertainty and culminate in a final season that remains remarkable in its ambition—not only for its era—for the entire history of scripted television.

After sixty-one episodes, *China Beach* took its final bow in July of 1991 and literally became television history. The series was a few episodes shy of syndication, and licensing fees for the soundtrack of golden oldies prevented a home video release for over twenty-two years. This window of time saw hundreds of other retired TV shows digitally reconnect with their audiences on streaming platforms and DVD, while the legacy of *China Beach* was relegated to word of mouth and dusty VHS recordings. Scarce reruns of the show on Lifetime and the History Channel held the only chance of discovering or revisiting *China Beach* until Time Life released the series on DVD with almost all of its music intact in 2013.

As someone too young to be a Generation X-er and too old to be a millennial, I wonder who still cares about *China Beach*, let alone the Vietnam War. *China Beach* is an artifact of the past, saddled with grainy video quality and an aspect ratio that looks askew on today's widescreen televisions. The present inability to watch it on a phone or a tablet will likely prevent millions from ever seeing it.

China Beach holds a monolithic presence in the TV medium. I see no equal and no parallel, nor one other emulation of the female experience during the Vietnam War. *Mad Men*, *Lost*, *The Wire,* and other luminaries of early-aughts TV seem like obvious descendants of *China Beach,* but time and scarcity have undermined its place in the genealogy of prestige television. *China Beach* co-creator John Sacret Young once said to me, "We as a culture have a short-term memory. It's like the earth is flat and *China Beach,* like Columbus, went over the edge and is gone." I can't deny Young's claim. I do cling to my belief that *China Beach* is a vital entry in the annals of television. Like a relic in a museum, it must be protected and preserved.

Any successes or shortcomings of *China Beach* are superseded by the fact that the show keeps the lessons of the Vietnam War alive, and asks vital questions about our history, ourselves, and where we are headed as Americans. Those questions are still relevant today, and, I believe, imperative. All the critical praise, award luster, and network squabbles seem petty in comparison with the sacrifices made by those who served in Vietnam. Let's see why *China Beach* matters.

And let's always remember the vets.

RBD

S.Sgt. Alvin Hendrickson

Uncle Alvin would drop everything to help anyone in need. He treated me like a grandson years before he had any of his own. Staff Sergeant Hendrickson retired from the US Air Force in 1979. He served in Vietnam during 1967-68, and returned for a second tour in '71-72.

Cpt. Mike Rowland

Amanda's dad was a steward of the law, his country, and community. A ringleader at church, political rallies, and service projects. A man to look up to. Captain Rowland served in the 1st Infantry Division — "The Big Red One" — in-country from 1967-68. The black scarf around his neck was a signature of the "Dracula" battalion. He passed away in 1998, four months after a lung cancer diagnosis. He previously survived Hodgkin's Disease in 1973. The Veterans Administration confirmed both diagnoses were caused by Agent Orange exposure in Vietnam.

"China Beach wasn't just another show with a straight, old, army guy shooting the shit out of stuff, running around, and throwing hand grenades, but it was a series about war."

- Troy Evans, Infantry Sergeant, US Army (Sgt. Bub Pepper)

ONCE UPON A TIME
IN THE EAST

SOUL AND INSPIRATION

War on TV, war in the movies. Mostly men on a mission, fighting for their country and whatever they believe is worth dying for. The 1980s brought a plethora of big-screen depictions of the Vietnam War dominated by testosterone and destruction, plus a similarly themed television series, *Tour of Duty* (1987). *China Beach* was the antithesis of this trend of masculine violence, focusing on a female army nurse navigating the aftermath of off-screen combat. It was an approach to the Vietnam War no other creator in Hollywood had attempted, a symbiotic vision from two men fueled by their separate passion, pain, and ambition. William "Bill" Broyles Jr. and John Sacret Young were accomplished writers with long pedigrees and a shared fascination with the Vietnam War. That's where their similarities hit the barbed wire of a DMZ.

Broyles brought the light, Young brought the darkness, and between them, the world of *China Beach* came to life.

***Dana Delany** (Lt. Colleen McMurphy):* **My impression of Bill was that he was sort of changing his life. I knew that he was a Vietnam vet, I knew he was incredibly charismatic, I knew that he had been a marine. I knew he was an unusual person because he had just been the editor of *Newsweek* and was highly educated. It was such an interesting mix to be a Texan, a Rhodes [Marshall] scholar, the editor of *Newsweek,* and this kind of tall, good-looking, Henry Fonda-type character.**

***Marg Helgenberger** (K.C. Koloski):* **Bill and John are both very bright and handsome guys. Bill, having been there and having served in the Marine Corps, whenever he would talk about his time there he would always get very, very vulnerable and his**

real sensitive side would come out. That whole expression—the thousand-yard stare—you would sometimes see that in his eyes. All wars are horrifying, but it seemed like that one was worse than others. No one really knew why they were there, and I think it was a time in his life that really changed him, and I think it made him who he became.

Broyles is a rolling stone that gathers no moss. He literally and figuratively climbs mountains, skis down them, and then moves on to the next range. After graduating from Rice University with a degree in history in 1966, Broyles studied politics and philosophy at Oxford University before he was drafted in '68 for United States Army service in Vietnam. American protests against the war were spiraling out of control, and instead of seeking deferment, Broyles made a conscious choice to enlist as a marine and served in Vietnam from November of '69-70. In conversation, he speaks calmly and gently about his time in the war with a subtle twang and total recall, taking immense pride in his work with *China Beach*. One fateful moment during his year of service planted the first seeds from which the show sprouted.

William Broyles Jr. *(co-creator and executive consultant)***: I went to China Beach in 1969. I was out in the field with my marine unit and came back to visit a couple of marines I knew who were there, medevacked to a naval hospital at China Beach. I walked in and I just saw this huge Quonset hut, this huge building. It was like that scene in *Raiders of the Lost Ark* when they take the Ark of the Covenant into the government warehouse and there are just boxes as far as you can see, and it's nothing but beds of nineteen-year-old kids. I had never been in such a concentrated experience of the cost of war and I literally fainted. I came to, and there was a nurse with smelling salts, and I just couldn't believe she did what she did every day, and that sort of image stayed with me, and that thought stayed with me.**

I was drafted; I didn't want to be in Vietnam. I joined the marines to get out of going to the army, and most of the people that I served with had either been drafted or joined up because they couldn't get a job, or because a judge told them to or go to jail—and here were these women who were there

Bill Broyles, in-country

because they wanted to be. They wanted to serve, they wanted to help, they went there to be in combat, and I just felt like these were stories I hadn't seen before.

Broyles approaches the war in his writing and conversation with dueling horror and humanity, making it as relatable and vivid as a Norman Rockwell painting. Mortar shells explode and bullets trace through the nighttime sky, while idyllic landscapes of rice paddies are filled with Vietnamese children riding on the backs of water buffalo. Broyles's time in Vietnam directly informed characters in *China Beach,* like the scarred and silent Dodger, played by Jeff Kober. Kober described Broyles as bright and sunny, if carrying the weight of Vietnam with him at all times. Broyles once said to him, "Vietnam doesn't exist in time. It exists almost in an alternate universe that is just a quarter-turn away from where I am at any point."

Concetta Tomei *(Maj. Lila Garreau):* **Bill was so emotional. He was like a big sponge, and he carried Vietnam with him. There wasn't a sixties song he could hear or a story he could tell or books he could read that tears wouldn't well up in his eyes. It never left him. He was emotionally absorbed and connected with that war, in the best and the worst of ways, really. It was just right at his fingertips—all those things that weren't there anymore.**

Broyles re-entered civilian life and worked for the Houston school district before he was drafted into another unexpected role in 1973, this time as the founding editor of *Texas Monthly* magazine. Broyles had no experience running a magazine, but his innate journalistic talents elevated him to editor-in-chief of *Newsweek* by the early eighties. Broyles introduced a sensationalist edge to the outlet, causing an uproar within the news establishment when he ran the death of Grace Kelly as a cover story. As controversy grew around Broyles, his memories of the Vietnam War began to stew. After Broyles' visit to the 1982 dedication of the Vietnam Veterans Memorial, he poured himself into researching the conflict. He reconnected with his former platoon members and mined the Vietnam War experience to extremes, claiming he has read every book on the Vietnam War ever written.*

A self-professed nomad, Broyles quit *Newsweek* at the dawn of 1984 with no backup plan, reflecting in a 1987 mountain-climbing article for *Esquire*, "I wanted personal achievement, not power." Broyles's wanderlust landed him in Hollywood as a late arrival, already in his forties, harboring the desire to tell a story of women in wartime. Broyles was a novice screenwriter with no credits, and a literary agent, George Diskant, paired him with John Sacret Young, who had his name on a number of television series and feature film scripts. Chief among them, a 1980 miniseries adaptation of Philip Caputo's Vietnam memoir, *A Rumor of War.*

John Sacret Young *(co-creator and executive producer):* **Bill had gone to this man named Scott Kaufer at Warner Bros., who was the vice president of comedy. They were talking about,**

*Innumerable unverified sources on the Internet say that Lynda Van Devanter's 1983 autobiography, *Home Before Morning,* was the inspiration for *China Beach;* however, both co-creators debunked this claim during interviews.

as I recall, a half-hour show set in a Saigon hotel where singers were coming and going, including women, but not necessarily women, and you'd have some craziness, and it would probably be a three-camera comedy. I don't think it ever got written. I said, "I think the idea of a Saigon hotel is cool, but for me, what would be interesting is to find another way to go at the Vietnam War...and what is that?"

If Young has a modus operandi, it is to "dig deeper." Every writer I spoke with from the *China Beach* staff recalled this mantra among a number of others that were immortalized in a rubber stamp set once gifted to Young. The near-unanimous opinion of interviewees was that Broyles was warm and affable, while Young was evasive and magisterial. Bill might slap you on the back after a draft or a scene. John might nod and ask for another approach. Broyles was the first of many to oblige Young and reconsider what *China Beach* could be, and his vision of a sitcom morphed into an hour-drama.

After a few days and a couple of emails, I was on the phone with Broyles and picking his brain. Young remained elusive and cryptic. After sixteen months of exchanging intermittent back-and-forth emails, I had to fly across the country to talk with him in person at the offices of Creative Artists Agency in Century City, California. I hadn't planned on footing any airfare for this book. It turned out I was just warming up.

I set up my recorder in a conference room and waited. Thirty minutes late, Young arrived with an air of whimsy and a knowing smile. A canvas bag was tossed over his shoulder, brimming full of papers. Included were letters from *China Beach* viewers of all walks of life, spanning fervent fans, armchair critics, and inquiring vets. A leather-bound tome documenting the creative journey of his pilot script acted as the Dead Sea Scrolls of the topic at hand. We talked for over three hours, and Young might have answered one of my questions directly. His memories of the show are incisive and peppered with asides and references to classic cinema and literature. He surgically critiqued everyone's contributions to the show, including his own. Young's countless stories relayed that he was incapable of compromise, all while pushing everyone who worked on *China Beach* to be better.

Nancy Giles *(Pvt. Frankie Bunsen)*: **John was a cool character with his wire-rimmed glasses and he always wore a little scarf around his neck, not like an ascot, but this casual scarf with his open shirt. He was this real groovy, cool guy, kind of like Steven Spielberg-ian. You couldn't always tell what was up with him.**

Michael Boatman *(Pvt. Samuel Beckett)*: **I just remember he looked very much "the auteur." He seemed like this sort of mysterious man who pulls the strings behind the scenes. [His hair] was just beginning to go grey, so he had a very distinguished look, and he had a goatee and this whole sort of Machiavellian glint in his eye. As I grew up and have run into John over the years and learned how warm and compassionate and brilliant he is, I sort of laugh at the twenty-three-year-old me who used to quake when he came around. I never knew what he was thinking, and he wouldn't let you know what he was thinking.**

Young has made a name for himself in Hollywood over the decades as an award-winning writer and producer. A more fitting description for him is an *artiste*. *China Beach* inherited its slow burn from a co-creator and executive producer who treats time as an afterthought. Years deep into our acquaintance, he was capable of taking weeks to reply to an email. A typical inquiry about a specific scene wasn't met with anecdotes about plot or dialogue, rather a detailed explanation of how it took all day to properly light a room or figure out an arduous camera shot. Pinning Young down for clarity feels like twisting a magician's arm to reveal the secret behind a trick.

It isn't that Young is smug, he is just that self-assured.

After adapting *A Rumor of War* and laboring over *China Beach* for four-plus years, Young was not done with the Vietnam War. He went on to pen a 2003 memoir, *Remains: Non-Viewable*, documenting the war's aftershocks on him and his family over the decades. A few good *China Beach* tales act as bonus material. Young is an early Baby Boomer who graduated from Princeton University in the thick of protests against the unpopular war that gripped his generation. He flunked multiple physicals and did not serve in Vietnam, then became fixated on the conflict when his first cousin, Doug, was killed in action during Christmas break of '69. Doug was like a brother to Young, and in a peculiar twist of fate, was serving in-country at the same time as Broyles.

Broyles authored his own collection of war stories in 1986, *Brothers in Arms.* The book is a personal reconnaissance mission recounting his return to Vietnam in the eighties to visit old battlefields and converse with his former combatants in the Vietcong and the North Vietnamese Army. As one of the first American vets to return to Vietnam, Broyles was determined to understand those he once fought against. Some vets came home and never spoke of their time in-country, while Broyles was doing everything he possibly could to relive it. Young and Broyles approach the Vietnam War from different perspectives, and both of their books further decode their dedication and motivations in creating *China Beach.*

The two men hit it off immediately despite their contrasting personalities, each admitting he needed the other for the project. Broyles lacked the television prowess to navigate the establishment and launch a series, and Young knew that a show like *China Beach* had to be bred in the veracity that Broyles possessed from his tour of duty.

Before *China Beach* was ever hatched, Young had formed a working friendship with the then-president of ABC Entertainment, Brandon Stoddard. Young recalled that the broadcast networks' infatuation with miniseries, stoked by *Roots* (1977), had begun to fade, and one of his passion projects was canceled before the script could be filmed. Young received a consolation pilot offer from Stoddard that was optioned by Warner Bros. Television, automatically blessing *China Beach* with studio support.

ABC was losing its edge in the mid-eighties and lagging behind its primary competitors, NBC and CBS. The 1986-87 season was especially embarrassing for ABC, with its highest Nielsen-rated show, the milquetoast sitcom *Growing Pains*, in eighth place. Pressure on ABC was mounting from outside the network establishment as well, with Fox developing its first slate of original programming, and basic and premium cable channels beginning to multiply, further fracturing a three-network hegemony that had ruled American television sets for over thirty years.

Stoddard led the effort to regenerate ABC's schedule and claim a new identity through viewpoints seldom seen on network television at the time. *Life Goes On* (1989-93) featured a working-class family with a teenaged son with Down syndrome, *Roseanne* (1988-1997) was a sitcom headlined by an overweight, obnoxious, nasal-voiced matriarch of an unruly, lower-class family, and *The Wonder Years* (1988-1993) rewound the Baby Boomer experience to follow a teenaged boy coming of age in the late sixties. Broyles and Young formally pitched their concept to ABC, and their drama following a US Army nurse through the Vietnam War was tailor-made for the network's makeover.

***Chad Hoffman** (then-vice president of drama series, ABC):* **It was obvious to me. It just felt different. Special. There was nothing on television that was like it, which I thought was really important and still do. I didn't see any downside at all, and I thought doing a show about women in war was a way to attract women to a subject they might not ordinarily be interested in upfront, and also as a means to get men who seemed to be attracted to stories about warfare. I wish I could say I had sweat bullets and labored over it and had nightmares, but it was a very easy sell.**

John Sacret Young directing an episode of China Beach

HAPPY TOGETHER

John Young and Bill Broyles had found an outlet for their burgeoning collaboration and began sketching out a blueprint of *China Beach,* resulting in a two-hour pilot episode. The pair retreated to Santa Barbara, California, to hash out the details between runs on the beach and throwing a football. Broyles's first-hand combat experience coupled with Young's screenwriting savvy birthed a rich collective of American personalities populating the fictional 510th Evacuation Hospital and Rest and Recreation Center, or in shorthand slang, the Five and Dime.

Young took the reins of *China Beach* as executive producer and screenwriter of the pilot episode, with Broyles designated as executive consultant—a spiritual sherpa who ensured the show was dyed in the wool with truth and reality. Young began writing the script with Broyles furnishing character and scene sketches along the way, who was pleased with the results: "It was like alchemy what John came up with."

> ***John Sacret Young:*** **Bill and I met and talked about a variety of characters. I kept going, "We can't do this straight forward. There's a tweak. The sixties were tweaked; Vietnam was tweaked." He was very good at saying, without saying it literally, "You can be dark, but we also need light, and light attached to music and light attached to the fact that experiences you had there were sometimes black comedy. You savor the comic moments because they were comedy. You savor the music because you needed the relief from either the boredom or the absolute terror of actually being in a firefight."**

On the cusp of forty, Young had already immersed himself in Vietnam lore while adapting *A Rumor of War,* interviewing dozens of veterans for his research and further deepening his bond with the conflict. A preproduction staff assembled, and veteran interviews continued to provide inspiration for the script—a sense of grounding reality was sacrosanct for Young and Broyles. Chad Hoffman recalled sitting down with Young at a restaurant in Cape Cod and realizing a ninety-minute draft of the pilot was missing something. ABC would pass for the moment and take a further look at a two-hour installment. Young was momentarily offended, then inspired to make something bigger and better. After a summer of intense work and back-and-forth with ABC, Young handed in a finished draft of the pilot just before Labor Day, 1987.

China Beach was designed from the ground up with army nurse Colleen McMurphy as the protagonist. An appealing, flawed archetype of midwestern America that is dedicated to serving her country and her soldiers. She is not quite the antihero that became prevalent in television a decade later with Tony Soprano, but it is hard to deny her as an ancestor of Don Draper in *Mad Men*—gifted, driven, and cloaked in self-loathing.

Young admitted to being absolutely territorial over the design of McMurphy, recalling, "I felt like I knew the person before I wrote the person." McMurphy was based on his copious research of Vietnam nurses, a Catholic girl he dated in college from Paoli, Pennsylvania, and his cousin, Samantha (Doug's sister). In a family tree full of boys, Samantha was one of the guys growing up, never backing down on the tennis court, or in a game of who could throw the football the hardest. Named in homage to the lead character in *One Flew Over the Cuckoo's Nest*, McMurphy works as hard as she drinks, and carries the warmth that a teenaged soldier would fall head-over-heels for. Young knew early on that everything began with this woman sitting on a beach.

China Beach was pitched to ABC as "a women's steam bath in the middle of a vast men's locker room," but the template resembles more of a classic western film. A frontier town on the edge of enemy territory, filled with eclectic personalities. Their lives protected by the strong, quiet lead role. Monument Valley was now Vietnam, Indians were replaced with the indigenous forces of the Vietcong, and no cowboy dwelling was complete without a saloon, an undertaker, a sheriff, and a prostitute.

William Broyles Jr.: **For me, *China Beach* was a way to explore the complexities of my own experience with the war and these characters, and also trying to recreate that sense of family that we had there: the range of experiences from**

the absolute horrors of things to the incredible sacrifices and dedication and love that people had for each other. War gives you a wider spectrum of human experience to explore than almost any other possible setting, from the horrors and the evil to the absolute love and beauty at the other end that you just don't experience in normal settings, and that was my idea and hope for this series when it started.

The casting process commenced, led by casting directors John Levey and Phyllis Huffman at Warner Bros. Television. Over the years, Levey's intuition has discovered a bevy of A-list stars, namely casting an unknown George Clooney in *ER* shortly after *China Beach*. As John Young and network executives began a cage match over the casting of Colleen McMurphy, the rest of the pieces fell into place with working actors who had yet to establish household names and a few gambles on green rookies.

With few screen credits to her name, Chicago native Nan Woods was cast as Cherry White, a nineteen-year-old Red Cross donut dolly from Iowa. Cherry is blond, petite, and transparent—terrified of this new world she has just touched down in. Her name alone announces purity, naivety, and virginity through a megaphone. Every avatar in *China Beach* has a motive, and she arrives in search of her missing older brother, Rick. Woods brings untaught fragility and gullibility to her character and establishes Cherry as the becoming babe in the woods of Vietnam.

The tail to Cherry's head is K.C. Koloski, a cynical, auburn-haired hooker from Kansas City. Sex sells, money talks, and K.C. had to be fluent. Born and raised in Nebraska, Marg Helgenberger brought her own legitimate midwestern flavor when she auditioned for the role. Levey remembers Helgenberger possessed an "adult authority and an open, charismatic, powerful sexuality," and was an early lock to portray the goddess of earthly desires in *China Beach*.

Marg Helgenberger: **A number of things compelled me about the script. I just found it to be very moving. I found the characters to be fascinating and interesting, and I loved the fact that women were featured in the Vietnam War. I don't recall anytime seeing anything else, television or film, in which women were the central characters, or pretty much**

in any war drama. Women were always sort of secondary characters, if any at all, so that was probably number one that just got my attention.

K.C. only has a few scenes in the pilot, but I knew that role had incredible potential because there was a lot more questions about her than answers. She was a mystery. Who was she? What does she do there? How did she get there? It just was a wealth of possibilities and potential, and I was very excited about it. I thought this was one of the best scripts I had read in a while at that point in my career.

I was on a soap opera [*Ryan's Hope*] for three-and-a-half years or so, and then I had done mostly episodic stuff. I did have a short-lived series before *China Beach* called *Shell Game*, so yes, this was definitely a big plus, and I was excited about it, and it just went really well. I remember I wore this one suit I owned to every single audition for this part, because I just thought it was good luck and apparently it was! I have no idea where it is; I gave that suit away a long time ago.

KC Koloski, ready for the next take

Every woman who gets paid for sex likely has a man in her life who is on a mission to remove her from the trade. In this case, the hardly known Brian Wimmer was cast as Boonie Lanier, the chiseled and borderline lifeguard/bartender/camp counselor of *China Beach*. Wimmer grew up on the slopes of Sundance in Utah, rubbing shoulders with Robert Redford and getting swept up in show-business as a utility player when the production of *Footloose* (1984) came to town. After a New York crash course in acting, he packed his Volkswagen Rabbit with everything he owned and moved to Los Angeles. Wimmer was a novice thespian when he auditioned for the role of Boonie. He based his take on the character of Lance from Francis Ford Coppola's Vietnam epic *Apocalypse Now* (1979), telling Young and Broyles: "He's a surfer who has seen too much, he's just freaked out."

Broyles drew characters from the polarity of personality that he saw within his own platoon, placing Boonie at one end and Dodger at the other. Dodger represents the spiritual cost of war, a boy numbed by the art of combat into near catatonia. Jeff Kober was the obvious choice to depict Dodger's internal struggle, even if he was more than a decade older than the character when he auditioned for the role.

> ***Jeff Kober** (Evan "Dodger" Winslow):* **Dodger was just such a sweetheart, and he was a broken individual who had a lot of strength, and if he pointed himself in the right direction, he could get things done. He had tools, but he was broken, and that's really how I saw myself, so it was a perfect match. Actually, I had the flu when I went in for my audition. I could barely speak, and they loved that about me as well; I almost couldn't get the words out. He was someone who had been in the bush for so long he had forgotten how to talk. They hired me for the pilot only; I was not a series regular.**

China Beach shies away from many television drama trends, namely having no true villain among its cast. The real enemy was the Vietcong, an omniscient threat camouflaged as civilians, or hiding in a network of caves and surrounding jungles. McMurphy needed a foil to clash with in both ideology and sexual tension. Dr. Richard "Dick" Richard is willing to reciprocate. When Robert "Bob" Picardo auditioned for the role, he read the lines of a barstool showdown between Dr. Richard and McMurphy. He brought his own props and a decade of credits in film and TV, far surpassing any other cast member in screen experience.

Robert Picardo: I remember at the audition scene, I did all the "don'ts and don'ts" of acting. In other words, you never bring props to an audition; it's just not done, but my recollection is I had a handful of raisins and I was tossing raisins up in the air and caught them once or twice in my mouth. Because It seemed so cavalier and so counter to what they were talking about, it was a risky thing to do, and I did miss one. [_laughs_] I guess it was a little high-wire risk to take my focus away from confronting her. There's really only a moment where he says, "You're absolutely right. Just be here, be miserable. By the way, if you want to help save teenagers, I'll be right over there." It was a way of looking like I didn't give a shit when I of course cared very much for her and what we were doing.

I was losing my hair at the time and I remember when I was cast in the job, the network edict was to "put hair on him," because back then, before Patrick Stewart helped change things in American television, you didn't really get to kiss girls if you were young and bald, [_laughs_] so the network's suggestion was to have me work in a hairpiece so that I could be, I guess, a more suitable, unresolved love interest for McMurphy.

Colleen McMurphy is the catcher in the Vietnam rye, and Pvt. Samuel Beckett tends to the ones who slip through her fingers in the graves registration unit (GRU). Preceded in reputation by his playwright namesake, Beckett had to carry a temperament beyond his years. A twenty-three-year-old Michael Boatman fit like a rubber glove. Boatman's first big break came with the Vietnam feature *Hamburger Hill* (1987), and he had witnessed firsthand the hushed emotional toll of the Vietnam War through his father and uncles who had served. Along with Bobby Hosea as Sweetness Elroy, Boatman was an icon for the black soldiers who served in Vietnam, accounting for 12.6 percent of American forces during the height of US involvement in 1969.* Rounding out the male counterparts of *China Beach*, Tim Ryan seized the role of Cpt. Natch Austin, a clean-cut bomber pilot with a daredevil wont that draws McMurphy ever closer.

---

*Butler, John Sibley, "African Americans in the Military" in *The Oxford Companion to American Military History*, ed. John Whiteclay Chambers III (New York: Oxford University Press, 1999), 9.

To rule all of these radiant personalities as the sixties met social upheaval, Concetta Tomei was cast as Maj. Lila Garreau. Forty-one years young and the senior member of the cast, Tomei was a relative newcomer to Hollywood before winning the role. A few years prior, she was a teacher in Milwaukee before beginning a second career in acting, performing on the stages of Chicago and Broadway before heading to Los Angeles. Tomei's taciturn delivery and starched class B uniform installs Major Garreau as the law and order of *China Beach,* stopping the buck every time.

Young and Broyles had spun an intricate web of characters, capturing unique, American vantage points of the Vietnam War. Tying all these personalities together was Colleen McMurphy—and a tense debate over who would play her nearly ended the show before it ever began.

IF 6 WAS 9

Colleen McMurphy is the river of *China Beach,* running through all other stories and characters, floating them downstream in her current. For a young woman volunteering as an army nurse in Vietnam, she's the embodiment of Kennedy "What can you do for your country?" values and the moral conscience of the show. She carries the qualities of a mother, a sister, and the sleeper candidate for prom queen all at once. Someone whose arms you wouldn't mind waking up in. God is on her side, and so are we.

She isn't Colleen, she's McMurphy. An immediate familiar. Our nurse.

In the role of McMurphy, Dana Delany was the franchise player of *China Beach*, leading an ensemble cast through four seasons and collecting multiple Prime Time Emmys and Golden Globes along the way. In conversation, Delany exudes a confidence that is cultured and urbane. She knew she wanted to be an actress while growing up in Connecticut, going home after school every day to watch classic movies, studying the acting craft while eating Fig Newtons. She loved films like *Singin' in the Rain* (1952) and *Oklahoma!* (1955), and gravitated toward the quirky supporting roles of females rather than the leads.

Delany later graduated from Wesleyan University and studied theater before moving to Hollywood. After an unfulfilling stint in the short-lived sitcom *Sweet Surrender* (1987), she was primed to enter the film world and not look back.

> ***Dana Delany:*** **Back then, you didn't do television. That was really looked down upon. You started in the theater and then you went to the movies. That was the plan, like everybody. Then, the world changed a little bit. I didn't want to do *China Beach*, because I had done three movies in a row. I was like,**

"Oh, I'm going to have a film career," and my agent told me I was a quote "fucking idiot" [*laughs*] because the script was so good for *China Beach*. And she was right.

The script was certainly one of the best things I'd ever read, in particular because it was from the female point of view, which was unusual, especially at that time. The character of McMurphy was so familiar to me. In many ways, McMurphy is the character that is closest to me that I've played; it's the one that I relate to the most, still, to this day. There were just too many similarities: Catholic background, stoic, kind of taking care of other people more than she took care of herself.

I grew up during that era, I related to Vietnam because my uncle had been a correspondent during the war, so it was something very familiar to me. Because I was relatively young, (I was like thirty when I read it, I think) every part that I was offered was always the wife or the girlfriend. There was always some scene where she was crying. The men never cried, it was the women crying. [*laughs*] I was so relieved to read it. The women I knew were very strong and stoic, so it was a relief where you had this character as I knew women to be. You never saw that on-screen, rarely on television at least.

Imagining any other actress than Delany in the role of McMurphy seems impossible, but John Young describes the casting process as "a rollercoaster ride that was not necessarily friendly to anyone involved, including her." It was a three-horse race for the role: Delany, Helen Hunt, and Linda Purl. Delany's competition had the inside track. Not only did they more closely resemble the strawberry blond that Young had imagined on the page, they were more connected and had stacked resumes. Hunt had worked with Young on the first show he created ten years prior, *The Fitzpatricks*, and Purl was Broyles's fiancé, known for playing Fonzie's girlfriend throughout the final season of *Happy Days*. Delany first crossed Young's radar when he saw her guest star on a 1985 episode of *Moonlighting* as a troublemaking vixen opposite Bruce Willis. Young recalled Delany arriving to their first meeting a day early, wearing cut-offs, a denim shirt, and a t-shirt underneath. He didn't recognize her and thought she was applying to be an assistant director.

> ***Dana Delany:*** **At that time, because I was a fledgling actor, I took auditions very seriously. I was in character as I was driving there. I just kept trying to imagine a Clint Eastwood character in a Western; that's how I saw her. John Young later told me he always saw her as Henry Fonda, but it was always a male character that we saw as the role model.**
>
> **I had to stay in character, and I remember waiting outside his office with his assistant and sitting there for almost an hour thinking, "God. How long do I have to wait?" I didn't know who he was, and he kept sticking his head out the door and looking at me and going back in. Finally, he came out and said, "Are you Dana Delany?" and I said, "Yes." He crooked his finger and said, "Come here."**
>
> **I went into his office and he said, "You know, you're a day early." I said, "What?" and he said, "Yeah, it's tomorrow," and I was so tense because I was trying to be Clint Eastwood. [*laughs*] He just started to talk to me to try to relax me, and we just had a regular conversation about what I had been up to. Then he said, "Well, you'll have to come back tomorrow," and I was like, "Ah!" I had to do the whole thing all over again and that led to a very, very long audition process before I got the part.**
>
> **It's one of those things where, of course, once I decided I wanted to do it, they didn't want me, so then I had to fight for it. It's like life, like any relationship. [*laughs*]**

Young took Delany out for a drink to discuss the role and proclaimed *China Beach* would be "huge." She laughed in his face. Still, Young gravitated to Delany as the ideal McMurphy. Purl fell by the wayside, and Delany and Hunt went in for film tests on the soundstage at Warner Bros. After hair, make-up, and cameras, ABC was still not sold on either choice and Young feared that a prolonged casting battle could send *China Beach* to development hell. During a meeting with the suits from ABC and Warner Bros., Young planted his flag in the sand. He declared, "You know what, we think it's Dana. We think she's the one, and if you don't want to make it with her, let's not make it."

***Dana Delany:* I was oblivious to most of that stuff behind the scenes, thankfully. I just kept showing up and trying to do my best. The fact that we actually had to do screen tests, which not many people were really doing that back then—rarely was that kind of money spent on that kind of thing. It was like old Hollywood in many ways, and it was hard, it was scary, but when you're that young, you're like, "Okay! Sure!"**

I do remember this. I think I had gone to the movie theater to try to chill out afterwards because I was just jittery from the whole thing, and then I lost my wallet. I remember going home thinking, "I lost my wallet...that's a good sign because that means I'm going to lose my identity and have a new one!" I tend to lose my wallet when something important is happening and changing in my life. Then I got the job, but it's that whole thing of "be careful what you wish for."

It's like, "Oh, I got the job! *Oh, I got the job*...now I actually have to come through."

ABC acquiesced to Young's bluff over Delany, birthing a series of stand-offs between the network and the executive producer that persisted for much of the series. I asked dozens of *China Beach* alumni about what it was like working with Young, and one in particular sums up his neck-deep conviction. Series editor Christopher Nelson reasoned why Young is his favorite collaborator of all, even though he is "completely infuriating and terminally tardy." Mining his memories, Nelson trailed off mid-sentence with a realization: "The other thing, too, that is probably a good thing to understand is that John *is* McMurphy. What's the word? Enigmatic."

The creative juices of Young and Broyles required an impartial conduit to the screen, and a trilogy of tall men with taller personalities was formed when Rod Holcomb was tapped to direct the pilot. Holcomb's resume included everything from *Battlestar Galactica* to *The Six Million Dollar Man*, in addition to pilots for *The Equalizer* and *Wiseguy*. Holcomb is described as everything from a "bull in a china shop" to a "big bear of permission" by the cast. Demanding while thoughtful, sharp while sensitive, Holcomb was the enforcer keeping an ambitious production like *China Beach* on the rails and under budget.

Young and Holcomb quickly found common ground on a series Holcomb had produced called *Harry O* (1974-76), an off-center show that shied away from succinct, happy endings and leaned into ambiguity with each episode's conclusion. A chromosome of *China Beach*. Holcomb is almost as self-critical as Young, ready to look back on a lauded scene with ways that it could have been better. Through reshoots, recasting, and post-production, the pair were unrelenting in their quest to make the best pilot possible. Production in Vietnam was out of the question for a litany of reasons, and a synthetic version of the country was captured in a two-day jaunt to Hawaii in November, 1987, before moving the production to California.

China Beach begins as "The Colleen McMurphy Show." Then, someone crashes the party.

Enter Laurette Barber, a USO backup singer from Paoli, Pennsylvania. An orphan grown up to be a man-eater. If McMurphy is a soft, minor seventh chord on a Steinway, Laurette is a screeching guitar solo pumping from a pawn shop Marshall stack. The two women form an ac/dc current, pulling each other in and out of their own voltages. Like Young and Broyles. The McMurphy and Laurette dynamic is the rocket fuel of *China Beach*'s blast off, and it failed to launch during the first days of principal photography.

Whomever was first cast as Laurette wasn't clicking with Dana Delany in the dailies, and a decision was made to change course. The initial scenes with McMurphy and Laurette were thrown out, the original Laurette was dismissed, and a replacement was needed as soon as possible. I pressed Young for the identity of the original Laurette, and he replied, "I don't know whether we need to talk about it, relieving people of duty. I don't know if the names are important."

Nearly two years after Young provided a non-answer, and days after this manuscript was finalized, I was able to confirm one Carla Brothers, an actress from Montclair, New Jersey, as the original Laurette. Brothers was kind enough to recall her brief experience via interview. Brothers was a stage actress working in New York—she received a call on a Thursday, flew to Los Angeles, and was in the casting offices of *China Beach* the following afternoon. Her screen test included the scene of Laurette singing a burned soldier to death, a scene she held a particular affinity for and never got to film. Brothers recalled the production in Hawaii as feeling "rushed," and wished she had more screen experience before tackling the role.

Dana Delany and Carla Brothers

Rod Holcomb returned from the troubled Hawaii shoot and sat down with friends and family for Thanksgiving dinner. The woman sitting next to Holcomb was new to town and owned a golden retriever that was a sperm donor at Holcomb's wife's seeing-eye dog school. The woman's name was Chloe Webb—the ideal Thanksgiving guest to curtail forced family interaction—and above all, the woman born to play Laurette Barber. It didn't take Holcomb long to realize this as the conversation drifted past canines and into Webb's recent work.

A few years prior to *China Beach*, Webb was an aspiring actress performing in *Forbidden Broadway* in New York, spoofing anyone and everyone in a Second City-ish stage revue. From adolescence, Webb was a restless soul, first drawn to music. She could play by ear and was in a high school rock band, finding trouble and getting expelled before graduating and attending the Boston Conservatory of Music. Webb switched her studies to acting after tiring of music theory. She also knew the psychological strain of war, as her father, a Korean War veteran, had committed suicide years prior.

Webb's theater experience later landed her the starring role of Nancy Spungen in Alex Cox's independent feature *Sid and Nancy* (1986). The film was an adaptation of the star-crossed, strung-out romance between Spungen and the Sex Pistols' bassist, Sid Vicious, played by Gary Oldman. Cox was taken with Webb's stage presence and cast her in her second screen role, with her performance garnering a number of accolades and awards from the National Society of Film Critics.

Sid and Nancy preceded Webb's reputation entering *China Beach.* She had depicted the existence of a wretch with electrifying personality, bringing charm to an irredeemable character. Pervasive heroin use and the constant screaming of "Fuck you, Sid!" throughout the film rattled the network suits, and Webb refused to sign on for any commitment past one season. A replacement for Laurette was direly needed, and all concerned parties were smitten with Webb.

Brian Wimmer *(Cpl. Boonewell Lanier)***: I remember showing up on set, we were at Zuma Beach. It was in the morning, so I reported first thing to the makeup trailer, and sitting in the chair is Chloe Webb. I was such a fan of hers that I turned around and walked out of the makeup trailer. The first thing I did was call my friend and say, "You're not going to believe who is on the show...*Chloe fucking Webb*!"**

> **It really hit me at that point. I had never heard of anybody who was involved in *China Beach* at that time, but Chloe Webb's on board? This thing is serious. This is intense. So I go back in the makeup trailer and I'm like, "Chloe, I've got to say, I'm like, a huge fan. I'm having a little bit of a hard time. I don't know if I'm going to be able to act with you," and she's just got this amazing smile. She looked at me and said, "You're going to be just fine."** [*laughs*]

Webb's rock 'n' roll lifestyle onscreen and off filled her portrayal of Laurette with an innate stage presence and unassuming effervescence, completing the ensemble cast. The Monday after Thanksgiving, Webb recalled climbing out of a helicopter and singing the Four Tops' "I Can't Help Myself" to a raucous group of extras at a makeshift firebase. The scrappy back-up singer seizes her moment of glory when the lead singer Georgia Lee (Gail O'Grady) is too sick to perform in the USO show. It's a near-riot scene as Webb stalks the stage and grinds to the beat, playing the horny mob like a fiddle. For an audience of actors being paid a stand-in wage, they come off as real soldiers savoring a break from the war through the sacrament of music.

Young crafted the character of Laurette in the image of singers from Holiday Inns he remembered from youth hockey trips to Paoli, PA: "You would see these people perform who were not very good, but they were out there trying." Laurette's curly red hair, scratchy voice, and unvarnished presence clashes with McMurphy in every possible way, resulting in an irresistible onscreen duo. Young and Broyles told Webb that her character was the heart of the show and McMurphy was the head, but Webb considered Delany as a bassist or a drummer keeping a beat that she could romp around stage with.

> ***Dana Delany:*** **Chloe is a force of nature. I fell in love with her; we just had this instant love affair between us. We were a yin and yang, which was completely right for the characters, and in life, we were very much yin and yang, and it's funny because we hung out together. This was before she was sober, but we would party together, and we just loved each other, and I loved working with her because you could just go anywhere in a scene and you knew she would have your back.**

Webb and Delany's real-life shenanigans translated to their characters' first meeting, when a long tracking shot eavesdrops on a late-night talk between the two. It's a sixties paradox of Mary Tyler Moore and Janis Joplin crossing paths and raising their brow at the other. The contradiction is explicit and enticing: McMurphy in a white t-shirt and dog tags, Laurette in a funky sleeveless mod dress. Mid-stride, they stop on the helipad, basked in blue light. They aren't so different now. The two size each other up and tempt a greater good that is unattainable to either individual. This moment underlines the necessity of solidarity among Americans in Vietnam, and in hindsight, the pitfalls of McMurphy going it alone. Holcomb, Young, and Broyles were all thrilled with the scene and knew they had lassoed the free spirit of the show. The brass at ABC were still not convinced. Delany's every move was nitpicked in the dailies, with complaints that her nipples were showing in this particular scene because she wasn't wearing a bra. Young, in protest, claimed she *was* wearing a bra, she was just really cold.

HOME ON THE RANGE

All the world's a stage, especially Southern California. *China Beach* spent four years bouncing between the beaches of Malibu, the Warner Bros. studio lot in Burbank, and a custom-made diorama thirty-five miles northwest of Los Angeles, to bring the Vietnam War back to life. Production designer James Newport was hired from the feature film world to construct and design the primary set of the Five and Dime from scratch on a plot of desert land in Indian Dunes. Home to productions including *M*A*S*H, The Dukes of Hazzard,* and *The A-Team*, the area was a popular and malleable setting for Hollywood in the eighties, with the ever-present risk of extreme weather disrupting filming.

Newport had avoided the television realm until seeing what Michael Mann did with the medium on *Miami Vice. China Beach* carried the sole directive of cinematic splendor—a challenge he couldn't turn down. When looking for inspiration in the Warner Bros. library, Newport came upon a limited series of Marvel Comics, *The 'Nam*, which became his bible for the overall look of the set.

William Broyles Jr.: **When I first walked on to the set, I literally thought I was having flashbacks; it looked *so* real and they had made it so beyond real. It was more real than my memories were. Everything—the costumes, the set design—it was just fantastic. I had had flashbacks and Vietnam dreams and nightmares and all this stuff, but after we started shooting *China Beach*, it was so real to me, I would start dreaming about the show. I couldn't tell which were my real dreams and which were dreams about the show because it had such a verisimilitude, such a powerful kind of reality to it.**

Scenes from the Five and Dime

A helipad surrounded by Quonset huts lies at the center of the base, a gateway to the oasis that all must pass through, dead or alive. The Jet Set is a watering hole with a jukebox, offering an escape from the chaos of the triage unit and the dread of the morgue. The dilapidated shell of a cathedral houses K.C. Koloski, moonlighting as an afterthought of failed French imperialism, the monetization of religion, and McMurphy's embattled Catholicism. A river snakes through the property as a natural border from civilian territory.

Like each character, the stage settings have their own fluidity. A large box fan pinwheels daylight at varying speeds into Beckett's underground lair, and panes of stained glass shine a revolving palette of colors down on K.C., depending on her mood. Gold being the first. Newport's set ended up as one big community art installation that other art directors and production designers could blow up and rebuild over four seasons of the show. After Newport finished principal construction of the set, torrential rains flooded the area, nearly destroying everything.

> ***James Newport** (production designer, first season):* **The next morning I drove out to the set with Bill Broyles. It was he that I worked most hard to please, for he knew what the set should look like. As we walked down toward the river valley it was evident that the destruction was immense. Our stately palm trees that we had planted on the perimeter were gone, washed away. The bridge had collapsed. There was debris everywhere, but amazingly – all the major structures – the Quonsets, the church, the Viet village – all stood in place. They had been buffeted and battered and a patina of mud and dust covered everything. And the river had carved a mean ugly scar where it had sought its original path. Bill turned to me and smiled. "Beautiful," he said. "The set's been to war."**

The set of *China Beach* was further broken in with memorable scenes of each character reporting for duty. Mjr. Lila Garreau commands a stage, backed by a gigantic American flag, offering a firm welcome to new arrivals, including Laurette Barber and Cherry White. Lila greets them in English, French, and Vietnamese and outlines the rules of the base. Lila is the mouthpiece of the war machine, caught between the powers above and their agents below. When not on camera, Concetta Tomei is the inverse of her character—vibrant, genial, and possessing a gift of supersonic gab.

***Concetta Tomei:* We were all like little kids in the sandbox and we were all going to play. We were all new players and we had all these toys, and the toys were jeeps and guns. It was like walking into another world, because John Young and Bill Broyles created that world for us. All you had to do was open your mouth and be in that moment. There was a lot that was brought. Lila was from the forties because she served in the Korean War. My dad was in the Navy in World War II, and my parents were always playing music from the forties, so Lila was of that vintage. I had a lot from my mom and my dad that inspired Lila, but then the writing gave us so much.**

***Michael Boatman:* Concetta is from Wisconsin and I'm from Chicago. Midwesterners, when they find themselves far from the Midwest, like LA or New York, we tend to stick together. It was lunch one day during the first season. I used to smoke at the time and so did Concetta (she's going to hate me for telling this story). We were standing out with Jeff Kober, who also smoked at the time. Concetta was, and remains, a staunch animal advocate. It's ninety-five degrees and incredibly hot, and Concetta is in her Lila outfit, perfectly quaffed, feeding these birds bread from the craft service table.**

Concetta's talking, cooing, doing all this sort of bird talk: [*softly*] "Look at these birds! Sweet babies, they're so darling and wonderful!" and someone brings up the fact that some serial killer of the moment had just been convicted and sentenced to life. Without transition, Concetta switches: [*yelling*] "Someone should cut his balls off! If I ever had a chance to kill that son of a bitch…" [*laughs*] She must have said "son of a bitch" five times in thirty seconds! It was the craziest thing I've ever seen. [*laughs*] I'm happy to be on her good list. She's Godmother to all my kids. That's a friendship I've grown to treasure.

Major Garreau's speech plays over another lasting image of the series, as the camera pans up from the feet of K.C. Koloski. She's leaning into a doorway, dragging on a cigarette, watching on with dismissal and defiance. Think of Lauren Bacall on the cover of a pulp novel. Irresistible, blood-boiling trouble. K.C. is the second lady seen in red, but unlike McMurphy, one look at her says she isn't here to save anyone. The room is suspended in dueling energies with the fairly new girls caught in between.

Liberty and justice for all on one shoulder, and the fleecing of America on the other.

Costume designer Paula Kaatz was responsible for outfitting each personality, further separating each character's identity from the other. Kaatz won a Primetime Emmy Award for Outstanding Costume Design for *China Beach*'s pilot episode and received three additional nominations for her work on the show. Costuming was like any other component of the series, fiercely debated, with even the length and style of the miniskirts scrutinized. In a show where dialogue is sometimes scarce, costume design is another voice singing in a wordless chorus.

> ***Marg Helgenberger:*** **Bill Broyles had said to me, "I have a pair of shoes that I got in Vietnam." They're called mules (that's a style of shoe) and on one shoe it said "Viet" and on the other shoe it said "Nam," and he said, "If they fit you, would you like to wear them for that scene? Then maybe they could do a shot where they start on your feet," which of course that became my opening shot, and then it became my credit shot for the first season or two. He was so excited about the fact I was going to be wearing these shoes [*laughs*] and they did fit! I mean, it was surprising, I guess I have a fairly common sized foot, but still!**
>
> **Then I had on that super-short dress; I never really worried about if my underwear was going to show or not, but I remember having to smoke cigarette after cigarette after cigarette. I kind of regretted smoking as much as I did in that scene, and throughout. Eventually I switched to just clove cigarettes or herbal cigarettes because it was just gross how much I was smoking. It's a bad, a terrible habit, and it's very unhealthy, but also it's appropriate for the period.**

K.C. is the most unlikely of characters to be spotted in the thick of the Vietnam War—a mélange of other entities—as arousing as Laurette, as inscrutable as McMurphy, and as cunning as the Vietcong. Her business model is neither liberal nor conservative, it is anarchic. She will sell anything to anyone, including her body for the right price. Helgenberger and Brian Wimmer establish delightful discord when their characters trade barbs and cutting eyes over a punch bowl, indicating an eventful past between them, and a detachment that reigns over any personal life K.C. musters outside of business hours. A true workaholic.

Cherry White is a surrogate set of fresh eyes trying to make sense of the base and all of its inhabitants. She treads lightly into K.C.'s domain as Alice in Vietnamese Wonderland. K.C. flashes a Cheshire grin behind her back, deciding whether she should initiate Cherry into the club or eat her alive. Each character is two-stepping in half time with another, trading partners like a square dance. When Cherry encounters Dodger, a hush goes over the barn as they stare at one another, both speechless at the nineteen-year-old on the other side of the bush. Cherry has hardly seen the world, and Dodger's seen too much of it. Everyone brought their own story with them to Vietnam, and *China Beach* is as much about the day-to-day war as it is about reconciling the present with the past. A page from the book of Bill Broyles.

The pilot immediately places McMurphy at odds with her co-worker, Dr. Richard. He's a self-absorbed, entitled gynecologist from New England who came of age in the fifties. The world was his oyster, and it's slipping away with the sixties. His wife Beth Ann, his kids, and his practice await his return home, while he pinches the rear of every girl in sight. A repugnant gentleman. Too clever to ignore.

John Sacret Young: **The purposeful goal was to make him a completely competent surgeon who was a complete ass, a man who hadn't wanted to be there, as opposed to the "volunteering" McMurphy. Opposites forced into intense proximity, yoked together, and finding an absolute reliance upon one another. A bonding beyond borders but one so difficult to translate into the "real world."**

Robert Picardo: **A lot of my character was borrowed from John Young. [*laughs*] This is going to be a tight rope to walk. There's a very sharp intellect in both of the characters, a very wry and dry sense of humor. There's a sense of sparseness in John's writing that I thought spoke really well to the urgency of the situations when we had medical emergencies. There's also a certain arrogance in John, and probably in me as well,**

that is in Dr. Richard, but underneath that, there's the soft underbelly that, under the right circumstances, you can see start to see unravel.

Another long shift brings McMurphy to nurse a bottle alone at the Jet Set. Dr. Richard makes his presence known, needling her over her self-pity and the fact that she made the choice to be in Vietnam. Silence speaks volumes throughout the pilot. Not here. Dana Delany and Robert Picardo deliver their lines through measured strikes, intent on ending the quarrel via technical knockout. Both too proud to back down, they keep swinging. As their inaugural debate escalates, their respective speeches play over the image of the other character absorbing the opposing argument and preparing a retort. The viewer walks in the shoes of a phantom bartender wiping off the counter, pretending not to pay attention. The bout results in a draw: an agreement to disagree.

Familiarity breeds contempt, and electricity.

McMurphy saves lives with Dr. Richard and sends the rest to Samuel Beckett in the GRU. He is an outsider by design in his race and occupation: a black man stuck with a job no one else wants. Beckett only comes to life in the presence of McMurphy, or when he is alone at work, using an overhead lamp as a spotlight for his grandiose epiphanies in a bunker of bodybags. Michael Boatman establishes his character with a Shakespearean soliloquy, declaring all the formaldehyde is turning him white, just as black is coming into style.

Dana Delany: **Michael was really a baby and didn't have that much experience. He was so sweet, and so wide-eyed and ready when we started. I didn't find out until later from him how nervous he was. You would never know it, ever, and I loved our scenes together in the morgue. His scenes were very much like a Samuel Beckett play, they were kind of elliptical and didn't really make sense, but they emotionally made sense. He had this gravitas underneath it all and he was perfect for the part, and he's just continued to work and do comedy. Nobody knew how funny he was. He was a serious kid at a young age—he got married early, had kids early. It's been wonderful to see in thirty years how people have turned out, basically. [*laughs*]**

***Michael Boatman:* The scene in the pilot where Dana comes in and actually introduces my character is always one of those standout moments for me. I just loved working with Dana. We had such a strangely intimate kind of onscreen relationship, and I think that was because the nature of Becket's job. She would come into the GRU to lift up Beckett's spirits, and sometimes he would do the same thing for her. It was an unusual relationship in that there wasn't necessarily sexual tension between the two characters. They were friends, and he sort of represented death and she represented life, to me. I think those two characters had such a great balance. To this day, people will tell me, "Boy, I really love that Dana Delany! Ooh man." [*laughs*] I am fully in agreement with them.**

Delany was fine-tuning her portrayal of McMurphy while network executives persisted in their complaints about her in the dailies. Young recalled feedback that Delany "wasn't pretty enough, didn't look good in a swimsuit," and wasn't capturing the essence of the character. Young responded by writing in an unscripted scene to shut them up, using soft light and a modern skirt made of a petroleum product that hugged every curve of Delany's body. The head honcho of Warner Bros. Television, Harvey Shephard, exploded at Young on the set, decrying the impromptu production cost. As a shouting match intensified, Delany passed by them in the outfit and caught Shephard's eye. Young claims he never heard another complaint from above about Delany from that moment on.

As *China Beach* made its sojourn from a concept to a screen product, it was marinating in the memories of Vietnam veterans. Bill Broyles had co-created the show, interviews conducted with veterans had inspired countless beats and twists in the script, and a Vietnam vet, Charles "Chuck" Tamburro, was flying one of the helicopters. Tamburro was more than familiar with the source material after getting shot down on two separate occasions while piloting a gunship. Stunts and aviation were no small matter—Vic Morrow and two child actors were killed in a chopper accident filming *The Twilight Zone: The Movie* several years prior on a neighboring set in Indian Dunes. As scenes were filmed on set, a final audit came from technical advisors who had lived through the war firsthand.

One key advisor was Jeff Hiers, Broyles's former platoon radioman in Vietnam. Hiers was later immortalized in *China Beach* when a recurring character was named after him in the second season, played by Ned Vaughn. Hiers and other advisors were re-living their Vietnam days through a grand scale re-creation of the event, and Hiers took it in stride, throwing his military know-how into the melting pot of *China Beach*.

> ***Jeff Hiers*** *(technical advisor):* **One of the main things I was able to do is to get these actors to lighten up, because they all wanted to portray it like they knew what the outcome was. When we were all over there, it was fun. It was light. Even in a firefight, you're yelling back and forth. It's like guys playing paintball. The actors, originally, they wanted to be downtrodden about it, so one of the things was to switch that around, because they think the reason they're over there at that point in time was that they felt they were doing heroic things, saving the world, and it wasn't until later that we find out we weren't.**

Bill Broyles, Jeff Hiers, and Shevitz

> ***Chloe Webb** (Laurette Barber):* **I paid a lot of attention because we had some vets around, and there were nurses who had been in Vietnam who were on the set, so I liked to ask questions. I'm kind of a connoisseur of human nature. It's different than if you're shooting in New York City or in the streets of London. You're just way the hell out of town and everyone is sitting around in chairs, so it was a really good place to get people to tell their stories.**
>
> **I had all these images from people that were there. I think in pictures, sort of with animals, especially horses and dogs, they think in pictures. When someone's telling me a story, I see the movie that they're telling me, but it's from their point of view—they are the camera. I had heard stories about people who had to give the morphine shots to their best friend who had lost his legs and stuff like that. I just felt like they were so close, so the people that were actually there on the set, it was like I was running their movie through me, for them.**

Digging into the creative process behind *China Beach* opens up wormholes straight into the lived experience of the Vietnam War, mutated by time and self-mythology. Broyles had offered hypnotizing stories from his tour of duty, and given that veteran accounts were the foundation of the show, I began tracking down more vets to talk to. The first veteran I talked to was a long- range reconnaissance patrol marine. He had never seen *China Beach* and requested I not use his name in print. He didn't want his service glamorized. Hardly anyone had ever thanked him for his service in the fifty years since returning home from his tour of duty, and Vietnam was something he, nor anyone else, had ever wanted to talk about. I thanked him for his service, and it felt patronizing. Insufficient. I kept talking to more vets and realized that a listening ear meant more to them than any pleasantry.

THIS MAGIC MOMENT

John Young envisioned the opening moments of *China Beach*, wrote them down one summer day in 1987, and never made a revision. He showed me the original page where his pilot script began, and we stood quietly, arms folded, as if we were looking at a painting in a gallery. I studied the words, picturing them in Technicolor. Young broke the silence: "I think about things that I've written, whether it's the best, the worst, whatever—and a lot of it is like looking at bodies that are in a coma. On the other hand, I look at this, and I go, 'For once, it was good.'"

The first impression of Colleen McMurphy is more than good. It is widescreen opulence masquerading as 4:3 eighties network television. A title card dissolves to a nondescript beach. Boonie Lanier looks on atop his lifeguard stand, playing harmonica, before he runs to assist McMurphy with her chair. The frame pans up her legs to a red one-piece swimsuit. She's reading a worn copy of Graham Greene's *The End of the Affair*. Aviators hide her face, and her bobbed brunette hair drips dry a few inches above her shoulders. She could be anyone, anywhere in the world, and the sight is mesmerizing.

The rhythm of solitude comes before all others in *China Beach.* The whoosh of wind, the crash of waves, next an industrial squall. The woman looks over her shoulder and bows her head, recognizing the noise of war that calls her to duty. The Bell UH-1 Iroquois helicopter, Huey for short, is heard but not seen. An indiscriminate courier, a vital member of the ensemble, propelling its own garbled language over everyone else. From the beginning of the series until its end, the Vietnam War is breathing down McMurphy's neck, whispering terrifying nothings in her ear. Our nurse's reply rarely comes in words, rather from the eyes and the movements of Dana Delany.

McMurphy swaggers through a dune with stone-cold confidence in her step. Sandbags and perimeter wire begin to line her path. Maurice Williams and the Zodiacs' 1963 pub closer "Stay" enters the field of sound before she enters a hut and changes into her scrubs. Outside, a rumble of screams and helicopter rotors builds. The door flies open. A gust of air blows her hair back. Unfazed, she squints through the blinding light to size up the day's work. Blood everywhere. Bodies without limbs. Some without pulses.

Underneath the collage of noise, you can still hear that familiar song.

***William Broyles Jr.:* "Stay" is the first word you hear in the series, and it was about characters of that age. The idea was to hit that from the beginning. We were all rock 'n' roll kids. We all grew up on Chuck Berry and Elvis and Johnny Cash and the Four Tops and that was the one thing we could take with us. The music was portable. We couldn't take our families or the room we grew up in or the home-cooked food, or our friends or our girlfriends...but we could take the music. That wasn't just a soundtrack, it was integral to the show.**

Two years after the Korean War ended in 1953, television sets were filling up American living rooms. Elvis Presley had impeccable timing in the summer of '56, gyrating on national television during a performance of "Hound Dog." Any preconceived notion of pop music was shattered in the moment. A huge backbeat and overt sex appeal were irreversibly injected into three chords and the truth. For almost a decade, a mushroom cloud of rock 'n' roll billowed through radios and turntables without any concurrent influence of wartime. Baby Boomers were the first generation to have rock 'n' roll soundtrack their teenage years, and that same music accompanied them to Vietnam through transistor radios and the Armed Forces Network.

***William Broyles Jr.:* It was the rock 'n' roll war; the music is what connected us to the world. We all had our eight tracks and we would go out on patrol, and at dusk we were digging foxholes, and everybody would be listening to music. As it got a little darker and dangerous, it all went off, and you were in the middle of the war.**

American troops began all-out combat in Vietnam in 1965, right as the Beatles were finishing their classic pop era with *Help!* and embracing experimentation that was as much aural as it was chemical. *Rubber Soul* and *Revolver* arrived next in the span of a calendar year as the war in Vietnam began to accelerate and complicate. Rock music followed suit. Brian Wilson traded his surfboards for polyphonic despair. Dylan went electric. It was like someone snapped their fingers and *everything* changed.

Mass media and wartime clashed head on, sensationalizing the civil unrest of Jim Crow laws, the Sexual Revolution, and antiwar sentiment, finding an unidentifiable breaking point somewhere in the vortex of the late sixties and early seventies. Men burned their draft cards in broad daylight, soldiers came home early in coffins, and a national blame game erupted. Americans had been sold the mission of stopping the worldwide spread of communism in Vietnam. They had also been sold color TVs just in time to watch vivid red hues of blood flow every night after dinner.

***Brian Wimmer:* I was born in 1959, so what I remember was they had this whole running body count thing: how many Vietcong were being killed in a day, how many Americans were being killed, and I remember Walter Cronkite had this running total kind of thing and then they would show a little bit of footage. It always just seemed so deeply mysterious. It was just weird, and it was something that kind of really got in my psyche early on in a very kind of weird, mysterious, something-we-didn't-talk-about kind of way.**

China Beach picks up its adaptation of the Vietnam War in late-November of 1967, with McMurphy crossing off the final days left in her year of service. America was mired in a cultural war back home that is absent at the Five and Dime. The overall mood is almost chipper—the war was still winnable. *China Beach* is rarely concerned with making a political statement on the justification of the Vietnam War, instead focusing on stories about the individuals who are embroiled in it. Protest music waits its turn, while golden oldies pump a breezy and soulful air through the tumult. Smokey Robinson and the Miracles, Stevie Wonder, Martha Reeves and the Vandellas, and more Motown artists cycle through the show's jukebox to go along with cold beer, beachside strolls, and pretty nurses to muffle the proximity of war. Aretha Franklin's "Natural Woman" adds some irony when McMurphy wheels a dead body out to the helicopter pad and fields a foul pop fly from the nearby baseball game.

The music wasn't confined to Motown in the *China Beach* pilot, with John Rubenstein's original compositions bringing a symphonic touch to the proceedings. Originally tasked with writing a theme song for the opening credits, the longing piece ended up being used towards the end of each episode to accompany a climax or revelation.

> ***John Rubenstein*** *(composer)***: I came up with the theme for the show that I still to this day play sometimes. I sit down at the piano and play it because I really like it! '88 was enough after the war so that the show was really a look back at a really terrible time, and the people in the show—the characters John Young wrote—didn't necessarily look at it like that because they were in the middle of it. So rather than write some sort of militaristic [*hums*] "Dun-da-da-dun!" I wrote about the sadness of dealing every day with death and missing home that was so far. Not only far in miles, but far in culture from home.**
>
> **If you're a medical person in the military in Vietnam in the nineteen sixties, you're dealing with horror on a daily basis, and that makes you sad, even if you're very up, very bright, and very articulate, and do your job with energy and with commitment, somewhere underneath it, you're being made to be sad. You're touching the sadness in your soul, so that's what I tried to write. There's a wonderful harmonica player named Tommy Morgan, he's the best harmonica player in Los Angeles in the studio, and I wrote many different scores and featured him wherever and whenever I could, and this was one of them. I wrote him a big solo and I loved that theme.**

Music is not mere decor in *China Beach*, it is the infallible unifier. Laurette needs a backup dancer for an upcoming performance, and McMurphy needs an extra hand on her final shift. A deal is made, and the two pull each other out of their normal gigs and into parts unknown. Colleen McMurphy is the alpha female. Too proud to not go first, and too proud to not go all the way. The nurse is dancing onstage behind Laurette, disguised in a wig, sequins, and miniskirt singing the Supremes' "You Can't Hurry Love" to a packed house. Bill Broyles recalled a number of flashy, polished studio musicians recording the backing track, riffing away. He cried, "Cut! Wait! You *have* to play it like a garage band."

Once Boonie calls out McMurphy, the entire bar begins to cheer for their nurse, and Laurette cedes the stage. McMurphy is overcome by the appreciation, steps forward, and submits to the feelings forcing their way out. Emotions, body language, and the music enter a trance. The Supremes track twists into Rubenstein's theme, the crowd noise fades, and the camera holds tight on McMurphy's face. Half laughing, half crying, fully cognizant of what Vietnam has given to her. Her hand covers her mouth, and she cries. "Dana has access to tears with a tremendous propensity. It's both awesome and sometimes even alarming," remarked Young.

Young had originally written McMurphy's display of emotions to come later, and his creative audible caused a heated disagreement between Young and Delany. Delany was going by the script, and wanted to save McMurphy's fireworks display of emotions until the very end. Both sides recalled leaving the stage for further discussion.

> ***Dana Delany:* You don't really enjoy it when your executive producer pulls you off the set and says, "I fought for you. I'm the reason you have this job." I said to him, "Well, I hope I had something to do with it too." [*laughs*] John was very much in control and it was his baby. He basically said, "Do it!" and I did it, and that was it. That was probably the biggest argument that we had.**

As McMurphy looks inward at her feelings and outward at her admirers, *China Beach* reissues a bulletin that there is a war on, and bombs start falling on the base. Everyone flees from the Jet Set and McMurphy and Laurette seek shelter in the medical ward, still clad in their sequined outfits. Like the opening moments of the pilot, choppers are still bringing in bodies. Laurette completes her end of the deal and helps McMurphy out in triage. She has no idea what to do, so she holds a charred soldier's hand and makes small talk with him. Through tears, tremors, and sniffles, she fulfills the man's last wish, and sings "Dedicated to the One I Love" to him as he dies.

***Chloe Webb:* So we do the scene and it's devastating. It's hard, you're just going full out, but the guy [was covered with] Corn Flakes, with coffee and molasses—that's basically how they make the burned flesh. So, as they're moving the camera around, and the close-up is on him, the close-up is on me, then it's on both of us. As he's moving around, as he's talking, the corn flakes and the molasses are cracking on his face, right? So people are laughing and they're eating the corn flakes, and making fun of the song because it's the end of the day.**

Everyone, the whole crew, is singing it together, and then they come back the next day and they're like, "We have to do it again." I was like, "Oh, are you kidding me? I can't even take this seriously anymore!" [*laughs*] That was brutal. Now, for the rest of my life, if it's a heavy scene—literally, as soon as I finish a scene like that, I put in earplugs and I walk back to my trailer on the outside chance I'm going to do it again, I don't want to hear what they're going to say! [*laughs*] It has never, ever happened again, but that was truly the scariest—just the idea of making something like that real again.

In the moment Laurette sings the man to his death, the sound of music triggers potent, unsaid revolution in *China Beach*. Laurette is finding the kind of strength she never knew she had, and she's giving it out freely to those who need it. She isn't onstage. She's in a dark Quonset hut, and McMurphy is in the audience hanging on every word. Laurette singing to the soldier sends the same message to McMurphy as the incoming Huey that interrupted her moment of peace on the beach. The war is demanding more from her. And she can't say no. The next morning, McMurphy sits on the beach, hair blowing in her face, commending Laurette for her bravery, and declaring that she's not going back to Kansas just yet.

The Vietnam War is where the nurse belongs.

John Young was so pleased with the scene, he took another stand against ABC when they wanted McMurphy's epiphany reshot due to the windblown hair across Delany's face. The fate of *China Beach* was soon in the hands of those same nitpicking executives, and a screening of the pilot episode determined whether or not the story of Colleen McMurphy and company would continue. If the network brass were tired of arguing with Young, they had an easy way out.

Christopher Nelson (supervising editor): **John and Bill were there, and they were nervous as cats. I said I'm going to stay and watch the film through the portal in the projection room, and they said, "I can't take this anymore, we're gonna go ahead and get a couple of drinks. We'll be back when it's over." I watched the show, everything goes fine, and when the lights come on, the room is really quiet. They just sit there and slowly they get up and walk out. Nobody's talking to anybody, and I'm just going, "Oh, fuck. They hated it."**

John Sacret Young: **We get a call: "The screening is done, you can come on up," and we come up and all these people, all the executives are standing in their doorways. Not one says a word, and you're thinking, "Disaaaster...disaaaster..."**

I

My bedroom rock record was inching closer to *Chinese Democracy*. Three years of conversations and research had piled up in my head and onto the laptop screen, and I wondered where it was all headed. Then, one book corrected my course—*War Torn: Stories of War from the Women Reporters Who Covered Vietnam*. I was so taken with these women's personal accounts, I had to see Vietnam for myself.

China Beach never filmed a reel of footage in Vietnam. Still, the war that raged on there is the lifeblood of the show. I had to taste the marrow on my lips. I had to see and smell the same rice fields and jungles that Bill Broyles had romanticized, minus the napalm. I had been willfully ignorant to the fact that I couldn't, shouldn't write a book about *China Beach* without seeing the real thing. The airfare was too affordable to pass up, so I booked roundtrip tickets from Nashville to Ho Chi Minh City for myself and my wife.

The locals still refer to Ho Chi Minh City as Saigon, so I will too. I asked a tour guide why they don't use the re-unified name, and she rolled her eyes with an embellished gag to declare it "ugly."

I woke up in Saigon after a twenty-seven-hour trek, and excitement edged jet lag for some food and adventure. I wiped the crust from my eyes and looked out at the city from the rooftop breakfast buffet of the Hotel Majestic. My senses were on fire. City life stretched eastward, far past the Saigon River, degenerating into a third world in the distance. A number of odors—wonderful and awful—collected below and wafted up my nose. I think I fell in love.

An ocean of motorbikes poured through the city streets, sometimes three riders deep on a saddle. They hauled boxes, small household appliances, toddlers, and anything else you can imagine. A car or SUV was a status symbol. When the street was gridlocked, the mopeds darted into oncoming traffic or rode on the sidewalk. Surgical masks shielded their lungs and nasal cavities from the poor air quality. The non-stop beep-beep meant nothing personal, just "make way, coming through." It took a day or two to not fear death or dismemberment while crossing the street.

Old folks lounged around in makeshift cafes, and everyone else was on some kind of mission, headed somewhere or selling something. The sidewalks were littered with little red and blue plastic stools that many full-size Americans would flatten into pancakes. I sat down on one for a photo, and an angry woman said to get out of her "restaurant." Entrepreneurs sold everything from Cokes and beers to fake Louis Vuittons and phở noodle soup cooked on the spot. Concerns over health codes, open containers, and traffic laws were nonexistent, most of all for the statuesque policemen situated on every corner.

Passersby held blank faces, some looking me in the eye, as if to politely, amusedly ask, "Why the hell are *you* here?"

Antique hotels like the Caravelle and the Continental stood in stacked grids of stucco, insulated with history, sharing a crowded District 1 with day spas, souvenir shops, and every other tourist trap imaginable. A couple of skyscrapers stuck out like American tourists. Mansard roofs and baroque cathedrals were accompanied by the smell of delicious banh mi bread and a healthy population of poodles, all stalwarts from a century-long French occupation. One bloody chapter of many these people and their country have weathered. I thought of John F. Kennedy, Graham Greene, and Walter Cronkite perusing the same sidewalks decades ago. If they could only see Saigon now.

One morning in Vietnam quickly told me that the country is as much at odds with itself as Colleen McMurphy. Vietnamese millennials seemed to carry no thought of their country's prior decades and centuries of war, preoccupied—no—consumed with making a living, their smart phones, and starting families. I saw them hang out at Starbucks, shop at H&M, and drink plenty of beer. The American dream, almost. Homeless beggars sat in front of Gucci storefronts. I was swindled into paying ten bucks for a coconut. Young women stood in front of massage parlors, making eyes and cheap offers. Was this communism, or a Confucianist, eighties Manhattan?

I kept watching. Wondering.

The War Remnants Museum was the first official taste of the Vietnam War. A big square of a building in the middle of a courtyard full of decommissioned Hueys, tanks, and bomber planes. Looped sound effects of falling mortars and screaming missiles completed the mood. Inside, exhibits forced a sobering Vietnamese viewpoint of their American War: pictures of Agent Orange victims, heaps of dead and mutilated Vietnamese, and newspapers from around the world undercutting the US justification of military action. One 4 x 6 photo was captioned: DESTROY ALL, BURN ALL, AND KILL ALL IS THE POLICY OF AMERICAN INVADERS. The victor writes the history books with their half of the truth, and so does the loser—both accounts hypnotic and heartbreaking. As crowds inspected the decaying vehicles of war outside, I watched urban life bustling on past the gate, oblivious to the forgotten time I was standing in.

I hardly crossed paths with any Americans during those two weeks, just a handful of vacationing Britons, Australians, and Malaysians. English is surprisingly prevalent throughout the country and every time I said, "USA," the Vietnamese perked up with wide eyes and a smile. It all felt friendly, if not genuine.

The US dollar and the Vietnamese dong were more pressing matters than any passé grudge. The only face on the currency of Vietnam is Ho Chi Minh, the father of Vietnamese independence. He is Vietnam's George Washington, Davy Crockett, and Obi-Wan Kenobi rolled into one, or at least the government would like you to believe. One can hardly walk a few blocks without seeing a mural of "Uncle Ho" looking down with kind eyes, a warm smile, and a wispy goatee.

Very little about Vietnam felt communist to me, maybe more of a capitalist demolition derby that is slave to a one-party rule. There are no elections, no guns, and income tax is mostly ignored, aside from what I was told about demands for money under the table from local police. No matter one's age, any form of healthcare or education costs dearly and must be footed by an average monthly salary amounting to $150 in American currency. A lot of people get sick with no cure except death. Each and every tour guide made sure we visitors were aware. For two weeks, I kept looking around and wondering how the hell any of these people could ever really get ahead.

I wondered what Uncle Ho would think.

I also wondered if things would be the same if my country had never waged a war there in the first place.

The author and a Huey in Saigon

PAINTED LADIES

Robin L. Cook
Bellingham, WA 98225

ABC Studios
1330 Avenue of the Americas
New York, NY 10019

To the writers of China Beach:

I am writing to express my appreciation for a segment of China Beach which I happened to see by accident. I tuned in to the end of an episode in which a nurse was on stage with a USO performer, and the gathering was fired upon. The two women ran to where the wounded were being triaged, and the singer, who was without medical skills, ended up holding the hands of two dying men. The next scene was of the same two women the following morning. The singer asked the nurse if it ever got better, if one ever got over it, and expressed her frustration and feelings of impotence. The nurse stopped her and told her, very directly and clearly, that it didn't matter that she couldn't "solve" anything -- the point was that she had <u>been</u> <u>there.</u> The nurse stated that although the dying man may have had a mother, a wife, or a sister, it was she (the singer) who had been there in their stead.

I am a critical care nurse who has left nursing because of "burnout", a kind of mortal frustration and anger. These scenes had a profound impact on me, and left me shaken and tearful. The nurse was offering the singer a perspective, an affirming way to handle the horror of her experience. I felt that I was being shown a way to handle the horror of my memories, a very clear statement that just by being willing to be there with another human being I had perhaps done something right and valuable. Some bitterness left me by virtue of being exposed to these scenes, and I feel compelled to write and at least <u>try</u> to thank whoever wrote them.

Most sincerely,

Robin L. Cook

June 11, 1988

Ms. Robin L. Cook
Bellingham, WA 98225

Your letter as much as any -- and we have received a great number -- made us feel what we are doing is worthwhile.

You expressed eloquently and movingly -- better I suspect than we could ourselves -- what we set out to do in the premiere of "China Beach," and our aspirations for it as a series.

Many of the women who served talked to us of their burn out from their time in Vietnam, their difficulty in putting it to rest, and how hard it was to knit themselves back together. They are making it and we hope you will continue to as well.

We are grateful to them for what they did, and we are grateful to you.

Sincerely,

J. S. Y. Young

John Sacret Young

JSY/av

WE'VE ONLY JUST BEGUN

On April 26, 1988, the *China Beach* pilot premiered on ABC to a national television audience of 18.4 million people. The responses were personal. Intense. Hundreds of thousands of Americans had served in Vietnam, and here was *this* version of *their* history on display. Barb Lilly, an American Red Cross volunteer who spent a year in Vietnam, turned off the show after five minutes. She seethed at the notion of a nineteen-year-old without a bachelor's degree serving in Vietnam as a donut dolly. The name alone of "Cherry" was an eye roller. K.C. Koloski joking that she had graduated from the Red Cross into prostitution prompted a change of the channel.

That same night, Rod Holcomb was at his house watching with his family and the phone rang. On the other end of the line was an angry man who had looked Holcomb up in the phone book just to chew him out: "What are you doing? What is this? You were never in Vietnam! What about the mothers? Shame on you!" Holcomb didn't say a word and let the man finish. There was silence, a click, dial tone. Holcomb stood frozen with the phone in his hand, speechless and unable to go back to the TV.

> ***William Broyles Jr.:*** **The real audience for the show, for me, was the women who had served in Vietnam, because that was my inspiration. I wanted them to realize it was just one big valentine to them, that this was an homage to what they had done, to honor their service and sacrifice. They meant so much to me when I was going through the war. We aired the pilot and I was expecting this outpouring of thanks and gratitude and I got this radio silence.**

Finally, I called a nurse and said, "What do you think?" "We hated it. We all hated it." I was stunned. She said, "You have us laughing, you have us drinking, you have us flirting with people, you have us wanting to go home." I said, "Well, wait a minute, that's all true!" [*laughs*] She said, "I thought we were going to look like heroes," and I said, "That's what makes you look like heroes, because you're so human," and she wasn't buying it. I was devastated, but after two or three episodes that changed, because they kind of got it. I think it is human nature just to want to see the good side of what you're doing and not to realize that the less-than-perfect side that you also have is what makes you human. No one could go through that experience and just be the same.

Jeanne "Sam" Christie *(Red Cross, '67-68; technical advisor)***: I heard from a bunch of the women and they were not pleased. I wasn't upset, because I understood it. I was far enough removed from it at that point. It depends on when people dealt with their Vietnam experiences. Some of them are just *now* beginning to deal with it. People were upset, and yes, I think one of the stupid things they had was Cherry trying to get the guys to talk. And we all knew, "Ask them about their weapons!" It's what we did sometimes, and it got the men to open up and talk to us.**

Linda Pelegrino *(Red Cross, '68; technical advisor)***: Of all the people that were over there, the Red Cross girls were sort of innocent and clean-cut. Did they have to name her Cherry? No, but I didn't think she didn't represent us well. The one thing about being over there is you had to be strong enough to say who you were. People tried to define you. There was the guy that saw you as the girl-next door, but there was the sergeant that saw you as his daughter, or a nuisance. We had a drunk, full-bird colonel say, "Yeah, the prostitutes are here." You got defined by a lot of different people a lot of different ways. To me, it wasn't surprising they used her character to define the innocence. Because, in all honesty, we pretty much were college graduates, right out of school, doing our thing. There wasn't a lot of us with life experiences.**

I was flipping through the pages of *In the Combat Zone* (1987) by Kathryn Marshall and couldn't believe my eyes. This oral history of women who served in Vietnam contains the memories of one Cherie Rankin. An American Red Cross worker who went to Vietnam, a virgin. Her brother was serving in-country, and although he wasn't MIA, she hadn't seen him in two years—and through her persistence, reunited with him in the middle of Vietnam. He was even stationed in Danang. Rankin also recalled two soldiers failing in their attempts to rape her, as well as guys in the bush who were hardly able to form sentences. They followed her around, staring. Like Dodger.

For all the impassioned reactions to *China Beach* that ensued for four years, the first impression from ABC executives was solemn quietude. John Young later realized their silence was an accolade—they were all collecting themselves after an emotionally exhausting experience. All parties remembered it differently, with a common denominator of big hugs and big tears. Brandon Stoddard was so pleased, he wanted to air the pilot right after the Super Bowl. Cooler heads prevailed with no additional episodes prepared, and an abbreviated season of six additional hours was ordered to air along with the pilot in the spring.

Young recalled not having a day off for six months, and he didn't want one.

***Chad Hoffman:* Everybody saw the same thing. It was just powerful, gut-wrenching, different, compelling, darkly funny, beautifully produced. No one had seen anything like this before on television and there was no question in our collective mind that we were going to put this show on the air. I came out of the screening and John was waiting. I remember it like yesterday; I picked him up and gave him a hug. It's just what you live for in those jobs, to have a moment like that. It all came together and through the talents of everybody and the risk-taking that was involved, it was an extraordinary screening. One of the best I could ever remember. It's just one of those pilots you looked at and you felt like the show had been on the air for a number of months, and not that you just put it together in a short period of time.**

Young referred to a standard bearing TV show like *Law and Order* as a sausage maker: "well done and well crafted" but "every episode is basically the same as the last one. They're great, but there's not a lot of afterthought." *China Beach* was going to be different, aiming to send an important message "without the bullshit of being self-important." Young and Broyles laid the tracks for a short and concentrated season, resolving to not make sausage, rather "a little movie every week." Broyles wrote the following episode as an absolute beginner, penning the first produced script in his storied filmography.

As writing and filming commenced, the president of Warner Bros. Television, Harvey Shephard, watched a trailer for the pilot episode set to John Rubenstein's wistful theme song. Shephard bemoaned it as too depressing, demanding that some rock 'n' roll was required to lift the spirit of the show during each opening credit sequence. To this day, Rubenstein is still dismayed that his theme was demoted, and Broyles recalled fighting the command before realizing Shephard was right. The consummate *China Beach* theme song was a mighty sword waiting to be pulled from the stone of the Motown Records catalog.

Hearing Diana Ross and the Supremes' "Reflections" before each episode of *China Beach* is akin to lighting a candle before making love, setting a mood for magic to happen. Hopes reaching for something fresh and fulfilling. Sometimes feral. "Reflections" was released during the Summer of Love, 1967, making it a timely selection to coincide with McMurphy's tour of duty. It is a Siamese twin of R&B and Beatlesque pop driven by shimmering bass and a hazy organ, full of bloops and bleeps foreign to preceding singles from Motown. Ross crooning about lost love, years passing, and the will to carry on aligns with both McMurphy's crusade and a nation looking back on a losing war. It sucked, and we survived. The rhythm section behind Ross kicks along with a snare and tambourine to get the blood flowing for certain episodes that range from meditative to morose.

***Christopher Nelson** (supervising editor):* **The credit sequence was so hard to cut, because you're taking a song and you have to make it fit this space exactly. What I hadn't known at that point in time was songs of that era (and until way after that era, actually) are all done live, and all those songs start off slower than they end. When it's done free and naturally and there's no click track or any kind of mechanical thing in there,**

> **they all become faster, so then it becomes harder to match the front end of the song with the back end of the song. I remember every time Diana Ross comes into sing, it's a pick-up, so she's coming in on the fourth beat of the previous bar, rather than the downbeat of the new bar. If you're trying to build a piece into there, I would literally have to find one note to be able to make the music cut into something else. I got it and went, "Oh my God!" and then Broyles would come in and go, "Aw man, I like this other phrase so much better than the one you have in there," and you feel like your head's gonna explode. [*laughs*] It's more complicated than you could ever imagine, particularly in film days.**

The rocksteady groove of "Reflections" meshes with Boonie Lanier leaning over his lifeguard stand and Beckett treading in the lone light of the morgue. When a two-bar break hits, it provides a few seconds to scan up K.C. Koloski's silhouette, making the "Show Me" State proud. The credits are a microcosm of the show, encompassing the contradiction of life among death that pervades each character. We see McMurphy screaming when she can't get her bloody scrubs over her head, then dancing in a wig and sequins, and closing the credits as she bows her head over a liquor bottle. She is every woman. This musical montage prepares the viewer for anything to happen, and never loses its gloss as the series evolves over four seasons.

China Beach's second episode "Home" aired on ABC the following night of the pilot, aiming to maintain momentum with viewers by sticking with what excelled in the first two hours: McMurphy and Laurette at the center of everything, leaning on each other. Written by Broyles and directed by Holcomb, the episode keeps the supporting cast on the peripheral, waiting for their cues as this world flowers.

Broyles has met prominent success throughout his screenwriting career by placing his characters in mystifying places, following their struggle to make sense of it all. *Apollo 13* (1994) has astronauts stuck in a space shuttle and *Cast Away* (2000) strands a man on an island with a volleyball named Wilson as his only friend. These scripts echo many of Broyles's own stories from *Brothers in Arms*; he had lived the part of a stranger in a strange land and understood how to make the story relatable. His first scene in "Home" crafts an uncomfortable moment and drops Laurette Barber straight into it.

A soldier is in a room, bringing the barrel of an M16 rifle to his mouth. All is quiet. We watch from an eagle-eyed view from the ceiling rafters, preparing for his brains to splatter across the plywood floor. A beat. His lips curl, and he blows into the instrument of death to create the sound of a flute, playing the notes of "When the Saints Go Marching In." Laurette looks on with an uneasy smile, and another audition for her live act goes kaput.

"Home" carries the prototypical plot of *China Beach*, placing McMurphy in a crisis and watching her moral code develop like an instant Polaroid. No snapshot ends up the same. When Boonie and Sweetness take the homeward bound Duey (Ned Vaughn) out for a final drink in the 'Nam, a Vietnamese woman (Elizabeth Lindsey) throws a grenade into the party. A firefight ensues and Duey, Sweetness, and the woman are hauled into the triage unit. McMurphy notices the woman is pregnant, right before discovering she also carried out the attack. Hatred takes over McMurphy when Duey dies, offering another side of the nurse we didn't see in the pilot.

William Broyles Jr. ("Home"): **I'm really proud of that first episode about enemies. John has often said that we based [McMurphy] on a classic western hero who doesn't say much and withholds everything, but in that episode I based her on John Wayne in *The Searchers.* She's angry, she hates that woman, and she's not sympathetic and nice at all. As a writer or as a creator, you have certain hopes and ambitions for a part, and then it's magic when an actor like Dana meets a role she was born to play. We could never write outside her reach, I could never imagine something she couldn't do. When you write something you have hopes for, sometimes you see the final result and you want to put a paper bag over your head. Other times, when you're blessed and lucky, it's beyond deeper, more complex, better than you ever thought it could be and that's what Dana did.**

Broyles's first script embraces the show's feminine tilt with subtle humor by Laurette giving McMurphy a ridiculous bouffant hairstyle to sport throughout the episode as she engages with her female adversary. A female VC attacker is a rare plot point in dramatizations of the Vietnam War, and thus an ideal approach for *China Beach.*

"Home" took on a new meaning when I was walking through a Vietnamese military museum, and I realized American GIs weren't just fighting Vietnamese men in the bush. A wall of black and white pictures showed women as young as teenagers and as old as grandmothers contributing to the communist cause: making weapons, hiding in trees with sniper rifles, entertaining soldiers with theatrics, and nursing soldiers back to health. The image of a tiny Vietnamese woman escorting an American POW with an AK-47 at her hip remains in my mind, staged humiliation or not.

Broyles's ironclad fascination with the Vietnamese opposition brings them from the tree line to arms-length, naked and spread eagle when the Vietcong woman goes into labor. Mother Superior McMurphy has no choice but to deliver the child, with Laurette behind her, cringing. The only dialogue is McMurphy screaming "Push!" between sadistic looks at the VC. Once the baby is delivered, McMurphy scrounges the compassion to let the woman hold her baby. McMurphy doesn't need to explain why she helped the woman, as a telepathic understanding between nurse and audience incubates.

There are long stretches of Broyles's script for *Cast Away* that find Tom Hanks's character trekking around an island alone with little or no dialogue. Words don't illustrate the struggle, and Broyles cedes this space to the actor in hopes they can convey an exchange with the audience through other means. Broyles's script for "Home" succeeds without dialogue in a more restricted space as the final five minutes of the episode tick away. McMurphy is alone, rocking the newborn to sleep. Yards away, we can hear Laurette singing the Four Tops' "Reach Out" to a crowded Jet Set. Both women back in their comfort zones. Sweetness begins struggling for air, and the Vietcong woman slinks out of bed toward him. McMurphy catches the scene out of the corner of her eye, rushing to restrain her until she realizes the woman is giving him CPR. Hatred cartwheels into forgiveness in McMurphy's eyes. The two women exchange a look, communicating with the universal bargaining chip of live and let live. McMurphy accepts the deal and pretends not to notice the woman leaving with her child.

***William Broyles Jr.:* You write it on the page and you set up the sequence and scene and you bring the characters into it and you say, "You're not going to have a word to say. It's gotta all be done by just your inner spirit and how you can reflect**

it in the way you look and feel—and the intensity of your concentration." I would never dream of writing a scene like that without Dana. Her ability, in her exterior appearance, to show the inner life of that character was incredible. We would sit in the room and write scenes, and I remember the first couple of times I was sure of something and she would take a pen and say, "I don't need to say any of this. X, X, X." It was like film school for me.

A few weeks after "Home" aired, Jim Caccavo, a former Vietnam veteran, and Paul Dean, a former war correspondent, tore "Home" apart in an editorial for the *Los Angeles Times*. They were both appalled that McMurphy let the woman escape with her baby. They were of the opinion that Cherry White was belittled as a one-night stand for soldiers, and particularly upset that Purple Hearts were handed out like Halloween candy from a lazy general, worst of all by mistake to the VC assassin. Amazingly, K.C. Koloski caught no flak. Dean and Caccavo have their own versions of Vietnam, and so does Broyles. They were all there, and that's the only thing that matters.

The opening pages of *Brothers in Arms* run in tandem to "Home," offering an unfiltered glimpse of warfare through Broyles's eyes. His platoon comes across an opening to a suspected enemy cave, and no one else wants to sniff it out. Broyles crawls through the pitch-black cranny with a flashlight, a gun, and a handful of C4 explosive. His sixth sense takes over as the underworld opens into a room. A human is sharing the same oxygen with him. Broyles whisper-screams in Vietnamese to get the fuck out of there and lights the fuse before fleeing. Broyles poses the same question in his memoir as he does in his first script: Does mercy come full circle?

The answer is not in "Home," or any other episode of *China Beach*. It is buried in the soil of Vietnam.

A MAN'S MAN'S MAN'S WORLD

So many television series from the *China Beach* era have been resurrected on the small screen, decades removed. *Dallas, Will and Grace, Twin Peaks.* The list goes on. There is money to be made in nostalgia, and nothing is sacred. Everyone else is doing it, which means *China Beach* won't. I kidded John Young over this, and he somewhat seriously said that if the show were to ever come back, he envisioned a network broadcast stage musical with all new characters and stories. I laughed, then realized it made sense. The pilot episode is not a manifesto for any episode that follows, it is the beginning of a grand staff for the series to compose itself within. There is a rhythm to the show, even in long rests of silence. McMurphy and Laurette dancing onstage says as much as Boonie and K.C. staring each other down over a punch bowl.

At the end of "Somewhere Over the Radio," denizens of the Five and Dime gather to send off Dr. Richard on his own R&R to see his wife. In the misty moonlight, they relish in the downtime, each holding a cocktail, singing Smokey Robinson's "The Tracks of My Tears." The jukebox isn't on, it's just their untuned, unaccompanied voices channeling in the air. Under the choir is dead silence, and the inherent risk a mortar might drop. This scene encapsulates the feel of the first season—a hootenanny—a gathering of bodies weaving folk tales into compact, accessible packages for consumption.

The storytelling machine of *China Beach* was never built to subsist on John Young, Bill Broyles, and Rod Holcomb alone. It would take a small platoon of the female sex behind the scenes to bring Colleen McMurphy and company to life on a perpetual basis with unfettered femininity. Young and Broyles knew that roles like McMurphy and K.C. Koloski didn't come around for women every day, and neither did the chance for women to write for such characters. The blacktop for their newborn series was laid, and then Young and Broyles did the craziest thing imaginable. They hired three women screenwriters with no writing credits to their names.

> ***William Broyles, Jr:* That was sort of what I did on *Texas Monthly.* I had no journalistic experience and everybody I hired didn't either. I think what those women brought was a sense of possibility, without any kind of jadedness or cynicism about what you could accomplish. And no careerism, really. They loved the idea of this show. It was really like Mickey Rooney and Judy Garland going out in the garage and saying, "Let's do a show." It worked beyond my wildest hopes, and you just look at those episodes and they feel completely like they could go on the air today, up against any of these great shows that I love watching.**

Thirty years of hindsight reveals that Young and Broyles possessed unearthly intuition. In the years since, over a dozen writers who began their career with *China Beach* ascended the ranks of the television hierarchy to executive producer roles. Regarding this collective success post-*China Beach*, Young joked to me, "At least some of them could let me stay in their guest house."

The first gamble was on Susan Rhinehart, a junior high school teacher working on a PhD, writing historical plays for her students to perform. She penned a script about the Vietnam War called *Goodnight, Saigon* and thought nothing of it until a friend entered her in the UCLA Samuel Goldwyn Writing Awards. Rhinehart won, and immediately joined the company of prior winners like George Lucas and Steven Spielberg. A number of phone calls afterward included Broyles with a job offer. Rhinehart shrugged with a laugh and said, "I don't know how they got me by the network. I had no credentials, nothing, and I'm not that good looking. I wasn't hired to be the pretty girl! I think Bill and I clicked and I made him laugh." Rhinehart is a fiery redhead who pulls no punches in a conversation. A choice ghostwriter for some of K.C. Koloski's greatest hits.

In the opening moments of Rhinehart's first screenplay, "Hot Spell," one can feel the energies that lifted off in the pilot, reaching for the stratosphere. K.C. lies caked in sweat, her mind moving from a turned trick to her next scheme. A sweltering day is made even slower by Lila Garreau's Dinah Shore record, and McMurphy flirts with Natch, pretty much *squatting over a water sprinkler.* Laurette cranks up Martha Reeves and the Vandellas' "Heat Wave" to drown out Lila's forties music, further amplifying these American voices clanging and banging together in a foreign land.

Young and Broyles had followed up on their pitch to ABC of a women's steam bath in the middle of a vast men's locker room by situating the shower stalls in the middle of the base. "Hot Spell" creates another place to congregate when a late-night mortar attack forces all of the women into a bunker. Caught off-guard and off-duty, each woman is augmented by costume design to further establish their personalities: Lila in her mink coat and mud mask, K.C. in business professional attire, Cherry in pajamas and rollers, McMurphy in a helmet and flak jacket, and Laurette in a bath towel.

Rhinehart's dialogue rings true between swigs of brandy from the flask and sing-alongs of the Shirelles' "Mama Said." The women complain about their hips and list off their qualities in an ideal mate, with every word laced with the hope they make it to see daylight. Every time Cherry speaks, it confirms how ignorant she is to the ways of the world. When McMurphy gets a hold of the flask, she takes a few long pulls before passing it on. Lila balks at the tell-all, then shows her sensitive side with a memory of a former flame in World War II.

> ***Concetta Tomei:*** **You could not phone those characters in. I was representing American nurses and it just had to be right. You couldn't be all military and all tough, because that would only have been one note for Lila, so I had to work sometimes opposite what the script said to find the vulnerability. You couldn't associate with someone that was just a tough-ass over and over again unless there was some other color in her personality or texture in her character.**

Women viewers can identify with this pillow talk, and men get a sneak peek at the ladies' night confessional. A mutual, beneficial exchange for all. Each female character was saddled with a stereotype in the pilot, and this is a crucial moment of realization that something far more intriguing than their surface is motivating them to be in Vietnam, placing their lives at risk. And for what?

The following episode, "Somewhere Over the Radio," drags the women out of the bunker and into the middle of the war for the first time. Major Garreau drafts Cherry and Laurette to join her on a trip into the bush to raise the spirits of a platoon, and it all goes awry during a firefight with the enemy. Their helicopter crashes and strands the women alone. Director Rod Holcomb marveled at the sequence: "I said to myself, 'I can't believe we just dropped a fucking gunship on the back lot of Warner Bros.'"

China Beach never shies from going meta, prone to naming characters after crew members and technical advisors, and reframing moments of cinema past. Ann Donahue's first and only script for the show borrows heavily from the plot of Francis Ford Coppola's *Apocalypse Now*, with Lila, Cherry, and Laurette encountering a platoon that takes orders from an unseen captain, later revealed to be an animal skeleton. Dan the Radio Man (David Marciano) sets the standard for an effective guest star by drawing out new emotions from each woman. His shattered mental state hints at a possible destination for Cherry's brother, the simmering mania within Boonie that Laurette is drawn to, and the boys in the bush that Lila never sees. The realizations within each woman are not pronounced, they are tucked in a three-part harmony hiding behind the verse.

With McMurphy and Laurette separated, "Radio" focuses on the circumstances that forge McMurphy's workplace codependency with Dr. Richard when they surgically remove a live round from a patient's body. Director Rod Holcomb foregoes any fancy camera work at the operating table, that he later popularized in the pilot episode of *ER*, instead relying on static shots, slow pushes, and the squish of organs being rearranged in the body cavity. Their mouths obscured by surgical masks, Delany and Picardo do all the acting with their eyes and hands to relay the tension, wiping the perspiration off the other with their elbows. When Dr. Richard wakes up with a bandaged skull from disposing the round, McMurphy treats him like any other wounded soldier as they joke about his burned patch of hair and bask in pregnant pauses.

There is tenderness, trust, and more to this story.

Boonie Lanier is more relatable than the doctor, and Brian Wimmer cracks the sheen of a happy-go-lucky lifeguard in the episode when he bares his soul to Laurette one night on top of the water tower. Mortars fall around them, resembling shooting stars. Boonie speaks about the war like an ex-girlfriend, the one that got away, barely noticing the woman in heat right at his side. Boonie is surfing a wave that will one day crest over his head. Laurette's face searches for a way to get him out of the riptide before it's too late. Every scene between the couple feels raw and instant, informed by a real-life kinship between Wimmer and Chloe Webb. They are both unmoored characters off-screen that bonded during the pilot and headed straight to Utah for skiing and snowmobiling once filming wrapped.

> ***Chloe Webb:*** **I really get energy off of the real world, and everything in nature is flawed. Everything in nature is kind of screwy and every daisy is unique and all that, so it's almost like you have more permission, I feel, to be yourself when you're outside. I think that is a really lovely quality of Wimmer's that he retains to this day. I wonder if it's from the natural world, like, we're so hooked into nature. For him, it's raft trips and fishing in Utah, and for me it's the sky and the animals. Maybe we wouldn't be able to hang onto it if we were sitcom stars where you have to be inside all the time, right? [*laughs*]**

Despite writing a strong outing with "Radio," Donahue was exiled from the show. Years later, she co-created *CSI: Crime Scene Investigation*, the long-running series that made Marg Helgenberger a household name as stripper-turned-crime fighter Catherine Willows. K.C. Koloski remains an impenetrable force throughout the first season. She seems unmoved at the bar when Boonie and Laurette flirt back and forth, and feels no guilt in leading on Cherry with lackadaisical efforts to find her brother. The dots connect between each character in these first eight hours, and K.C. is the outlier, bound to the almighty dollar. Her sole emotional link is to the donut dolly, as decreed in the first rough character sketches as read by John Young:

> *"Pollyanna, a donut dolly come to do good.*
>
> *Irreducibly innocent. Makes the eyes roll. She doesn't understand number one and number two.*
>
> *If she could think anyone bad, they could qualify, ('whatever that means'), yet there are moments her charm is in her intransigent naivety.*
>
> *When all else is turned to shit, her brightness is a buoy to hold on to.*
>
> *A prostitute, she was getting the shit kicked out of her in Toledo, or Kansas City, beat up by her pimp, wanders into Red Cross. Uncle Sam is her pimp now and works right next to Pollyanna."*

China Beach took its share of criticism from viewers and veterans alike over the fabrication of K.C., not to mention a scene of the character driving a red convertible through the dirt roads of Vietnam in "Hot Spell." Bill Broyles insisted the character was based off someone he knew in Danang. They didn't sell sex—they sold Nikon cameras, Illuminated Bibles, and anything else for the right price. Broyles claimed he received numerous complaints, then, a letter from a vet asking, "Hey dude, how did you know about my car?"

Later in 1988, Broyles was in the *Los Angeles Times* sniping back and forth with producers from the other contemporary Vietnam series, *Tour of Duty*, who had accused *China Beach* of being sexist and unrealistic. Broyles fired back, "Our women are much more real as characters than the men of *Tour of Duty*," claiming further, "And as far as our technical details go, I would put them against anything on TV or film."

(TV's '60s: War and Remembrance: 'Tour Boosts Role of Women After Success of Beach, November 30, 1988, Diane Haithman, *Los Angeles Times*)

The first season takes one step back with "Waiting for Beckett," setting a precedent in outing the weaker episodes of the show's four-season run. There are exceptions, but when hours are crafted outside of the usual hive mind of writers and directors, the soul of the show tends to get lost in translation. Terry McDonell's only script and Kevin Hooks's sole directorial effort fall flat with an episode that hardly moves the plot and its characters forward. Michael Boatman and Nan Woods march in place with worthy performances that have no upward lift for either of their characters. The episode is exposed further by the following hour "Brothers," which continues the trials of Beckett and Cherry with more effective storytelling.

"Brothers" marks the debut of another key voice behind the scenes, Carol Flint, who had previously entered a ten-week unpaid internship under John Young. Flint was finishing up a Master of Fine Arts, intent on a career in theater and academia, eager to look over the shoulder of a professional writer. She didn't own a television and didn't buy one until the *China Beach* pilot aired. After interviewing a number of Vietnam veterans for research on the pilot script, Flint was offered a co-writing opportunity with Rhinehart on the episode "Brothers," and eventually penned eighteen more hours and produced the final season. The episode has the advantage of being directed by Young, who knew these characters better than anyone, and was able to juggle them all adroitly.

Jeff Kober: What I learned from watching John was that the voice of a show has to come through the mind of someone. For better or for worse, his stamp was on everything. They used script colors when you have new pages, and they have a whole wheel of colors, and rarely do you get through the wheel once. We went through it _twice_ on some scripts because he kept changing things, and his way of changing things was extraordinary to watch. He changed things by whittling down. Less dialogue was always more powerful, especially for a character like Dodger. The less he said, the more powerful it was when he did speak, and the more powerful his listening became. [John's] writing is enigmatic, and when you have people so committed to bringing a reality to it, the enigma of the dialogue gets filled up with stories that are more universal. The less that is said, the more ability one has to fill in the blanks with their own experience, so it becomes a more powerful emotional experience for anyone who is watching.

The bond between McMurphy and Dr. Richard gets a peek from a new angle when the doctor returns from R&R in Hawaii, dejected that his wife is abandoning underwear and embracing the Sexual Revolution without him. The audience watches from outside the window, prying. Delany's facial expressions reach further into feeling than any dialogue can express, allowing McMurphy to feel rapture without regret for once. She's elated to have him back. Picardo and Delany again sublimate their characters' relationship beyond doctor and nurse, leaving a curious aftertaste.

Cherry's desperation to find her brother Rick leads her into recruiting Dodger to track him down. Jeff Kober's confidence and deadpan demeanor is as convincing as it is amusing: "You should have asked me sooner." Cherry and Dodger are a stark pairing. A glass of lemonade chased by a Guinness, and never is enough. Dodger wasn't forged as a permanent character, and Kober's stellar performance in this episode likely earned his promotion to the main cast in season two. Dodger finds Rick (Fredric Lehne) with ease, tracking him down to a nearby opium den, Cherry and McMurphy at his heels. Rick is hugging a rifle, dazed and confused. He doesn't recognize his own sister and thinks she is a prostitute. In one swift blow, Dodger knocks him out and Cherry is forever sullied.

Young's featuresque cinematography debuts in "Brothers," maximizing the pulsing urban blight of Vietnam as McMurphy and Cherry stalk Dodger, and later capturing a lonely overhead shot of Beckett playing basketball with two fellow black soldiers he is desperate to fit in with. Omar (Glen Plummer) and Fluke (John Marshall Jones) only want to use Beckett and the GRU as a hub for moving drugs back to the states. The army has used them and their race as pawns in the war. Omar and Fluke want to return the favor. Later, a crane shot eases up and out to magnify an expanding field of spent shells, with the peer pressure on Beckett meeting no end. Omar and Fluke ingratiate Beckett, and he struggles to choose between fitting in with the people who look like him and doing the right thing. An individual conflict that still feels relevant in 2018. Undeterred, Beckett rises above and Michael Boatman continues growing into a grounding force of the show.

"Brothers" stands out as the most confident episode so far, a revolving carousel that offers everyone some space to reach outward. Young breaks out his beloved crane shot once more at the end for an elephantine panorama of the ensemble running out to a tank full of wounded soldiers, bringing it all back home. By the end of "Brothers," the first season of *China Beach* is already down to one episode—an encore performance—to close a circle that began in the pilot.

John Young directing "Brothers"

SATISFACTION

The spring of 1988 found the hearts and souls of *China Beach* camped out in the brutal desert of Indian Dunes. It was rustic and uncomfortable. An ideal place to bond. Chloe Webb described it best: "We didn't have trailers, we had 'honey wagons.' They were the size of, like, a small bathroom. Instead of a tub, there was a little bed and a piece of particle board with a mirror. If you were lucky there might be a TV that doesn't work, and a slab of foam that looks like a couch. No one liked being in them, so everyone would sit on the stairs smoking, drinking coffee, and shooting the shit with each other."

As the first season of *China Beach* came to life during long nights and grueling days in the desert, a family unit came together that has remained pat thirty years later. The interpersonal drama of an ensemble cast in a television series seems inevitable, but in the case of *China Beach*, hard work and dedication eclipsed bacchanalia and melodrama. The objective was simple: Make the best six hours of TV humanly possible and hope that the show would come back for another year.

And upgrade from honey wagons.

Dana Delany: **We all felt like we were one, that we were working together. There was certainly no bad behavior at all, and really, no egos that I can remember. If there were, they didn't last long. It was a different time in television because we would shoot twenty-four-hour days. We would see the sun come up, and you loved it. You wanted to be there; you didn't complain, because you felt like you were doing something that mattered. Not to be pretentious, but it just felt like "this is pure" and I don't think you could get away with that these days. It was hard when that was over because you felt like you were giving 100 percent of yourself.**

Marg Helgenberger: Dana worked very hard and had more scenes than any of us. She never complained; she is a trooper, a hard worker. Sometimes we would get re-writes at two or three in the morning, or whatever. I can't even remember if we had a fax machine, it was that long ago! We had one phone. There were no cell phones, just one landline on that Indian Dunes set that worked [*laughs*], and I do remember being on that one landline with John Young at three o'clock in the morning going over rewrites.

William Broyles Jr.: Marg was an absolute joy, and really, her character was one of the least developed that we had. I just knew she had to be in there and she just made it completely her own. She was always incredibly prepared, every right note. It was like having this instrument that you could just write whatever you wanted for it and it would play it the first time. The thing about her and Dana that I loved was they would come to the set and they would never look at themselves in the mirror, ever. If we liked the way they looked, then they were glad.

Jeff Kober: It was all so real, and you know, *China Beach*, it was really like a family, it was one of the best experiences I've ever had, in terms of everyone pulled for everyone else and we did it all together. There were no prima donnas. We all felt it. With actresses like Dana and Marg there, just filling up the space with their own sense of reality and their own sense of commitment to the work, it was in a sense simple to just live that reality.

Robert Picardo: We were legendary among crews. [*laughs*] I made shirts for everybody when we finally wrapped that said, "Let me sleep," and then on the back, "I just wrapped *China Beach*." We were pretty famous for long hours, especially in the early episodes. We literally had one twenty-four-hour work day.

Brian Wimmer: We were at Indian Dunes and it would be snowing and I would be in shorts! We had a scene where everybody is in a swimming pool, and we arrived on set and there was three inches of snow on the ground. The problem was that you would breathe and steam would come out of your mouth, so we had to suck on ice cubes to keep our breath from venting out like that. The hardest thing to do in the world is acting when you're cold because you're so tense.

The shooting would go into the next day. Oftentimes I'd find myself coming home from work at the crack of dawn while traffic is going the other way and I'm just getting off work. This is TV? This isn't TV. We had feature-film people coming on board going, "I've only shot a few features that take this much time."

Marg Helgenberger: The stories that we told were based on real stories that we brought to life, and with every episode we felt so compelled to get it right, to tell these stories with the right amount of compassion and truth and vulnerability. When you have that as your basis for the thrust of the show, it's amazing. With some shows, it's just "let's move on, let's go" and they're more kind of masculine and fast-paced—and this show took its time. You felt awarded, like, "Wow, I got this great gig and it just keeps getting better," and it did.

Michael Boatman: I looked forward to being at work with everyone. There was a lot of laughter, and over the course of a four-year series, you go through events in other people's lives. You meet their children; sometimes you meet their parents, their spouses, their ex-spouses or the person they left their spouse for. All sorts of things, so we really bonded.

Concetta Tomei: We didn't want to leave any stone unturned and John Young and Bill Broyles and all the writers worked hard in helping those actors just get to those places they needed to be and that's how lucky it was. It's like having Shakespeare; it's all done for you if you just let it go and get out of your own way and let that writing and those words and those moments inform you. Then you're home free, then you really have nothing to do with acting—it has do with being and living—and hopefully you've done your job well enough that it's believable.

William Broyles Jr.: We would sit around as writers and say, "Okay, who can write a scene with the fewest words of dialogue? Okay, who can write a scene with only the words yes and no? And now, who can write a scene using only the words yes and no, and yes has to mean no?" [*laughs*] Things like that, as writers, you could do because you had this cast that could do anything.

Jeff Kober: With acting, you can work your ass off to make shit up or you can just be real, and the cost is you go through the emotional life of the character. The payoff is that you get to go through the emotional life of the character and they get to capture it on camera. That's a gift for the actor, that's a gift for people watching it, and to really underscore it with what I believe everyone was committed to. It was a gift and a thank-you to the men and women who were in the experience themselves. No one was going to phone it in because this is an experience that so many of our veterans and the USO and nurses had. To not play it for real felt too cheap to even consider.

Chloe Webb: It changed you and you were a bigger and better version of yourself. Even as actors, the situation made us *not* competitive and weird. The situations and the people we were playing made us into an ensemble that would literally take a bullet for each other. It feels pretty real to me all this time later. Every day, at least when I was there, there was no bullshit, really. No infighting, people bored, "we're not curing cancer." I know everybody was really young, but it had this psyched feeling. You were just psyched to be there, psyched to do it, to try anything.

Brian Wimmer: We would be in the middle of this insane scene where people have no legs, stuff being blown up and shit everywhere, people covered in blood, and these guys at lunch would be laughing and telling jokes and singing; it would become like a Broadway musical. Every lunch was like that, and this is where I was just in awe of all my coworkers. That was so not me, I just sat back, and it was the greatest ride. Picardo seemed to be the center of that energy. He could sing, he could dance, had amazing comedic timing, and he could

whip the place up into a frenzy. People would come from the studio to have lunch on the *China Beach* set because of the entertainment.

When *China Beach* made it to air in April of 1988, it was an instant critical success, maintaining a modest following with consistent ratings, if never riding the top of the TV zeitgeist in its 9PM Wednesday time slot. By the time all eight hours of the first season aired, the show received a second season from ABC and garnered multiple Emmy awards and nominations, Golden Globes, and national media attention. The ensemble that formed only months prior had made a joint trip from working actors to bona fide stars.

Dana Delany: **Here is a perfect example of when it was so clear that television was changing, because I was in Cannes in France at the film festival and I was there with *Patty Hearst*, which I had been filming while I was doing *China Beach*. I was at a few parties and people kept coming up to me and talking to me about *China Beach*. I think it had just premiered, and I said, "What? Why are you talking to me about that TV show? I'm here with a Paul Schrader movie!" and they kept wanting to talk about it. That's when I realized it really made an impression, and I was really surprised by that. I remember Mike Figgis was there, he wanted to talk about it. Roger Ebert was there, he wanted to talk about it, and I thought, "Okay, maybe there is something in this television show." I realized it was different.**

Robert Picardo: **Right before *China Beach* was the era of the nighttime soap opera—*Dallas*, *Falcon Crest*, all of that stuff in the early mid-eighties, and that was an unfortunate time for me. That kind of acting and that kind of material is something that has never spoken to me. Sure enough, I never appeared on *Knotts Landing*, nor would I have thought necessarily I was going to be in a war drama. That was a very heady time for me, to be playing a character role on *The Wonder Years* on Tuesdays at eight o'clock and then a dramatic leading role on Wednesdays at ten o'clock on the same network. I went from bald, goofy character guy one night to a well-quaffed leading man in a drama the next night. That was a dream to have that.**

Concetta Tomei: It was a life-altering experience. I flew around the United States a lot to pick up awards. They would send me because Dana was always working those hours, and if I had a free day off they would just send me on a weekend; she needed those weekends to rest. I'd go to Atlanta and I'd pick up an award with the nurses and with veterans and they always said that this was the show that helped them to heal. We all knew that this mattered a lot, that this was a huge responsibility, and I think all of us took it very seriously.

Brian Wimmer: I didn't really get it. I didn't know how the machinery worked, that's how much of a rookie I was. I didn't understand the whole fame thing and nor was I really interested in that. The second I got any time off, I would fly back home to Utah and hang out with the same buddies I always hung out with, and there was not much pep up about it. I would go to these award ceremonies and they were really stupid. They seemed so fake, like, everybody clapping for themselves? It seemed so vain. It wasn't until later that I kind

The cast and crew celebrating the tenth anniversary of China Beach

of caught on: "Man! I could have done something with that!" [*laughs*] I wasn't really expecting to do all that, it was just something I was checking out.

Chloe Webb: I've been nominated for stuff, but it's always as a guest star. I'm always the bride and never the bridesmaid in real life, but for some reason I'm always the guest star. The guest star award was on a different day—not the real Emmys, like the night before—and it's old school, more like the Golden Globes. Everybody's just at tables, there's no cameras, people are getting toasted, and it's definitely the funner one. [*laughs*]

By that point I was sure I was on another job, so I just remember borrowing a dress and showing up. I wasn't real well-versed in what was happening. I was like, "For sure, [Teresa Wright] is going to win, right?" and then some person I never heard of before or since won over both of us, and she came up and she was just like, "I was so sure you were going to win," and I was like, "I was so sure *you* were going to win!" The thing is, it gave me the proper attitude toward awards forever. [*laughs*] You know, you just can't get too wrapped up in it.

Kober, Wimmer and Webb reunited

Michael Boatman: I've done a lot of comedy since *China Beach* and it's great to make people laugh, but it's really great to touch people's hearts and make them think and see beyond politics and beyond whatever your stance on war is. These were human stories, and they're still happening. Are we going to be a society that honors these sacrifices that people make? I think *China Beach* helped bring that home for a generation of people (like me) for whom the war was just something that happened a long time ago. We talked about a really unpleasant time in American history, and yet humanized it, and made people feel they could understand it from a human standpoint as compared to a political one.

Jeff Kober: We were all very proud, we were all very thrilled, and I think I speak for everyone, or at least nearly everyone, that what really mattered was that veterans would come up to us on the street and say, "You got it right." Whatever awards were given, that was still the best review. I might say this differently if I had received an Emmy, [*laughs*] but the only review that counted was the veterans'.

UP, UP, AND AWAY

As a child of the eighties, I remember Chloe Webb's work in comedies like *Ghostbusters 2* (1989) and *Twins* (1988), where she holds court with luminaries like Bill Murray and Danny DeVito. She carried a childlike disposition, full of idiosyncratic zest. She was a grown-up I wouldn't have minded hanging out with. Her voice, her eyes, and her screen presence were as quirky as they were memorable. It was a revelation to explore the dramatic depths of Webb's work in *China Beach* and *Sid and Nancy* as an adult—no longer was she the eccentric character actor popping in for a cameo—she was top billing as an Andy Warhol portrait come to life.

Much like her character on *China Beach*, Webb can't be pinned down or categorized, nor is she content to remain in one place too long. Time is always fleeting with her, making each second of her company and presence more precious. Eight hours of Webb portraying a scrappy lounge singer from Paoli, PA, in *China Beach* isn't enough, and neither was any amount of time I spent on the phone with her.

An hour into our first conversation, I began sweating in my seat, realizing I would not be able to cover half of the questions I wanted to ask her. It had taken over a year of convincing and the behest of John Young to get her to talk to me. It was clear interviews were neither a custom nor a priority for her, but she was personable, tangential, and above all, disarming. Many of my pointed questions about *China Beach* were turned around for me to answer, or Webb would talk about her love for animals, nature, or her work as a licensed equine therapist for veterans suffering post-traumatic stress disorder (PTSD) through saveawarrior.org.

It took another six months to get ahold of her again and ask the rest of my questions.

Webb's aura commandeers a good portion of the first season, even supplanting Colleen McMurphy into the number-two slot at times. I gather that no one expected this development, nor did anyone complain. The only way to quell this maelstrom of a woman was to give her character laryngitis in "Brothers," and she still manages to steal the show when she lip-syncs to a warped tape of chipmunk vocals and demonic growls during an audition. Laurette is a dashing comet lighting up the night for everyone around her, and the first season finale, "Chao Ong," watches her cruise on to the next galaxy.

"Chao Ong" forms one big wall of sound with Young's plotting, Bill Broyles' dialogue, and director Christopher Leitch's finishing touches. The first season finale dials into what has worked best in the series so far by surrendering the stage to McMurphy and Laurette and letting them do their thing. Both women have sensual appetites that they can't whet with their respective beaus. Living quarters are cramped, so they run to the beach for another brand of self-amusement. Laurette strips her clothes off and darts into the ocean, tossing her bikini at a giggling McMurphy.

McMurphy's laughter recoils as she fails to lift her shirt over her stomach. All of the tension settles into her loins, her shoulders, and her jawline, while the same repression is beaming out of Laurette's every orifice. Dana Delany's face prods the viewer to wonder what dispatch the Vietnam War is hissing in her ear. John Young read me his early notes for the lead character in *China Beach*, and McMurphy was shackled before she even had a name.

"Nurse evac, likely Irish-Catholic.

Full-blooded, 360-degree emotions after work. Doesn't go into a corner. Goes out with the guys, drinks.

Her privacy is rigidly selective. Her emotions come out. Her inside is her outside except for that way deep down wall where she has learned almost perfectly to hide behind."

The crude work-up of Laurette is more uncertain, still spanning the skinny-dipping divide.

"Betty, USO.

A gorgeous, overwrought hunk, a middler straight from the Holiday Inn.

She thinks she's great. She's not, but she is here. She's a rebel, an early protestor, but one without portfolio. She overthrows herself into everything 100 percent.

Raucous, perhaps black?"

McMurphy finally quenches her libidinous drought when a fit of passion with Natch turns into a soiree. Through clever editing and conversation, *China Beach* slipped a sexual marathon past network censors and lived to tell the story. The script for "Chao Ong" left director Christopher Leitch with even more room to get creative. He was intent on capturing the cost of life from the war that he saw on the six o'clock news in the sixties. There would be more blood, more guts, and more slaughter. There would be Nancy Sinatra. Leitch spotted a vague scene in the script titled "USO Show" and was determined to draft performers who had once toured through Vietnam entertaining troops. Comedian Johnny Grant appears to crack some jokes, and Sinatra performs her number 1 hit feminist anthem "Boots," looking hardly a day older than she did twenty years prior.

***Chloe Webb:* I was so gobsmacked to even talk to Nancy Sinatra because I remember watching her, [*sings*] "These boots were made for walkin'," and just how cool that was. I was completely starstruck, and then she starts talking about taking her kids to see *Sid and Nancy.* Oh my gosh, she was the coolest. It was one of those moments. I just think that actually standing behind her in the white boots was pretty much like a career high [*laughs*] just because it was just so cool. I know the word cool is overused, but she was the coolest. That was pretty cool.**

Laurette's exit is built around bum-rushing the USO tour when it passes through *China Beach*. Laurette angles for fame at the side of the stage, unable to climb over the wall of showbiz on her own. Her options dwindle to a prodigal return to Paoli. Laurette's dilemma matches Webb's offstage situation at the time—both women following their instincts, conflicted about letting go of a good thing. Webb couldn't bring herself to watch the show after her departure, and claimed she is now slowly catching up with the DVD release.

"Chao Ong" brings all the women together at the Jet Set for some drinks to take the edge off. Laurette is undeterred, intent on opening a salon when she gets back to the States. McMurphy needs a drink after losing a corpse (which is explained away later) and Cherry's disillusion over her brother hangs in the air. They down beers and razz Dr. Richard to the tune of Martha Reeves and the Vandellas' "Nowhere to Run." For a second, Vietnam doesn't seem so bad.

Happy endings are hard to come by in *China Beach*, but McMurphy convinces Johnny Grant to give Laurette a spot on the USO tour. One too many goodbyes pile up, then certitude settles in as Laurette and McMurphy ponder their separating paths at the beach and sing "The Letter" by the Box Tops. Who will the Lone Ranger be without Tonto? Laurette offers one wish, for McMurphy to keep taking chances. There was a tight window of storytelling opportunities with Laurette, and K.C. Koloski feels like a missed connection. One prior meeting between the two in "Brothers" has Laurette muted with laryngitis, and a final kiss-off between them in "Chao Ong" hints at a dream team that could have been.

***Chloe Webb:* Both Marg and me turn up in the same dress, and I just thought it was the funniest fucking thing ever. We started really laughing and then we were kind of hugging because I was leaving, and they were like, "Stop! Stop! Don't do this! We're not on camera yet!" As if we're going to run out of feelings for each other. Towards the end, Boonie was double-timing us and that wasn't really a problem. I really like that last scene, where it's a certain kind of, "We're bigger than that little catty shit." [*laughs*]**

As Boonie and McMurphy escort Laurette to her helicopter goodbye, their jeep breaks down and they seek refuge at an orphanage. Leitch wanted to pack as much meaning and emotion into Laurette's farewell as he could and revisited an intersection of his own life and the aftermath of the Vietnam War to frame the character's send-off.

***Christopher Leitch:* After film school, I was traveling with the National Endowment of the Arts and teaching elementary school kids Super 8 filmmaking in Gulfport, Mississippi. I had every kid make a little movie. One of the girls wanted to make a documentary about her dad and where he worked, which I thought was lovely. I had no idea where he worked, but I went**

with the kids to film it, and he made wooden prosthetics for returning Vietnam vets; his place of business was right outside the big military base. The entire shop was lined up with all these limbs hanging from the ceiling everywhere. A soldier sitting there, some nineteen-year-old boy.

In those days, they didn't have high-tech material. All prosthetics were made out of wood and hand-crafted, and that's what this man did. And the kicker: he was deaf, so his daughter had to speak to him in sign language! This had a profound effect on me at the moment, so when I saw this in the script, I really wanted to try and recreate that: the fog of war, the consequences of war to the refugees, the innocent, and everything. I wanted Chloe to walk into the set, not knowing what to see, so that she could experience these kids and the consequences of stepping on landmines and being shot at.

Laurette, McMurphy, and Boonie sit in the room, holding orphans in their lap, putting off a final goodbye. *China Beach* began with the nurse and the lifeguard on a beach—two lonely shepherds—soon to be touched by a guardian angel. Laurette brightens up the first season, and more importantly, the two people who needed her the most. When silence and dialogue run their course in *China Beach*, music takes over, and Laurette ekes out the words to the Beatles' "With a Little Help from My Friends." Laurette flew into Vietnam thinking that she wanted fame and fortune, and every following scene proves she just wanted somebody to love. Somebody to love her back. Laurette grew up an orphan, and here, she holds a little Vietnamese version of herself in her lap, before chasing down her destiny. Her voice quivers through the verse, unable to finish the song. Boonie makes his peace with misty eyes and a warm smile: "Chao ong."

The keys of John Rubenstein's theme hit, and it is about as warm and fuzzy as *China Beach* will ever get.

***Chloe Webb:* I remember asking the little kids that were there if anyone was an orphan, and what did they think it would be like being an orphan. I wanted to think about the kids' perspective: "What would it be like to be the kid?" because you're still playing the scene with another actor; you're not**

just singing to an extra. I don't like to think of it like that. I remember this little girl said, "That I wasn't forgotten," and that just moved me so deeply. It moves me now, thinking about it. I think that I personally was sad to be leaving all my friends and everything, and just that feeling that people do forget you, they do. The idea of trying to sear into someone's mind that there will always be someone for you—it might not be me, but there'll always be someone—is a thrill.

Goodbyes are ruthless in *China Beach*, and once Laurette Barber is gone, she's never heard from nor spoken of again. Webb's departure from *China Beach* was contracted from day one, and she surmises that if an offer was ever made to return to the show, it never made it through her constant turnover in agents. A string of her free-spirited representatives were prone to join the Peace Corps or up and move to a third world country. Plenty of opportunities to bring Laurette back over the course of the series are left unfulfilled, and Laurette's fate is left to the imagination. John Young said the truth of Irish storytelling would find Laurette back at the Holiday Inn, while Webb prognosticated that Laurette is now living in Africa on a micro-loan, helping needy women monetize beaded bracelets and basket weaving.

Dana Delany: **Chloe did not return, which is shocking when I think about that. She was such a huge part of the show. It changed the dynamic, definitely because she is such a force. I remember Bill Broyles saying to me, "How do you feel that Chloe's not back?" and I said, "Well, It's different, that's for sure. In some ways…it's calmer," [*laughs*] It just took a different tone, that's all, and I think that's when McMurphy came more to the forefront.**

At the end of "Chao Ong," McMurphy is right back where she started from, at the beach, alone. Everything is different. It is dusk, and McMurphy is standing, studying the fine line where the ocean meets the sky. She isn't buried in a book, trying to escape her reality. She is embracing it. McMurphy peels off her clothes, garment by garment, and walks into the tide, ready for whatever it may bring.

The rhythm of silence resurfaces in Laurette's place, and it is deafening.

II

One morning, I was sitting in the lobby of the Hanoi Opera Hilton, people watching, taking it all in. Bonnie Raitt and Jim Croce propelled a string of roots and rock through the spacious plaza. A television show had brought me to this unlikely place, yet the Vietnam War was the only thing on my mind. I was excited to visit another Hanoi Hilton later that day, an infamous prison where American POWs, including Senator John McCain, were held captive for years on end during the war. I homed in on an aging American couple headed out the door with a tour guide. He was a vet coming back to see the country he once fought in fifty years ago.

I listened to "I Can't Make You Love Me," and an unsettling feeling was at odds with Bruce Hornsby's piano. That gorgeous piece of unadulterated Americana was destined to play in that room at that moment, whether or not that vet or my country had ever stepped foot in Vietnam.

The *other* Hanoi Hilton looks like hell on earth. The Hỏa Lò Prison was inherited from the French occupation and put straight to use during the Vietnam War. Now, it's a trophy on the mantle of a proud totalitarian government, open for daily tours. I didn't like standing in those dank, black cells for even a moment, and I shuddered at the thought of the years that some people have spent there. Prisoners could breathe the same air as the city dwellers and see a glimpse of daylight through small windows barred with steel, a solace as much of a scourge.

Former American occupants are advertised on banners in an outdoor courtyard, and Senator McCain is the centerpiece, not to mention a returning visitor every few years. I turned and saw another set of banners displaying a timeline of America and Vietnam making diplomatic amends, presidents 42-44 smiling and shaking hands with Vietnamese leaders. It was all a surreal sight, the mathematics of time and politics not quite adding up.

Later that day, my wife and I were in a cab with a particularly chatty driver. We mentioned we had been to the prison, and he exclaimed, "John McCain!" He described how McCain had been shot down over Hanoi once upon a time, crashing into a pond he couldn't swim in, punctuating every sentence with, "John McCain, he very lucky." His version continued, describing how the Vietnamese saved McCain's life by pulling him out of the water. The cabbie kept repeating, "He very lucky." I thought about how McCain stayed in that shit hole "Hilton" for five-plus years afterward. Torture, starvation, interrogations, forced statements for propaganda. I suppressed an uncomfortable, dismissive laugh.

Some luck.

My wife and I kept repeating the words "very lucky" to each other, half joking, half realizing it wasn't Vietnamese spin. The cabbie was right. McCain was lucky the crash didn't kill him. Lucky he didn't drown. Lucky he made it home. Many would kill for his luck. It's not for me to say what the veteran in the lobby or Senator McCain got out of returning to Vietnam, but I know what I did. Perspective.

In the following days and weeks and months, I found more reasons to believe we are all very lucky.

YEAR OF THE MONKEY

THE BEAT GOES ON

Paul's Boutique. Pinkerton. De La Soul is Dead. Many of my favorite records are those second statements from artists where they reach into a lower register, sacrificing the formula that made them. The opening hours of *China Beach*'s sophomore year pack away much of the preceding humor, sequins, and Motown 45s. In their place are crisp, unmarked boxes to cut open. The second season would either succeed on its own terms or die trying, both fates beating obsoletion. It was an act of rebellion to shift moods with the audience, and *China Beach* was no rock band, but a spoke in the wheel of a broadcast network that could be replaced after a few duds.

As Laurette Barber would say, "Let 'er rip."

"Men, women, love, sex...what's it all about?" Dr. Dick Richard asks in the opening seconds of the two-part premiere, "Lost and Found." Daylight fills an empty medical ward, and a rolling dolly shot creaks over the floor tiles to find this year's model of McMurphy playing dead, sweating and slumbering on a gurney. Too tired to make it to the beach with a book.

McMurphy's power nap is cut short as Dr. Richard plays recordings from home and brags about his sons who are learning to flush toilets and play football. The sound of an approaching Huey outside interrupts their ritual of bickering. Just like the opening moments of the pilot, the doors are blown open by the thunder of the rotors. McMurphy is not alone this time. Dr. Richard stands by her side, and the space between them will be a central theme of this new season of *China Beach*.

In the summer of 1988, *China Beach* was in a creative vacuum and required more stories, more characters, more everything to fulfill a lease on life of seventeen episodes, but not until a six-month Writer's Guild of America strike came to an end that August. John Young and

Bill Broyles hurriedly cowrote "Lost and Found" to expedite production, and the two-part episode was scripted, prepped, filmed, and cut together in just over one-hundred days for a late-November airing. Directed by Young, "Lost and Found" portends a season of devastation while rebranding the show as a slower, more deliberate rhapsody than its predecessor. 1967 is winding down, and the coming new year is a trojan horse loaded with bloodshed, rigged to pour down in sheets on Vietnam.

This minor key change is just a sign o' the times.

"Lost and Found" is a sad bastard ballad that demands repeat listenings to sink in. It's gloomy, draining, and strung together with Young's sparse dialogue and distinct imagery. Young loves to shoot scenes through windows, including an extra frame in every episode he directed. When Young peers through an opening, it implies a more intimate look at something we viewers shouldn't be present for. For the voyeur, observing confidential conversations and body language is as gratifying as it is unjust. Our judgment and fascination of the specimen is magnified nonetheless. Young has written extensively in his memoirs about one particular window from his New England youth. When playing tennis with his siblings and his cousins, his father was a shaded figure on the other side of the glass, downing drinks and building critiques of their performance. The longer the match, the more painful post-game analysis.

The watcher in the window holds power.

Young's camera sits outside McMurphy's window in surveillance. Laurette left a gaping hole within our nurse's intramural realm, and we observe Natch Austin fall in backwards, kicking and screaming. Natch was first inspired by the magnetic, thrill-seeking spirit of Bill Broyles, and McMurphy is head-over-heels trying to wrangle him. Natch has been grounded from flying after a psychological evaluation, and now he is another one of the boys McMurphy can fix. Natch's smooth lines evaporate and he writes off their dalliance as a sortie, graduating McMurphy's attraction to an obsession when he returns to his station.

Licensing music was the biggest hurdle to *China Beach*'s home video release, with a tiny fraction of songs replaced by similar soundalikes. "Lost and Found, Part 1" is the victim of the most significant edit to the series on DVD, wiping out an entire scene due to a creative impasse. Struck from the digital record is Dr. Richard speak-singing the chorus of the Beatles' "Hey Jude" as he escorts McMurphy to a helicopter en route to surprise Natch with a visit. The Beatles' catalog is notoriously expensive to license, and the condescending tone of Dr. Richard wasn't palatable to the rights holders, ultimately terminating the sequence.

McMurphy is taken aback by Natch's indifference when she shows up at his door, and they continue pedaling a cycle of almost breaking up and making up. Young recalled emulating George Stevens's giant close-ups of Elizabeth Taylor and Montgomery Clift in *A Place in the Sun* (1951), barely shading half of Tim Ryan's face as McMurphy and Natch lie on the bed, sorting out their wants and needs. McMurphy later awakens from their rendezvous to find Natch's wedding portrait tucked away in his belongings.

Dana Delany has steered McMurphy through an emotional rollercoaster so far with brilliance, and here comes the free-fall. McMurphy scorned by a lover. This betrayal prompts the nurse to explode at Natch. Her eyes stab like daggers and the insults drip off her lips in a key moment affirming Delany's ownership of the character. Now, the pilot's face is a half moon, the veneer of a divided man claiming he has already asked for a divorce from his wife. McMurphy flees back to China Beach to get lost in her other affairs: work and alcohol.

McMurphy isn't the only one treading water in the new season. Dr. Richard's marriage is fading by the day, and a visiting commander is pressuring Lila Garreau to clean up the base and expel those without an official purpose. The bureaucratic BS trickles down to K.C. Koloski when Major Garreau delivers an eviction notice, revisiting their own version of the ruling class against the bourgeoisie. K.C. isn't standing in a doorway smoking this time, she's between outfits in her underwear, openly challenging the major. Oh, and a war is going on in the background.

"Lost and Found, Part 1" crawls and plods, then ends on an uncharacteristic cliffhanger for the show when Dr. Richard informs McMurphy that Natch has gone missing during a mission. A roof of anger and resentment collapses into her own house. The first hour of the new season has room for improvement in its excruciating pacing and receives a mulligan for a production short on time to recalibrate.

The disappearance of Natch strangely coincides with an exit of sorts for the character's muse behind the scenes. Bill Broyles offered his final *China Beach* writing credit with "Lost and Found," holding the vague title of executive consultant for the remainder of the series. The cast and crew recalled Broyles's presence from this point on as sporadic at most, while his presence loomed over the proceedings with significance, if distance, from then on. Broyles began work on *Under Cover* (1991), another ABC series that was co-created with Young, to seek some autonomy and a platform to prove himself. As the storytelling devices become more elaborate and exciting over the course of the series, one must wonder what the co-creator's voice and sensibilities would have offered to the rest of the canon.

William Broyles Jr.: **I've asked myself [why I stopped writing for *China Beach*] often, because I was so proud of it. I think I was just interested in doing something on my own, and it took me a long time to do anything that was remotely as important to me as that was. Often, I wish I had just stayed with the show because it was an opportunity to do something amazing, and at that point, film was at the top of the food chain. Only when you look back do you realize that there's nothing in film that's as good as this, so I regret not staying with it longer. I wish I had. I wish I had, because I love all those people. I started a magazine called *Texas Monthly* back in the seventies, and those are the things I'm most proud of—and I left that too. I'm kind of a nomad.**

John Sacret Young: **[Bill] wasn't a guy that was in the trenches of the 24/7, he was sort of a leader who came in spectacularly at specific times. He was an officer. We were grunts, in a way. We get along famously, but how often do we see each other? It's been, I don't know. We really like each other, we really respect each other, but there's a certain savviness: "Guess what? I'm on my path and you're on your path."**

"Lost and Found, Part 2" further cracks the funhouse mirror that the Vietnam War was reflecting off during the first season. Personalities aren't dilated, they are drawn and quartered.

McMurphy returns to Natch's room in search of catharsis, only to face the other woman—the wife—Maggie (Jana Marie Hupp). The lighting in the room is careful to cast no shadow upon this wholesome, curvy blonde with nothing to hide, employed at a grocery store. McMurphy's face conveys a mortal wound—Natch had sought out a woman who was nothing like his wife. Maggie corroborates Natch's claim that he has asked for a divorce, only to flog McMurphy's mindset further and collect more sympathy for each woman. The nurse bites her lip as she hugs the crying woman she has cuckolded.

The Jet Set offers McMurphy sanctuary, and she assumes her position on a barstool. Young stages the isolation and intrigue of a living and breathing Edward Hopper painting. Bottle and glass at hand, the nurse is a stone gargoyle merging with the smoky bar lights. Innocent of malice, except towards herself. McMurphy isn't drinking, she is swallowing the fermented poison by the mouthful. The liquid vaporizes through her pores and into the room's atmosphere, at odds with the Righteous Brothers' hopeful analog undercurrent emitting from the jukebox.

We pity the fool who interrupts McMurphy, and Dick Richard enters with a bag of golf clubs.

This scene is a twisted take-two of the pair's first argument at the bar from the pilot, akin to a song on a live album that's louder and drunker than the studio version. Fury builds in the room as the camera inches closer to Dr. Richard's face, as he compares the trials of life to the breaks on a par five. McMurphy snaps. She breaks his 3 wood over the bar and screams, "I can't drink it away, and you can't golf it away." McMurphy reserves a special brand of anger to take out on the one person closest to her. The person who will forgive and forget an outburst. An exercise of next-level intimacy.

***Geno Escarrega** (co-producer, "Lost and Found"):* **I was on the set and it was heart breaking. Watching that performance, you literally felt she was having a breakdown. It was amazing. When they said "cut," I was behind the camera, and I'm thinking, "Oh my God, this is hard to watch," and Dana looked over and kind of smiled and winked. It sent chills down my spine.**

Ten hours deep into the series, the viewer has been able to form a private bond with McMurphy by observing her work, her relationship patterns, and her ballooning dependence on alcohol. The buzz of Laurette's providence is wearing off, and McMurphy is self-medicating after every shift and any crisis. *China Beach* allows the audience to decide when McMurphy's dumb pride and reckless behavior goes too far. Then, she keeps going.

"Lost and Found" continues to give and take from the nurse. Dodger is found face down in a creek the next morning, on the verge of death. During a blood-soaked surgery, McMurphy and Dr. Richard lose Dodger's pulse on the operating table, and McMurphy massages his heart back to life. To break the tension, a crew member hid under the table to grab Delany's hand on a false take. McMurphy's momentary joy in saving Dodger is interrupted by a tsunami of wounded soldiers flooding into the ward, as Lila, Cherry, and Boonie do all they can to stifle the onslaught. The keys of John Rubenstein's theme sneak up, and McMurphy stands in the middle of the storm to collect herself before changing into a fresh pair of gloves.

***Jeff Kober:* The question I was asked more than any other question when I would travel around during the *China Beach* years (and after) was, "What's Dana Delany like?" She's a diamond. The scene that I remember most is the scene where she finds Dodger and he's all shot up and collapsed before he was able to make it back into the compound. She screams for help and she's just so completely *there*. It was amazing to me to watch her work and to be present with her.**

Dana and I traveled to Vietnam during the Writer's Strike in '88 because the production was held back. It was thirty days after Vietnam opened to tourism. We flew there for a ten-day tour. She's an adventurous woman with a huge heart, and I'd do anything with her at any time. I love Dana to death. And working with her, it was *easy*. She's willing to throw herself into it and go wherever the scene takes you, and that's the way I like to work. There's no planning it out, there's just doing it.

Dana Delany: I remember there was an earthquake in California when we were shooting the show. I was living in Venice in this little apartment on the beach and I was so into my character. [_laughs_] I think it was the middle of the night and all the lights were out. There was no power, and I walked out into the hallway and I said to everyone, "Okay everybody, it's going to be fine, be calm," as I'm helping people out to the sidewalk. And you know, you just get into it, you start believing it all. I still feel like I could save somebody if I needed to.

John Sacret Young: In terms of Dana, we psychologically and emotionally had a connection that was a little like the character. It was often without words, or with very few words. You could say, "Well, you're going to move from this room and pick up the glasses and think about throwing them out the window," and she would make it her own. She would carry an emotion in every half step and moment.

Kober and Delany visit Vietnam

> ***Dana Delany:*** **[John] and I got to work at such a level, sometimes he wouldn't even talk. He would look at me and give me a gesture. His hand would go "less," which I always appreciated. His direction was always, "Go deeper, dig deeper." He'd say that to the actors, he'd say that to the writers, and I think that's a really good direction. We always have more depth in us.**

Another day at the office sends McMurphy to a last resort of prayer at the empty church K.C. has evacuated. The show's credits remind us at the dawn of each episode that McMurphy clings to her faith in one hand and a bottle in the other. Laurette is no longer around to draw McMurphy from outside of herself, and Natch has betrayed and deserted her. McMurphy's faith and community are on the edge of an abyss, threatened to be consumed whole. The final moments of "Lost and Found, Part 2" are her Hail Mary of desperation.

Young returns to the same window shot from the first part to observe a small act sparking a violent period of Darwinism in the show. McMurphy's guilt over Natch can't be drunken away, so she confides in the one person who won't judge her. K.C. Koloski. The two women from opposing sides of the tracks have hardly spoken in the series so far, and here they take one enticing step toward the other. Somewhere in the shame of marital infidelity, K.C. scrounges a grin from McMurphy. Our nurse inches further toward the light at the end of the episode, sitting at Dodger's bedside, holding his hand. Dodger squeezes back, and it is all that McMurphy needs to keep hanging on. The episode ends on McMurphy's smile, the lone beacon in a stormy bay.

"Isn't that final image, in a sense, what the show is all about?" remarked Young.

"Lost and Found" is protracted and draining throughout its two parts, unapologetic in its quarter-time rhythm, dominated by droning, sustained whole notes. This continuation of *China Beach* isn't a warm welcome into a new season—it is an ultimatum to either climb down in the foxhole or go back to the world.

Opposite page: Delany taking in the real China Beach

DO YOU LOVE ME

The second season of *China Beach* unfurls, and a tonal change is expounded by an influx of new faces onscreen. The show was rarely content to repeat itself and wasn't about to replace Laurette Barber with another ol' USO singer. Personalities cycled in and out of Vietnam on an annual basis as politics and attitudes evolved, and true to life, *China Beach* was no different. The first season builds a physical and emotional fortress for McMurphy and company, and the second season pours foreign entities into the moat that surrounds. Only the worthy will scale the wall and join the knighthood.

Each new season of *China Beach* is demarcated by a special guest star, and an eventful 1968 in Vietnam calls for a journalist to document the mayhem. Portrayed by Megan Gallagher, Airman Wayloo Marie Holmes is a Texan weather girl from the Armed Forces Network, looking to transition into broadcast journalism. She is a plucky brunette bombshell sticking a microphone and a camera in everyone's face, aiming to package their story into her resume. The Vietnam War marked a time when many female journalists trekked into the heart of combat on their own dime, their reporting often at odds with government spin and a military that feared being undermined. The character of a female journalist in Vietnam was ripe with promise.

Making her debut in "Lost and Found," Wayloo is stonewalled by everyone except Dr. Richard, who consents to an interview after pulling a piece of shrapnel out of Wayloo's posterior. Gallagher and Robert Picardo hit it off on day one and remain close friends thirty years later. The pair introduce their characters with amusing back-and-forth and innuendo that vanishes when Wayloo joins McMurphy and K.C. in the shower stall. *China Beach* can be considered a high-stakes poker game of personality, and most of the second season feels like

Gallagher, Picardo, and Mimi Leder filming "Crossing the Great Water"

Wayloo is out of her chair peeking at cards instead of surveying the room and reading body language.

> ***John Sacret Young:* Our problem with Megan Gallagher wasn't Megan Gallagher. It's very difficult to write for reporters and to have them be part of the fabric. They are in many ways observers, and we started her as a one-liner joke of this sort of silly woman coming to a wacky world. There's a certain growing gravitas to the role, and to Megan, and yet how are you really going to incorporate this reporter who is "apart" as well as "of"?**

Lydia Woodward was another new girl to the show, albeit in the writers' room, penning one of Wayloo's better arcs, digging into the past of Boonie Lanier in "Twilight." Kevin McCarthy guest stars as Wayloo's father, a glad-handing congressman who shows up to award Boonie a Navy Cross. Intent to succeed on her own, Wayloo has kept her powerful patriarch a secret. What Wayloo doesn't know is that Boonie and Dodger have actively covered up Boonie's killing of a rogue marine who had a habit of killing innocent Vietnamese civilians. This plot successfully strikes at the true-to-life gray moral areas that soldiers and journalists shared in Vietnam, all squeezed by institutional pressure from the military.

The cast with new faces, Gallagher and Giles

Wayloo and McMurphy finally click in "Twilight," sharing gripes about their fathers and drunkenly tap dancing into the night. McMurphy opens up to the journalist like she hasn't before, signaling that Wayloo wasn't figured out in the writers' room until it was too late. By the time Wayloo realizes her big scoop is merely being taken advantage of by her father and his political allies, the truth sours her outlook and attitude. The military doesn't want a messy investigation, so Congressman Holmes doles out a medal, poses for a picture, and promptly choppers out of 'Nam. Wayloo realizes she is a culpable tool of government publicity, and Boonie is stuck living a certified lie. "Twilight" offers little resolution, and to the tune of Tommy Morgan's sad harmonica, salvages Wayloo and exposes the source of Boonie's inner conflict.

Nancy Giles was another newcomer to the cast as Pvt. Frankie Bunsen, a girl Friday who pinballs around China Beach with a number of temp jobs. Giles recalled auditioning with no script and winning over the casting directors with stories from her stage and improv work in New York. Giles got her start on the silver screen in a cameo with Tom Hanks in *Big* (1988) and expected her acting career to progress with a role in a sitcom. Instead, *China Beach* stretched her dramatic facilities further.

***Nancy Giles:* They had an idea for this kind of awkward girl who was in the army almost by accident that was sort of trying to find herself, and find her identity. She was African American and so tall and had such short-cropped hair that sometimes people from behind thought she was a guy. [*fainting laughter*] That got a little tiresome for me, but eh, whatever. It didn't happen that often. It was a little intimidating and also kind of wonderful because I felt like we grew together, Frankie and me, which was kind of lovely.**

Giles seized the role of Frankie and relocated to Los Angeles, having no real grasp of the character she was hired to portray. She had never lived outside of New York, nor driven a car, and had to go to department store driving school mere days before her character was to drive a jeep into the Five and Dime. Giles is as versatile as Frankie in real life, now a regular contributor on *CBS Sunday Morning* and often seen as a political analyst on cable news. It's no coincidence many of Frankie's top moments come as a DJ for the Armed Forces Network. An orator with biting wit, Giles once commented on her performance as Frankie at a 1990 Paley Center panel, saying, "I couldn't really find a black woman who sort of wandered from job to job to base my part on, oddly enough."

Frankie shares a few of the same developmental struggles with Wayloo in the opening hours of the season, later hitting her stride in another Woodward script, "All About E.E.V." *China Beach* tests out the absurdist side of war with Stephen Baldwin guest starring as Chuck Berry. Not *that* Chuck Berry, but another Chuck Berry who *believes* he's that Chuck Berry. Woodward was known to chain-smoke in the office ("There's a period piece for you," remarked Carol Flint), otherwise fitting in with a growing cafe society of budding female screenwriters. For all of Woodward's bizarre scripts, she gave off the austerity of a strict school teacher in our interview. Woodward was unwilling to engage past the surface, and only eased up when I impressed further upon the peculiarity of her work.

***Lydia Woodward:* I was living out on the west side and driving to Burbank every day, which gave you a lot of time in traffic for your mind to just go anywhere. I think things would literally pop into your head while you're on the way**

to the office or on your way home at night. I was never a huge watcher of *M*A*S*H*, but it was a great show. I'm aware that they did a lot of stuff with that one character who kept putting on dresses and stuff as if he's trying to get himself out of the army. I don't know if that had any influence in my deep-seated consciousness, although the Chuck Berry wasn't particularly trying to get out, he just thought he was Chuck Berry. Played by one of the Baldwin brothers, I believe.

Nancy Giles: **Steve Baldwin was kind of a pain in the ass. He was the least known Baldwin brother and I feel like he was trying to really make a name and show that he was his own man. I remember all of this kind of obsessive yakkety-yakking about "this has to be the perfect guitar, this guitar has to be strung a certain way, I need to do this, I need to do that," and he didn't really play the guitar. He kind of faked it, you know? But somehow as kind of obnoxious as he was, it was sort of this sweet story.**

Beckett and Frankie quiz Chuck on life and liner notes, and his flawless score convinces Frankie to sing "No Particular Place to Go" with him at an upcoming luau. Frankie comes into her own in a flashy, gold gown as she and Chuck bring down the house. The Chuck Berry gig has the escapist, feel-good vibe of the pilot while allotting some much-needed R&R from the toll of war.

Dennis Farina is another guest star in the episode who parachutes into China Beach as the famous, mustachioed, Silver Star Colonel, Edward E. Vincent. Wayloo wants a high-profile interview, K.C. wants his money, and Lila Garreau wants to outrun her menopause diagnosis from Dr. Richard. Lila finally gets her shot at love during a re-staging of an iconic moment of cinema. Concetta Tomei recalled the cast and crew waiting an entire Malibu morning for a wave to knock her character down during a beachside stroll with Farina. The cameras rolled.

Concetta Tomei: **So, Farina takes off his gun belt and jumps in. He grabs me, and it is right out of *From Here to Eternity*, only it's *China Beach* with Burt Lancaster and Debra Kerr. We're lying down and all of a sudden he grabs me and kisses me as water is rushing over us. I kept thinking,**

"Wait a minute, did I not read the end of the scene?" It's like an *Annie Hall* moment. You're listening to yourself and you're thinking, and you can't answer yourself because the film is rolling. I kissed him back and it was really hot and heavy. They said, "Cut! Print!" And I said, "What? Farina! That was not in the script!"

I went along with it because I thought I must have misread the script. He said, "I always wanted to do that scene," and I said, "Well, you got it! Alright?" Everybody knew Farina was going to do that except me, and I guess that's what made it so real. It was really hysterical. Everybody started laughing and I said, "Oh, you guys, you assholes, you were all in on this!" But they got it, they printed it, and I didn't have to do it again because once you go down, if you don't have a good first take, you get out, get dried off, and do hair and makeup all over again. I said, "I thought I was the major here!" He pulled rank on me, but it was a lot of fun.

"All About E.E.V." proved Woodward could camp on the fringe of reality, and also capture an authentic Vietnam dilemma in "Twilight." A satiating crossfade found in the best hours of *China Beach*. Woodward became a key contributor to the show and continued delivering essential episodes throughout the series. Draftees weren't always so successful. *China Beach*'s carte blanche with rookie screenwriters dissipated in the second season, and Warner Bros. TV boss Harvey Shephard insisted on more proven writers to join the fold. Behind the scenes of *China Beach*, a war of attrition perpetuated. Trial by fire determined if a writer, director, or producer was fit for the team. Mid-episode firings weren't unheard of.

***Robert Picardo:* They had a British director who was kind of old school, who was hired to direct and fired by about day three. He was directing it, to me, like a *Starsky and Hutch* episode: You do the wide master, you shoot a jeep role in, and then you cut to the people getting out of the jeep. I mean, all of the interesting stuff we were doing on *China Beach*, suddenly we were back to the mid-seventies in style. I pulled him aside and said to him, "Sir, most of what my character says has a different meaning. He either doesn't mean it at all**

> **or he's being ironic. If you're shooting me close in a three-quarter cowboy, you don't know whether I mean what I mean or not." He said, "Oh dear boy, don't worry," and whenever anybody says, "Oh dear boy, don't worry," my advice is worry. [*laughs*]**

Bill Broyles's exit from the writers' room demanded another capable, towering voice to tell stories in *China Beach*. John Wells was a promising and unproven thirtysomething on the Warner Bros. lot with his eye on comedy and a pilot under his belt. Wells had seen the *China Beach* pilot episode before the first season was complete, and a successful interview with John Young led to a writer-producer role with the show. Wells recalled, "*China Beach* was the place where I really felt that I could be the writer that I wanted to be, and it was very difficult to produce, so there was a lot of producing that's learned in trying to do something that's virtually impossible to do under the financial constraints that we had."

The hiring of Wells was a blue-chip investment for the show that paid off handsomely, with Wells's initial writing credits accompanying the five preeminent hours of the second season. Wells gained a reputation as an easygoing sergeant who listened to headphones in his office and managed a vast whiteboard to track character arcs. By the fourth and final season of *China Beach*, Wells was the co-executive producer of the show. Wells's stint on *China Beach* preceded his destiny as a television magnate, executive producing *ER* (1994-2009), *The West Wing* (1999-2006), and creating a healthy number of cable television mainstays including *Shameless* (2011-). A close study of Wells's work on *China Beach* exhibits the populist leanings of Broyles and the idiosyncrasies of Young, welded together with Midwestern practicality.

Another offstage hire at this time completed an all-star squad of writers and producers who ushered the show to its end. Mimi Leder entered the corps of *China Beach* directors after a stellar debut episode, "X-Mas Chn. Bch. VN, '67," and was later promoted to producer. Like Wells, Leder entered *China Beach* with scant credits, going on to establish herself as an irreplaceable contributor, eventually directing more episodes of the show than anyone else. Leder became popular among the cast and crew as a stage boss that was patient, thoughtful, and able to move a camera with finesse, once more proving *China Beach* was a land of opportunity where raw talent could thrive.

MORE TODAY THAN YESTERDAY

China Beach is full of posers. Great company or not, sooner or later, the audience must second-guess everything they have come to know about a character. The staccato dialogue, the soundtrack, and the interpersonal drama is a cover up for the real reward, packed deep within each individual's layers, only gifted when the sweaty, naked person hiding inside the rubber clown suit is laid bare.

Who plays dress-up the most? K.C. Koloski.

When I referred to K.C. as a prostitute, John Young bristled, quick to reference journalist Horace Greeley's famous capitalist maxim of, "Go West, Young Man," turn it inside out, and gift K.C. her own dharma.

Go East, Young Woman.

K.C. is a godless goddess, pledging sole allegiance to get rich or die trying. Upon her immaculate conception, K.C. was a one-dimensional outlier. An entrepreneur peddling sex, drugs, and glamour while everyone else was dutifully serving their country. The character had dubious historical grounding and could have (and should have) gone terribly wrong. In the hands of other writers, directors, or actresses, it likely would have.

Marg Helgenberger is one of the most successful television actresses of this young century after fifteen seasons of playing forensics expert Catherine Willows on *CSI: Crime Scene Investigation* (2000-2015). That doesn't mean she rests on her laurels, nor does she forget her roots. As I type this sentence, Helgenberger is finishing up an Off Broadway play and frequently runs into Chloe Webb at an acting class. Webb said, "I don't know any other actor that has made as much money as her and been on TV for that long who is just exactly the same as the first day I met her. [She's] just completely a hometown girl and I think that that quality was, like, so not what you would normally put on a prostitute."

Helgenberger isn't nearly as measured as her character, but maybe as intimidating. Only time warmed up our rapport, just as it did with her character and audiences thirty years ago. Helgenberger was matter-of-fact, conservative in conversation until her thoughts on Bill Broyles moved to the failed policies surrounding the actual Vietnam War and the rejection of our veterans when they returned home.

As the second season hits its stride, K.C. Koloski begins to lose her aura as a Mona Lisa Madame and initiates an evergreen push and pull with the audience. K.C. will always be the femme fatale smoking in the doorway, and until the final moments of *China Beach*, she finds ways to sneak out of that long shadow. K.C.'s wants are material, and as she is humanized with each episode, her needs become the great unknown mystery of this woman.

> ***Marg Helgenberger:*** **The writers wrote it that [K.C.] wasn't one note, that's what was so fun about that show, and most of the actors on the show would say the same thing. They kept just throwing stuff out there and seeing if we could handle it. On the other hand, it does get you spoiled, especially when you're a young actor and you get this choice part. You think all these choice parts are going to keep coming your way and things are going to continue throughout your career, and it's not necessarily the case.**

"Lost and Found" puts McMurphy through the ringer, and "Limbo" follows right behind to threaten what K.C. holds dearest, besides her money. Control. Written by Carol Flint and directed by Dan Lerner, the episode places a shortage of penicillin at the center of the story to wreak havoc on all that surrounds: Dodger needs it to fight an infection, a nearby village is suffering without the medicine, and Boonie is willing to strike a deal with K.C. to replenish the supply. Boonie and K.C. shared a punchbowl stare-down in the pilot, and with Laurette removed from the equation, they resume their Argentine tango.

K.C. is all business, bargaining with Boonie to help her launch a beauty salon, thus giving her an official role at the Five and Dime. As Boonie and K.C. ponder the prospects of business and pleasure, Boonie discovers that K.C. is actually stealing penicillin from China Beach and selling it to the VC. Her heel turn is complete, and yet he still loves her: "The only time I think about going back to the world is with you." A subliminal message. Never quit on a Koloski.

Throughout the episode, Lila searches for a Karen Koloski to deliver news of her father's passing. There is never a doubt Karen is K.C., and it is surprising that a less obvious pseudonym wasn't used in an otherwise cracking script by Flint. K.C. has one-upped Lila by opening a salon, and the major evens the score by revealing that Karen Charlene Koloski came over as a civilian secretary in October of '65. K.C. squirms as her origin story is spoiled, and deflects the news of her father's passing.

She hated him anyway.

In these few seconds, Helgenberger joins Dana Delany as a Chaplin-esque master of quiet communication, dialing into her character's mainframe to remain calm and collected during a worst-case scenario. Fresh skeletons dragged out of her designer closet. K.C. Koloski is human after all, blurting out that her father abused her. K.C. now ceases to be a small-time shyster: she's vulnerable, and she's running from something. Just like Boonie. Just like McMurphy. Only K.C. could escape "Limbo" more sympathetic.

No one is denied humble pie in *China Beach*, and Dr. Dick Richard is served generous portions throughout the second season. Bob Picardo is famous for playing another wise-ass doctor for seven seasons on *Star Trek Voyager* (1995-2001), but Dr. Dick remains close to his heart and conscience, and the actor is still able to recite select monologues from his character. Picardo was an ideal fit for the role, once a pre-med student at Yale University and draft eligible as the Vietnam War was ending. Discussing his work on *China Beach*, Picardo wasn't as self-deprecating or playful as portrayed on set by his collaborators, rather deeply thoughtful and analytical of his former role all these years later.

Picardo was fondly referred to as "The Great Suggester" of *China Beach* by his colleagues, prone to bring ad-libs, props, and jokes about male-pattern baldness to the set. As Dr. Dick's personal life implodes throughout the second season, Picardo was an active participant in the demolition of his character's ego.

Robert Picardo: **There was a famous, old Arthur Godfried episode where this kid is being interviewed, and the kid says something like, "When Uncle Charlie comes for the weekend, my mom makes me sleep in the kitchen, but you know, he's**

really not my Uncle Charlie," [*laughs*] so I took that old story and pitched the writers the idea that Dr. Richard finds out about his wife's affair through his young children's stick drawings that they sent him. Then, Dana turns to me and goes, "Who's this Uncle Doug?" That was another idea I pitched to them and I think it was a fun, sort of oblique way for McMurphy to tweak Dr. Richard.

"X-mas Chn. Bch. VN, '67" marks a transitional moment for *China Beach* with John Wells's first script, Mimi Leder's directorial debut, and Dr. Richard's pivot from a future pariah of the #MeToo movement toward a sympathetic family man. Wells begins a long tradition of redrawing the set parameters of the show by threatening the doctor's marriage and pushing him closer to McMurphy, with the weight of the Christmas holiday elevating each moment.

It is Christmas Eve morning. A ceasefire is in place, and all is silent. Most of the Five and Dime has headed out for some R&R at a Bob Hope show, and the doctor steals a kiss on the lips from McMurphy under some makeshift mistletoe. Her face shows shock and a hint of pleasure before realizing the innocent custom. All of the comfortable silences and snug static between the two now takes on a different meaning. While McMurphy and Dr. Richard mull a workplace fling, the Vietnam War and the holiday spirit eddy around them.

***Robert Picardo:* We were killing time by trying to remember the lines to the "12 Days of Christmas," meanwhile the helicopters land, the bodies come in, and one young soldier has been shot in his penis. He's very concerned about what's going to happen after that. As I said, we'd been trying to remember the lyrics to the song. So he says, "Am I gonna be alright, doc?" I say, "You have a temporary limbic kenosis of corpus cavernosum." He looks at me blankly, and I said, "A cartridge in your pear tree," which I got on the air! [*laughs*] That is an example of one of my line suggestions that made it to broadcast.**

The lone holiday special of *China Beach* might be the most action-packed. Instead of a Christmas vacation, all hell breaks loose as soldiers, orphans, and even animals flood into the medical ward. Pressing Wells for inspiration of his script, he confirmed with a laugh that the raucous stories all originated from veteran accounts. Children screaming, a wild chimpanzee, and a drunk Santa Claus firing a grenade launcher on the helipad all contributed to long nights of filming that stretched into the early morning hours of Leder's first episode.

> ***Concetta Tomei:*** **We were in the operating room and Mimi was directing and all these Vietnamese kids were being brought in—and pigs—there was this pig named Sugar! It was the sweetest pig, but if pigs get anxious, they start squealing and they start crying. It was like two in the morning and we did this take over and over again. The children were crying, poor old Sugar was having a fit, and the more she squealed, the more the children cried. I think Mimi just wanted to get it perfect. I said, "We'll get it, but I can't take this anymore! This is breaking my heart. These kids are killing me! We get one more take because I can't do this anymore," and I never said that again in all those three-and-a-half years of *China Beach.***

> ***Chip Vucelich*** *(series assistant director):* **We were rehearsing in the GRU with Michael Boatman, and there was some of the noise that just happens on a stage. Mimi yells out, "I want it quiet! I don't want to hear an apple box rake the floor! I want no noise, nothing!" Everything got *pin-drop quiet.* The poor craft service guy has no idea that just happened. There were one or two beats and you hear [*yells*] "Hot dogs are ready!" and everybody burst out in laughter, including Mimi. It was such a great way to break the tension. [*laughs*] I'll never forget that. I looked at her and thought, "Oh shit," and she was laughing as much as everybody else.**

As a wounded soldier begins fibrillating, McMurphy performs CPR as a priest reads the patient his last rites. It's a classic *China Beach* moment: the catcher in the rye double-teamed by the grim reaper and the voice of God. Wells's penchant for snappy dialogue is a highlight of the episode as McMurphy's temper builds over the calm scripture of the holy man. Each dissent from McMurphy is met with divine reasoning. Only a group of carolers busting into the room prevents her from exploding at him. Another life slips through McMurphy's fingers, and into the hands of Pvt. Samuel Beckett.

> ***Jan Richardson, née Wyatt*** *(Army Nurse Corps, 1969; technical advisor):* **We had several patients come in at once that we didn't know were coming, which a lot of times you didn't. They were all in just bad shape, and we got to work on them. The next day, the priest came down and he said, "Why wasn't I notified of these guys coming in?" I'm not a Catholic. I'm not really anything, and I said, "I thought you might want something *live* to pray over." I got transferred out of the emergency room to post-op, which was like twenty-five beds of ICU. We nicknamed it "the pit." [*laughs*]**

Beckett is now training Frankie on yet another job. His golden rule: "Nobody dies on Christmas Eve." As they work the holiday away, a Vietnamese woman, Mai, (Elizabeth Lindsey) visits the GRU looking for the body of her brother. Keen-eyed observers will remember Lindsey from the first season episode "Home" as a pregnant Vietcong guerrilla, and here the actress is reimagined as a delicate local who bonds with Beckett in the coming episodes. As a funeral procession commences for Mai's brother, it's a reminder that the Vietnamese paid a vicious price in the war too. Some were communist, some were fighting alongside the Americans, and a million, maybe twice that number, were killed in the crossfire. Mai succeeds in bringing Beckett back among the living, while representing all of the Vietnamese civilians caught in the middle of the war.

Dr. Richard and McMurphy receive a momentary break from the casualties, and he recalls the comfort of Christmas traditions at home with a pleasant disposition: the smell of a spruce tree and home cooking that is dispersing as he speaks. The doctor is a romantic, a family man underneath it all, and McMurphy is a single, independent woman in need of company. Life on the other side of the world barrels on without them, binding the doctor and the nurse tighter in their isolation and occupation. An expectant silence takes over as they stare at the mistletoe above, before Boonie and company kick in the door with drinks and fake snow.

The relationship between Dr. Richard and McMurphy will never quite be the same.

Robert Picardo: **My stock and trade as an actor (if I've had one) is to play characters that the audience does not like at first, and then they grow to like them in spite of a negative impression. The audience sees the guy trying to hold up a mask that he now no longer understands or believes in, so, you see the cracks in his former identity as it's kind of falling apart. [Dr. Richard]'s whole life basically crumbles while he's in Vietnam. He's kind of dismantled and has to rebuild himself after that, and he's made into a better man in the crucible that is Vietnam. Richard didn't deserve McMurphy early on, but the man he becomes did.**

The side effects of Stockholm syndrome inch McMurphy and Dr. Richard toward equilibrium. The prototypical girl-next-door reveals her self-destructive habits with each episode, and Dr. Richard's prickly charm and humor becomes more endearing over time. In director Mimi Leder's second episode, "Crossing the Great Water," Picardo continues stripping his character down to the quintessence of the man hiding in plain sight. After a box of mutilated wedding pictures and love mementos arrives from Beth Ann, Dr. Richard's only escape is his work, and he pours himself into helping the indigent locals. He is a handyman of the human body with no tools, at his wit's end.

Robert Picardo: **Dr. Richard is falling apart because his wife is leaving him, and he's presented with a kid with bubonic plague, and he can't cure the bubonic plague with an aspirin. He doesn't have anything and he just kind of falls apart. I remember that Carol Flint wrote the script and I say, "I don't belong here, I belong back in Boston. Passing out diaphragms, teaching my kid to ride a two-wheeler and sleeping with my leg over my wife." I remember that line twenty-five years on, it was so perfect.**

Dana Delany: **The thing I love about Bob is he's a true actor's actor. He loves, loves acting, he loves what he does, and he comes from the theater. Early on, I said to him, "You are a prop actor!" It was so important to him—his props. He was very organized and in every scene, he had to have his props in line and ready to go, which in theater, that's your job, to make sure it's all there, and I loved watching him work with these**

props in a masterful way. I also loved the relationship and how it emerged. Yes, at the beginning it was that doctor-nurse thing where the doctor is lording it over the nurse, which, is like life. Then, eventually it becomes clear that he's starting to develop feelings for McMurphy, and I just think that was so great how that came about.

Picardo hits all eighty-eight keys of his character in "Crossing the Great Water," reaching an apogee after a little girl with a heart murmur dies on the operating table. Words fail his losing streak. In a grievous rage, the doctor drives golf balls into a minefield until he sets off an explosion, desperate for the smallest, most insignificant victory to celebrate. Beth Ann, the kids, the country club, and the private practice are slipping from his grasp, and Dr. Richard Richard is on the other side of the world, standing at an operating table opposite McMurphy.

Less of a dick, more of a man.

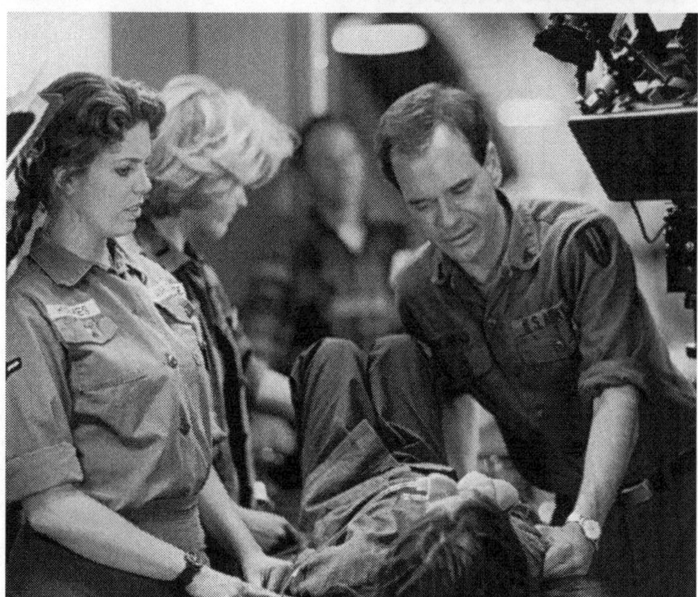

Behind the scenes of "Crossing the Great Water"

WHEN THE LEVEE BREAKS

China Beach waits for just the right moment to slam the meteor of K.C. Koloski into the calm earth of Colleen McMurphy. Planned or not, the gravitational laws of the show first set forth by John Young and Bill Broyles pre-ordained it as an inevitability. The founding of McMurphy and K.C.'s dysfunctional sorority coinciding with the Tet Offensive is more than an astrological occurrence—it is an event of biblical proportions for *China Beach*. Looking at the entirety of the show and the very war it was dramatizing, this epochal moment inexorably alters the course of both sagas.

On January 31, 1968, the North Vietnamese Army and the Vietcong staged a surprise nationwide attack on South Vietnamese targets and American military installations. An annual ceasefire for a celebration of the new lunar year was interrupted by geysers of communist firepower ejaculating from caves, wicker baskets, and anywhere else the guerrillas could hide.

Charlie's end game was to cause an uprising in South Vietnam and topple the American opposition from within. Two prolonged battles persisted just south of the DMZ in Khe San and Hue, with most other attacks quashed within days. Tet ended up a military failure for the communist cause, and a psychological snakebite on the United States. American tolerance for death had begun disappearing during 1967, and Tet gaslighted the brushfire of protest. Four weeks after the Tet Offensive began, Walter Cronkite offered a best-case scenario for the war on national television: stalemate. The venom of doubt circled through the veins of America until the last marine left Saigon in 1975.

Tens of thousands more American soldiers still had to die.

***Susan Rhinehart** (co-writer, "Tet '68"):* **Tet was a huge event, but given the logistics of the show, you could never write Tet the way you might have wanted to. You would have to go back and make it more male-dominated. When I wrote "Tet," it was more in service to the ongoing storyline than anything about the battle, the Tet Offensive, even though that was the background. You couldn't stop in the middle of this TV series and now do—Ta Da: "The Tet Offensive as it meant to everybody sitting at home" because it had to be only as it meant to the people there at *China Beach*. You couldn't go too far. You're telling Cherry's story, or you're telling Wayloo's story… just with more bombs going off.**

China Beach captures the massive scope of the Tet Offensive by fracturing the story into different locations as the attack commences: McMurphy and K.C. are barricaded in an officers' club, Cherry White rides out a firefight with a new donut dolly in a bunker, Samuel Beckett is taken captive by Mai's Vietcong brother, and Wayloo and Boonie race around the Five and Dime to dodge the shelling.

Director Steven Dubin's first of three directorial efforts for *China Beach* is admirable, utilizing each character effectively within an overarching story. Dubin conceded the successes of the episode to his collaborators, professing that he meticulously prepared for the shots and angles he wanted, then trusted the cast to take it from there: "The amazing thing about those actors is they just did it. They knew who they were, they knew how they behaved, they understood the risks that their characters were in. It wasn't that hard because they were so good."

Lawrence, Kansas, is only forty miles away from Kansas City, Missouri, but the crooked paths of McMurphy and K.C. converge into one, ten-thousand miles away in an empty officers' club. K.C. begins acting erratically, tearing the dining room apart until McMurphy notices track marks on her arms. Two sly lines of dialogue out K.C. as a heroin addict, and McMurphy assumes the role of moral authority. Tet ravages the world outside, while two gladiators battle it out in their private coliseum. The women insult one another, proclaim they would have hated each other in high school, and find a nutty form of common ground by trading old pom pom and twirling routines on top of the dining table. It is a passive-aggressive confrontation that literally dances around outing a main character on broadcast TV as a junkie.

Marg Helgenberger taps into an unseen barbarism of K.C., laying a guilt trip on McMurphy for all of the advantages she had growing up. Words come to blows, and McMurphy lands a roundhouse on K.C., knocking her out for the night. Dana Delany did not gauge the stunt correctly, and accidentally sent Helgenberger into Christmas break with a bone bruise on her chin. Helgenberger's lasting memory of the scene is a crew member screaming for a medic. The McMurphy and K.C. relationship is born here in this petri dish, with the pair bringing out the absolute worst in one another.

McMurphy and Laurette 2.0, this is not.

John Wells: **I loved writing for McMurphy, obviously because Dana's so talented, but I loved writing the K.C. and McMurphy scenes. They had a rhythm together that they developed over time; you could write these back-and-forth scenes with them that almost took on a musical quality. It was kind of like watching jazz performers try and top each other.**

Dana Delany: **Marg's such a rock n' roller, and I sometimes worked scenes with her and I would watch what she was doing and think, "Wow, how did you even come up with that?" She was such a natural, an instinct actress. It takes a while to really know Marg. She is loyal, and funny, and just *game*. She goes out there and lives life fully, and takes risks and chances, and I feel like I sort of stay in my house more and read books and think about things. [*laughs*]**

It was kind of perfect in many ways because McMurphy was Catholic and Midwestern, and could be somewhat moralistic, and then to have her play against K.C. who was… also Midwestern [*laughs*] but from a different perspective of a business woman. I have vague memories of our characters sitting together, philosophizing with a bottle of booze between us and always coming from different perspectives and yet somehow meeting in the middle somewhere, begrudgingly, and I really liked that relationship.

Adapting the magnitude of the Tet Offensive to the TV screen was a tall order for the show, coinciding with another creative challenge:

Cherry White, in good company

the misdirection of Cherry White. Once Cherry accomplished the objective of finding her brother in the first season, the writers' room had an identity crisis to address. The market of jaded women in *China Beach* was crowded, and Cherry wasn't wired for the renewable resource of good vibrations like Boonie Lanier. Cherry also lacked the calluses of K.C. and Dr. Richard that could be picked away, as ideas churned how to progress.

In "Lost and Found," Cherry has grown up overnight and lays out the rules to the new Red Cross volunteers: no geographic bachelors and no crying. Later that day, she takes the fresh donut dollies to a USO show to cheer up the soldiers and eat C-rations with them. When the firebase is attacked, it hardens Cherry even further. Later that night, Cherry is dinner drunk at a fancy banquet full of endless toasts, and she interrupts the self-gratification, decrying the current state of the war. The soldiers have inherited the brunt of it, and those above them have disowned the reality. Even Major Garreau can't argue with Cherry's indictment of the hypocrisy. It's a provocative moment that moves Cherry toward maturity, defiance, and a dedicated stool beside McMurphy at the bar. Imagine that.

Cherry's proclamation turns out to be a pump fake, and she is not reborn as the grand marshal of civil disobedience. She's just the senior donut dolly—until Tet. After an all-nighter of gunfire, morning comes and Cherry steps outside the bunker to soak in the bliss of rain and daylight. Somewhere above, the solution to Cherry's cloudy future materializes. She is enshrouded by white light, and an incoming explosion wipes her from the earth.

> ***Dana Delany:*** **This is where *China Beach* was ahead of its time. You didn't kill off a regular character back then; you just didn't do it. It was a shock to everyone, including us, and Nan, obviously. It was effective because these are the consequences of war. She was so innocent and beautiful and young.**

> ***Michael Boatman:*** **They made great, devastating television out of it because in one of the very first shows I can recall to use that device, they killed a main character. Now, that's sort of a big thing, you see it on *The Walking Dead* and all kinds of shows now, but back then it was pretty much "this character is a regular" and you sort of have an innate understanding that "oh well, they'll be around next week," so you know nothing too bad can really happen to them. [*laughs*] Well, they took the sweetest girl-next-door you could possibly imagine and then [had] her die in the middle of the Vietnam War.**

> ***Jeff Kober:*** **[Nan] had a really hard time dealing with the way that people on the show approached the work, which was to make it real, and I think that her character was challenged by that and I think she was challenged by that, and yet in the pilot we had such a beautiful experience together. It was very real, and we had a really strong connection, and really, she was wonderful to work off of in that. Even you mentioning it right now brings up literally almost tears. It was all so real, and *China Beach* was really like a family.**

> ***Dana Delany:*** **I do remember we had a shower scene, early on. I was very much in that phase of "I want to be real and go there" and I think that in the shower scene I had very little clothes on. She was very prim and proper, not really enjoying it that very much. [*laughs*] All I remember is how young she was. Where is Nan Woods these days? Do you know?**

John Sacret Young: She went back to Chicago, I was told. I actually tried to find her at some point and failed, which I regret. There were certain difficulties. At some point we started to talk about, "Well, did women die over there? Is there a way to do that that seems authentic and surprising or shocking?" It led us to deal with that, and I would say I never regretted the decision, the story choice.

I think when you're doing the show and you're in the hot bed of twelve and fourteen and sixteen hours a day, I maybe should have been, or could have been better able to reach out to her and see if she had concerns in her own life that were affecting things. I don't think she was ever unprofessional, but let's say "starchy" might be the word. We were having communication issues. She wasn't fired, but once the story idea came up, it fit, and that led to the decision. Those decisions are never easy, and in a series, they happen.

Michael Boatman: It sort of sent an existential shock through all of us, which the brilliance of John Young and Bill Broyles, I would imagine, was exactly what it was meant to do, to sort of to say, "Look, this is war and this is what happens and it can happen to anybody." The bad part of the story for me is we lost contact; I never saw her again, never communicated with her again. We hadn't traded phone numbers and there was no such thing as social media back then, and so when she was gone, she was just gone.

I would venture to say that because of our nearness in age at the time, we were probably the closest to each other at that time, and so when she disappeared, it was really kind of shocking and devastating, both as a character on a show and as an actor. I never heard from or about her again, and she's someone that I think about all the time, especially when I look at the first season of *China Beach*. It's a little scary, even now with the advent of social media; I've found people who have dropped out of acting or the business, but in her case I don't know what happened. I obviously wish her well and hope she's living the kind of life she wanted to live.

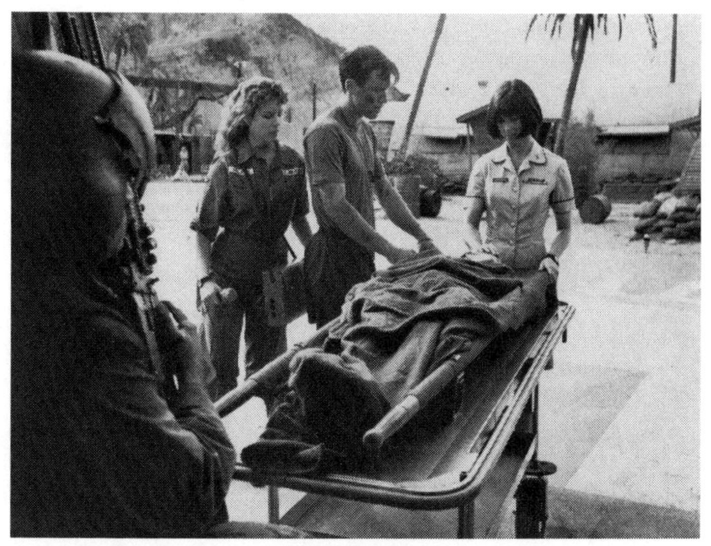

"Bye, Cherry."

Not one person I spoke with from *China Beach* remained in contact with Woods after she left the show. The actress snuck out of Hollywood and has no further screen credits to this day. The death of a screen character coinciding with the end of an acting career and public life is a stunt worthy of Andy Kaufman, making Cherry's death all the more riveting. I spent more time than I would like to admit trying to find Nan Woods, desperate to document her memories and feelings regarding her work on *China Beach*. An interview request eventually reached her through a chain of contacts. Woods respectfully declined to speak on the matter, and her side of the story will remain missing from this record.

> ***Rod Holcomb:*** **Nan was so unsure about who she was. I didn't have to talk to her very much because she embodied a lot of what the character was successful at, in her simple approach to the work. I had conversations on the set with her about her inability to grasp what she was involved with and I thought, "I don't want to fool around with that." I just encouraged her to tell her that she was doing a good job and it was a blessing from my standpoint as a director to have somebody who was**

> **playing the role that was sort of written for her. I always got that questioning in her face and in her eyes about what she was doing. She wasn't really sure she wanted to be an actress. She actually said that to me: "I'm not sure I'm good at this."**

"Tet '68" reaches for its end as Cherry's body is choppered back to *China Beach*, her face sticking out of a bodybag and glistening in the rising sun. An angel in the dirty snow. Director Steve Dubin crafts a classic sequence of the show with a series of draconian shots anchored by Cherry's frozen profile. The cast gathers around Cherry's body on the helipad, using only their faces and body language to relay their grief. Marg Helgenberger recalled channeling the freezing morning air into K.C.'s heroin hangover.

One by one, characters recede to their stations as Wayloo's camera crew documents the death for outsiders to witness, leaving McMurphy and Boonie to mourn over Cherry's body. The picture is poetic: the first two characters we met on *China Beach* are the last left grieving. Boonie bows his head, trying to keep it together. The Vietnam War sends one more silent telegram to our nurse, awaiting a reply. McMurphy only scowls. The air is still, the camera hardly moves, and the scene feels like being stuck in a wooden pew at a funeral, pondering the final destination.

Nan Woods' eyes hold a hesitancy and fragility in *China Beach* that unites all other components of her character, and "Tet '68" closes them forever. The actor's own doubts about her talents and her work informs Cherry with perfect pitch and a believability that reaches past fiction and pathos, into the wonderment of what is performance and what is real life. Upon reviewing an early episode of *China Beach*, John Young remarked to me, "I see again why we thought Cherry's storyline was finite. I wonder if we could've come up with a new beginning, another left turn, but it so easily could've violated the character she personified." Removing Cherry from the abacus of *China Beach* resembles the prior subtraction of Laurette Barber. This time, innocence is slain in lieu of atom-splitting energy—and everyone feels it. The loss of Cherry reflects the erasure of faith in a winnable war and places a face on the cost of lives being spent in Vietnam. Cherry's death feels like the major event that Tet demands to be, successfully dividing both *China Beach* and the Vietnam War in half with a violent tipping point.

WE CAN BE HEROES

"There was a bunch of kids sent off to do a fucking dirty job, and most of them probably couldn't find Vietnam on a map before they got there. They were just kids. We asked them to do something and they did it. Let's shut up and let people start telling their stories again.

I think that's what China Beach *did. That's a powerful thing."*

-Susan Rhinehart, series staff writer

Two days before *China Beach* ever aired, William "Ziggy" Siegesmund wrote John Young a letter. Ziggy was thrilled at the prospect of a portrayal of the Vietnam War that focused on something more than the usual sideboard of napalm and bleary-eyed GIs blasting their way through the jungle. *Platoon*, *Apocalypse Now*, and *Full Metal Jacket* were sensational successes of eighties cinema yet enforced a damaged caricature of Vietnam vets.

Like Bill Broyles, Ziggy knew there were other stories to be told about the experience. In mid-1969, Ziggy volunteered for military service at a time when protests were raging through city streets in America and the military presence in Vietnam was at its peak. Ziggy had a shaky marriage, a young daughter to provide for, and few exciting job prospects in Milwaukee, Wisconsin.

Vietnam it was.

Fate determined Ziggy would not venture into the bush for search and destroy missions, and he was reassigned to China Beach for bar management. It was a coveted position in the rear, and the sergeant at the reassignment center asked him if his dad was a senator. Ziggy had been hanging around pubs since he was sixteen and knew the booze business inside and out, remarking he was more of a psychotherapist than a barkeep when soldiers came in to air their grievances. GIs on R&R coped with survivor's guilt, received Dear John letters from home, and Ziggy poured them drinks and offered a listening ear.

April 24th, 1988 William A. Siegesmund, Jr.

Mr. John Sacret Young
"China Beach"
Warner Brothers Studios

Dear Sir;

Congratulations on your up and comming hit, "China Beach". The reason why I am excited is because I was stationed at the China Beach R & R Center as a Club Manager in 1970.

I have been writing down my experiences for the past year trying in vain to write a story of my personal story while being stationed at China Beach R & R Center. I felt it would have made a great movie, even better than M.A.S.H.! It is finally time society is willing to accept the Vietnam stories that have been introduced to the public.

At China Beach, we all were part-time "psychologists" helping fellow G.I.s with there personal problems and conflicts and would do anything to insure the G.I.s a good time. I have countless humorous stories and memories and many displeasing tales of my own.

I was married before I entered the Army. My wife and I had "off & on" relationship. It was on "off" so I joined the Army wanting to go to Vietnam. I rationally concluded my pain would at least end. When I finally got to go to Vietnam, our marrage was "on". Then I felt guilty and didn't want to go. After a few months at China Beach I received my "Dear John" letter. I was an emotional mess.

I really have some great stories and if you ever need some ideas, please don't hesitate to ask.

The very best of luck with "China Beach", I know it will be well accepted and you can count on me to help promote it.

Sincerely Yours,

William A. Siegesmund Jr.

William A. (Ziggy) Siegesmund, Jr.

William "Ziggy" Siegesmund

Ziggy returned home, divorced, and was unable to maintain contact with those he had served with. Everyone else wanted to move on. His memories remained. It's one thing to watch Boonie Lanier brood about his displacement between life and war on the TV screen. It's another to hear Ziggy's voice shake on the other end of the phone line. He still grapples with Vietnam dreams and shame over not being in the thick of guerrilla warfare with his men: "We all sacrificed, but I didn't sacrifice as much as those guys, you know?"

Ziggy recalled writing Alan Alda in the eighties to ask if *M*A*S*H* was about the Korean War, or if it was really all about Vietnam. Alda personally wrote him back and mentioned *China Beach,* which was set to premiere days later. Ziggy's subsequent letter to Young was promptly answered, and he was invited to Los Angeles to assist the show as a technical advisor. Brian Wimmer was waiting on him at the airport when he arrived. Memories of the real China Beach flowed through Ziggy as he answered questions about the colors of the drapes in the old mess hall and other minutiae to help reconfigure some semblance of the once real thing. When K.C. Koloski opens a salon on the base, the details came from the actual salon Ziggy remembered at China Beach. Ziggy's memories of sniper fire mistaken for live rounds in a barbecue grill also inspired a scene in "Where the Boys Are." Ziggy's trips to California included an annual seminar called "Vets Day," held at the beginning of each season of the show, where

Brian Wimmer, Ziggy, and Bill Broyles

veterans shared their experiences with the cast and set a tone of consequence for the coming episodes.

> *Dana Delany:* **We didn't have any hookers there, [*laughs*] but they were telling us stories and I was in such awe of them. [I was] terrified of playing this part, just terrified, because I thought, "How can I possibly imagine going through this? I've never had anything in my life like this, nothing that was as horrific as what they went through and witnessed," and I remember I said nothing through the whole thing.**
>
> **Bill Broyles told me later that he was concerned about me, that I had said nothing and asked no questions. This is before we shot anything, and he was like, "Huh. Maybe we did make the wrong decision." But if I feel overwhelmed or I feel like I don't know enough yet to ask a question, I'll just keep my mouth shut. I won't ask a question to ask a question. By the second season we had them back to do our boot camp and I had a million questions because I had shot enough to know where I still had holes and didn't understand things: "What was this like, what was that like?" It just evolved like that.**

As the second season wound toward an end, John Young recalled a point where he was malcontent with the product beginning to resemble sausage. *China Beach* took risks when things got too comfortable, and when the shock of Cherry White's death wore off, the show again took drastic measures by abandoning its format entirely.

The result is the landmark episode, "Vets."

"Vets" opens up with the standard *China Beach* credits set to "Reflections." Afterwards, a woman is sitting in a dark room, speaking about how she was the only daughter in a family with four sons, and how she had never seen her father cry until she went off to war as an army nurse. It's a similar story told by Colleen McMurphy, and this woman even looks like a slightly aged version of the character: brown eyes, bobbed brunette hair, and a soothing voice.

A montage of snapshots from Vietnam flickers by, and John Rubenstein's theme takes over. Smiling nurses and soldiers emerge from plumes of smoke, playing games, and posing on tanks. I could almost swear that Boonie Lanier incarnate is in one of the photos. A voiceover from Dana Delany explains that actual nurses from Vietnam will be telling their own stories in their own words. The woman who looks just like McMurphy is Diane Carlson Evans. One might presume Evans was just like Ziggy, one of many "Vets" excited about what *China Beach* was doing with its platform.

One couldn't be further from the truth.

In 1966, Evans volunteered to be an army student nurse, shortly after her brother and a number of her 4H Club friends were drafted for service in Vietnam. Evans recalled not knowing much about the war at the time, and after volunteering at a Veterans Administration hospital in Minneapolis and bonding with the vets, she was sold on joining up and going to Vietnam. She broke the news to her parents and had a nice portrait made for them. Evans knew she was heading into a war zone and might not return.

Evans finished basic training, and from August of 1968 until August of '69, served her country in the Army Nurse Corps with pride and without obligation. After days that could stretch to twelve or fifteen hours, Evans returned to her room and listened to Joan Baez on her reel-to-reel recorder while writing letters home. Music was her outlet, claiming it is what made life bearable in Vietnam. Evans didn't drink or use drugs, and avoided most of the parties at the officers' club. After returning home from the war, Evans married, and never replaced her husband's broken television because the six o'clock news showed nothing but Vietnam. She had lived through it and was uninterested in reliving it on a nightly basis. Twenty years later, she was visiting her parents and first crossed paths with *China Beach*.

She was livid.

> ***Diane Carlson Evans:*** **Mother said, "Diane, are you watching *China Beach*?" and I said, "What's that?" Because for me, China Beach was China Beach in Vietnam, for R&R near Danang. Why would my mother know about that or ask me anything about that? She said, "Well, it's a television program." My mother was a nurse and worked a three-to-eleven shift, so she was not watching it, but Dad was watching it, and my mother said Dad sits there and cries because of Dana Delany. He thinks he's watching me in Vietnam because the likeness was so significant.**
>
> **I thought, "How dare they do this to us, and portray us like a bunch of bimbos," and Dana Delany with her t-shirt**

> **on—I was in Vietnam for a year and we never wore t-shirts! And the drinking and all of the above and the prostitute… they portrayed the Red Cross women like a bunch of flaky airheads, and all the Red Cross women there had to have a bachelor's degree. They were college graduates, like us. They weren't nineteen-year-old bimbos. Then, one of them was named Cherry. It was like, "Why do they have to do this?"**

Evans immediately wrote to the production office of *China Beach* and demanded they stop exploiting the service of Vietnam nurses. Evans was not just a concerned veteran. She had founded the Vietnam Veterans Women's Memorial Project five years prior, leading an effort to place a monument honoring women veterans on the National Mall of Washington, DC. Many Washington insiders were opposed to the women's memorial, and Evans had become accustomed to a fight. Every time a bureaucrat told Evans that the memorial would never happen, she dug her heels in deeper.

In addition to resistance from the political establishment, Evans was sensitive about the portrayals of veteran nurses in the media. *Platoon* made light of a nurse giving a wounded soldier a blow job, and she felt *M*A*S*H* dehumanized women with a character named Hot Lips Houlihan. For all of her frustrations, she did appreciate *M*A*S*H* for bringing attention to Korean War veterans. Evans is still fiercely protective of all whom she served with in-country: "My soldiers that I took care of were as brave and as good and as heroic and courageous as any other veteran or soldier who has ever served in any of our wars. These were amazing men, and I am very defensive of them. This thing about 'the greatest generation'? Well, wait a minute. Mine was the greatest generation too."

China Beach had not only earned the ire of Evans and her deputies. ABC was up in arms over strained budgets and a contentious creative concept that had been pitched by John Young. Twelve episodes deep into the second season of *China Beach*, circumstances demanded that *China Beach* play some financial catch-up due to a budget that was constantly stretched thin by music licensing, paying overtime to the crew, and having two helicopters on call during filming. The typical solution was a "bottle show," an episode on a minimal budget, confining a couple of characters to a certain location and relying more on dialogue and less on pizzazz to move the story and the characters forward.

Instead of trapping McMurphy and K.C. in a bunker, *China Beach* abandoned its episodic format for a concept juxtaposing scenes from the series that were informed by (or coincided with) real life events, as told by Vietnam veterans. The kernel of the "Vets" concept generated from John Wells's work as an intern on the feature film *Reds* (1983). Directed by Warren Beatty, *Reds* recreates an early twentieth-century love triangle steeped in communism, splicing in interviews with actual witnesses of the event. ABC had no interest in straying from the weekly format of *China Beach.* Young and his team proceeded anyway, flying in dozens of vets for interviews, all filmed by the renowned cinematographer Vilmos Zsigmond (*The Deer Hunter, Close Encounters of the Third Kind*).

Jeanne "Sam" Christie *(Red Cross, 67-68, "Vets")*: **I came back home in '68, and we had, as women, the luxury of never saying anything. If we weren't around for a year, it didn't matter. People didn't know we had gone off to Vietnam. It was a luxury to be able to hide it. Most of us just buried it for many years and didn't say anything. And here I was, twenty years later on national television, talking about Vietnam.**

I will never forget when we were shooting ["Vets"]. They were asking me questions, and I don't remember what the question was. I made a comment about women who did not understand Dear John letters and the impact they had. I was angry about that, I was angry at American women for doing that to the guys, because they did not realize many of these guys would get the Dear John letters and they would go out and blow themselves up, and I said something in that vein, that regard. There was dead silence from the crew that was around me. It was like, "Oh my God, what have we done? What did we ask her?" Then it was like, "Okay, let's move on to the next typical donut dolly topic!" They were blown away. I just remembered that reaction, that they were shocked, that there could be that much passion still in somebody those years after.

One Friday afternoon, Diane Evans received a call from the *China Beach* offices, inviting her to do an interview for "Vets." She scoffed at the offer while someone on the other line pleaded their case. Evans hung up the phone and consulted with her advisors, who unanimously said her stories needed to be heard.

Diane Carlson Evans: **When I arrived in Los Angeles, I took a cab to the hotel and I'm all by myself and I go into the elevator, and guess who's in the elevator but Dana Delany. She looked at me and I looked at her and we were stunned. It was like looking in the mirror, and it was just uncanny. The first thing out of my mouth was, "Well, Dana, you don't have any wrinkles, but I do. I earned mine," and she laughed.**

It was amazing, and I loved Dana. I loved all the cast, but Dana was really down to earth, and they made it clear to us—nurses and all of us women who had served in Vietnam—how proud they were to meet us and how proud they were to do the program, to highlight our service. So despite all the Hollywood crap that I didn't appreciate, I felt like these people are genuine.

The filming of "Vets" was as physically and emotionally demanding as the harshest evening at Indian Dunes, with hours of interviews conducted under high-beam studio lights. Dana Delany recalled sitting on the floor and letting the war stories wash over her, while writer Carol Flint remembered wrapping interviews for the episode and waking up the next morning just inside her apartment door with her coat still on. Young said "Vets" was filmed without a script; he sent the footage with a few notes to editors Randy Morgan and Christopher Nelson, directing them to piece it all together and find a story. A few weeks went by as the first two acts came to life. "Vets" was a gambit during an uncertain time that could have crippled relations with the network, with the president of ABC Entertainment, Brandon Stoddard, soon to be replaced by Robert "Bob" Iger. The wandering spirit of *China Beach* stood eye-to-eye with the reactionary fear of the network.

John Sacret Young: **I was arrogant. In my conviction, I didn't like the network trying to say no to something I believed so worthy and so well done. They feared people wouldn't get it, would be confused, would turn it off. I didn't believe that, but also didn't care about their panic. In fact, [ABC] made me fight harder for something I believed so legitimate and important. It was a *High Noon*.**

I'm on the phone with Brandon, who was a tremendous supporter, and he said, "Well, you didn't tell me. You can't do this!" [*laughs*] I said, "It's kind of late now. We're sort of into

it." When it was done, he said, "Come on over, but I'm not going to put this on the air necessarily," and we took the first or two acts cut together. He turned towards the television set in his office, he looked at it, he turned around, and he had tears in his eyes. He said, "You're gonna make me put this on the air, aren't you?"

Throughout the episode, an eclectic gathering of nurses, doctors, Red Cross volunteers, USO performers, and Ziggy weave their memories in and out of scenes from *China Beach*, and a mosaic of blood, sweat, laughs, and tears congeals. Not knowing what to expect from the episode, Evans sat at home with her husband, crying her eyes out. She was touched by "Vets," and driven more than ever to keep fighting for the women's memorial. Post-"Vets," Evans and Delany stayed in touch, and Delany helped raise funds for the memorial by appearing at events and donating props from the show, including her field jacket for auction.

Delany made another trek to upstate New York to assist two other "Vets," Tom and Nellie Coakley, with a women's memorial fundraiser. Delany stayed at their house, and after a parting breakfast, the Coakleys drove her to the airport. Later that day, Nellie heard the song "Reflections" emanating from their living room. She discovered her ten-year-old son curled up on the couch, watching *China Beach*, weeping, "I'm never going to see her again!"

Diane Carlson Evans: **I identified with Dana Delany, obviously, because she was the nurse and I was the nurse. One of the things I did like about the portrayal was that Dana always looked like we looked in Vietnam. Forget the t-shirt, but she was focused on her patients, she was compassionate—everything was about those patients. She cared about them and that's the way we were in Vietnam.**

We were the youngest nurses ever to serve in wartime, the average age of a nurse in Vietnam was between twenty-two and twenty-five and we were just left out there to hang and dry by ourselves because we had very little support from the older nurses. They just turned us loose, and like Dana portrayed, we learned fast and we were quick, and we were brave. To me, she looked very efficient, and she appeared very brave and she was very compassionate. For me, those were the

qualities and characteristics of the women I remembered in Vietnam, and why I wanted them to be recognized.

Dana Delany: **The women who had been in Vietnam were very, very weary of us, and Diane was one of them. I think she eventually saw that we were taking it seriously and we only wanted to tell their story in a truthful way, a respectful way. Once we got past that, she asked me if I would help with the Vietnam Women's War Memorial, so I got more involved with her personally.**

It was so strange how similar she was to McMurphy in many ways, even though John Young did not know of her when he wrote the pilot. She was focused on getting this memorial and getting the women honored in the same way that the men were honored at the Wall, and she made it happen. She did not back off, and I met such wonderful women during that time period, and then to actually be there when it was unveiled was really moving.

As Evans reflected on her *China Beach* experience, her mixed feelings led to an appreciation, believing the show aided her mission in raising awareness for the women's memorial. "Vets" never mentions

Diane Carlson Evans and Dana Delany

the cause, but Evans recalled support and donations skyrocketing after the episode. Evans and her deputies continued their work, and the Vietnam Veterans Women's Memorial was dedicated almost four years later, a rock's throw from the Wall, on November 11, 1993. A sculpture of three nurses comforting a dying soldier pays tribute to the women veterans of Vietnam. Two of the figures bear a striking resemblance to Colleen McMurphy and Frankie Bunsen.

"Vets" garnered a Peabody Award and multiple Prime Time Emmy nominations, although Nielsen ratings dipped to their second-lowest point of the season. Years after *China Beach* went off the air, the interviews conducted for "Vets" were entered into the Lyndon B. Johnson Presidential Library, further cementing the legacy of the episode. "Vets" stands as one of the premier hours of *China Beach* for its ingenuity and content, and continues the show's fabric of ambiguity by refusing to specify whether certain events or characters are coincidental or not. Every vet has a story that is all their own, and "Vets" is remembered for placing a shining light upon them.

The real life "Vets" are spread far and wide across America, and it was a thrill to speak to the select few I could find. A quick realization was that many women like army nurse Christine Schneider had already departed this plane of existence. Questions swim in my head over whether the Vietnam War had shortened their lives, and what *China Beach* meant to them. I wish those ladies were still with us, sharing their lives and inspiration.

"Vets" will have to do.

Vets Day

WHO'LL STOP THE RAIN

"There's nobody else, man," says Boonie Lanier to Samuel Beckett. Toward the end of "Lost and Found," Beckett stands, stammering in front of a quiet crowd of mourners in need of assurance, faith—anything to cope with their grief. Countless wounded boys were brought in on choppers the prior day, and most of them didn't make it. There isn't enough room to display the remains, and Beckett looks at what is left. A row of empty combat boots.

The words find him.

Beckett gives each pair of boots a name. He remembers them all. Where they came from. Each one matters, each one counts, and each pair of their boots must be walked in. The eulogy is absorbed by the mute, dour faces of McMurphy, Boonie, and Dr. Richard. The afternoon sun gives the smoldering profile of Wayloo Marie Holmes a golden honey glaze. K.C. Koloski is moved to tears. With arms wide open, Beckett holds the *China Beach* matrix together for a moment, giving everyone else the wherewithal to make it another day in the 'Nam. Michael Boatman does more than ease his boyish character further into the skin of a sage. Boatman unsheathes the four-year mission statement of *China Beach* in one breath.

Walk in these boots. We must.

Beckett's ordination into sainthood comes later in the season, during "Promised Land," directed by Michael Rhodes. Rhodes fit like a round peg into the board of *China Beach* when he was hired in the second season to direct "Where the Boys Are." Rhodes had crossed paths with John Young at the University of Southern California film school two decades prior, not knowing what to make of Young's self-possession: "I directed something early on that John wrote involving a guy who committed suicide by running further than he should on the beach. He would over-stress himself intentionally and roll over and die. I thought, 'Jesus, what does this mean? What is John thinking about?' It was a fascinating thing, but I couldn't get into what it was. John wouldn't explain it, but he liked what I did with it."

Rhodes has a penchant for ambitious cinematography, the kind of painstaking labor that could take an episode of *China Beach* well into overtime. Perhaps that is why Young hired him to direct a number of episodes—Rhodes was going to go the extra mile and get it right. Rhodes's exposure to the Vietnam War was limited in the late sixties, but he later documented one of the more horrific events of 1968 for his film-a-week class, following Young's suggestion to track down one William Calley at a nearby speaking engagement.

Calley is infamous as the only convicted killer in the My Lai Massacre on March 19, 1968, when American soldiers mass-murdered up to five-hundred Vietnamese citizens, spanning the elderly to the infant. Calley's life sentence for taking twenty-two Vietnamese lives was whittled down to three years house arrest by the mid-seventies. The massacre was kept a secret from the American public for over a year until it was exposed by a whistleblower. 1968 was the white elephant gift that kept on giving. Rhodes's first episode of *China Beach,* "Where the Boys Are," is a lighthearted affair surrounding a haphazard prom for all the guys who are missing their own back home. His second episode strikes at something more personal: another American nightmare that followed just two weeks after the My Lai Massacre.

On the evening of April 3, 1968, Martin Luther King, Jr. ended a speech to a crowd of people in Memphis, Tennessee, telling them, "I may not get there with you, but I want you to know tonight that we as a people will get to the promised land. So I'm happy tonight; I'm not worried about anything. I'm not fearing any man. Mine eyes have seen the glory of the coming of the Lord." King's voice had grown to a roar, and he tore himself away from the podium, as if in mid-sentence. He disappeared into the curtains behind him as the crowd cheered. At thirty-nine years of age, he had so much more to teach the world and his country, and it was all stolen away when he was killed the following day.

Nancy Giles: **I was seven when he was assassinated. I knew who he was, in the way that a seven-year old does. That was a really weird year because there were so many violent things**

that were going on and what I remember the most is the day of his funeral. It was a really sunny, beautiful day and I wanted to go outside and play. I'm from a family with six brothers and sisters and my mother insisted, "No one is going out to play." We had to sit inside and watch this funeral.

Five days prior to King's death, President Lyndon Baines Johnson announced that he would not seek re-election in the coming fall. The wake of the Tet Offensive and his management of the Vietnam War had sealed his fate as the leader of the free world. King's killing fueled the national unrest, and King would soon be joined in death via assassination two months later with Robert F. Kennedy. Leaders were disappearing, and faith and confidence were brittling across the US, while Ho Chi Minh's disciples kept a white-knuckled grip on their dream of reuniting Vietnam. *China Beach* continues blazing a treacherous path through 1968 with the inescapable chapter of King's killing in "Promised Land," examining the fallout and placing Pvt. Samuel Beckett in the middle of it.

Michael Boatman: **People cite that episode to me all the time and it was certainly one of my favorites, but doing it was awkward, and it would probably be awkward today because you are suddenly talking about race, and no one's ever comfortable about it. No one's ever *been* comfortable about it. I don't think people are comfortable about it now, and all of a sudden there was a moment where I was aware in a way that maybe I hadn't been before: "Oh, all of my friends, my coworkers are sort of looking at me as 'black guy.'" Not in a derogatory sense, but a sense of "What's he thinking? How does he feel?" and I don't know if they were actually thinking that. It's what was going on in my head at the time, but I suddenly was very aware of a separation.**

The opening moments of the episode find Beckett in the GRU, reflecting on his year in Vietnam coming to a close. Director Michael Rhodes pushes the camera past the slowly spinning box fan, bringing us up close and personal with Beckett for a farewell address to his departed audience. Boatman is a consistent and reliable dramatic force in the role of Beckett, able to animate an empty room full of the deceased, while much of his post-*China Beach* success has come from lengthy stints on sitcoms like *Arli$$* (1996-2002) and *Spin City* (1996-2002). Boatman is a lively conversationalist, and Beckett's hysteria is the by-product of Boatman suppressing his inner light.

Beckett bids a hungover McMurphy farewell after a string of drunken and forgotten attempts the night before. The two characters played wonderfully off each other in the first season, and this tender moment exposes a missing link of the second season where Beckett has been divorced from the rest of the main cast, occupied with Mai, or hidden away in the GRU. Beckett stands on a tarmac, waiting to go home until an epiphany sends him back to China Beach. A joyful reunion with Mai at the Jet Set is cut short when Frankie informs them that King has been killed.

> ***Michael Boatman:* I remember John Sacret Young saying something to me before we shot that episode, like he wanted Beckett to feel under a spotlight. He actually didn't need to say it, because that's exactly what happened. I felt whenever your character is the focus of an episode in a show like that, it's great. It feels great for your ego and you worry about "Can I rise to the challenge?" but that one was easy because there was already so much emotion around the topic that it just sort of played itself. In a way, it was easy to play because the events are unfortunately still relevant.**

> ***Concetta Tomei:* It was almost twenty years since King had been shot, and yet when we started filming this episode, it was as if it was yesterday. There was kind of a solemnity, not a lot of joking around the set because he was such an admired warrior, such a hero, and such a respected man that it was almost hushed, coming in to do a lot of those scenes and wanting some kind of justice to be done.**

"Promised Land" writer Patricia Green recalled finding a rumor within her research of black soldiers in Vietnam revolting upon the news of King's death, lighting a match for her story when a tank of black soldiers crashes through the fences of China Beach, dejected and on a mission to mourn the passing of King. A solemn evening of grief is shattered when a gang of rebel rousers led by Corporal Whitlow

(Richard Tyson) rushes into the Jet Set to celebrate King's death. Jerry Lee Lewis blasts from the jukebox, and Whitlow decries King as a traitor. Boonie shuts down the bar before a race riot erupts. Tyson is delightful and devilish in the guest role of Whitlow, bringing a natural southern snarl from his roots in Mobile, Alabama, seen elsewhere at the time portraying odious characters in the films *Two Moon Junction* (1988) and *Kindergarten Cop* (1990). The black-hat bad guy is a welcome rarity in the gallery of tortured *China Beach* characters.

After a night of acrimony, Whitlow's crew marches through the Five and Dime with Confederate flags and an effigy of King. The black soldiers stew in segregation. Among them, guest stars Mykelti Williams and John Marshall Jones, reprising his role of Fluke. "Promised Land" is a more confrontational take on the typical *China Beach* offering—an invitation to look back, then take a look around. I see the Ku Klux Klan and Neo-Nazis marching through Charlottesville, Virginia, in the summer of 2017, and a woman who died protesting their presence.

China Beach can feel dated from time to time, but "Promised Land" hasn't aged a day.

"Brothers" aside, the explicit topic of race feels absent in most plots of *China Beach* until "Promised Land," while the American minority experience is carried by Beckett and Frankie throughout the series on a macro level. Beckett works a job that no one else wants, and Frankie cycles through different jobs, searching for stability. When *China Beach* chooses to address race relations directly, the results are haunting, and somehow still alive and well in America.

The tensions between black and white escalate throughout the episode until Whitlow confronts Beckett in the GRU. Boatman and Tyson hit all their marks, and words turn to action. Whitlow pulls out a gun, and the two men wrestle over it. It's a vision that could be found on any given city block in 2018 America. The sight is as infuriating as it is poignant.

Beckett and Frankie weather the racism from Whitlow and his crew, and are also displaced from their own race when their black brothers want revenge. Whitlow is bound and gagged, prepped for a lynching after Fluke is found dead. Beckett refuses to participate in the violence and offers his own life before Whitlow's. Frankie stands with him.

Nancy Giles: **Beckett and Frankie were both unique and not the norm of what you saw for black characters. We weren't stereotypes, and that meant a lot to us. There was some lovely nuance about how Frankie reacted and Beckett reacted, and how some of the other guest characters reacted, and we got to see the clash. It's not pretty, but it's the truth, because everybody doesn't think alike. What was cool about an episode like that was you got to see different shades of black. It's very important storytelling, and it helps to break stereotypes.**

Michael Boatman: **You know at the end of that episode that things can't be the same, because the country wasn't the same after that, but that's what was great about that show, to me. Unlike shows today, even dramas, it's very strange to me that there's just certain things that don't get talked about anymore. Race is certainly one of them that doesn't get dramatized.**

China Beach reaches its highest notes while finding some shape of morality within a schism. Here, everything is exactly as it seems—an anomaly of the entire series. "Promised Land" reinforces the best qualities of Beckett and Frankie, the worst qualities of their aggressors, and leaves little room for realizing much else. McMurphy stands for equality, Major Garreau doesn't pick sides, and K.C. is out of sight since there is no dollar to be made. Writer Patricia Green earned a Humanitas Prize for her script, and Boatman's performance is among his best in the series. Yet, something remains missing at the episode's end.

Racial tensions boil over so quickly in "Promised Land" that the loss of King becomes an afterthought until Beckett and Frankie follow in his steps and extinguish the vengeance that their black brothers demand. Whitlow remains unredeemed, and a two-part episode may have been required to allow Beckett or Frankie to confront the perpetuation of his hate. *China Beach* proved early on in "Home" that the enemy can be humanized via shades of gray, and "Promised Land" refuses to reach outside of black and white. Today, more can be done to bridge the gap between races, and "Promised Land" is a fine example of that perennial challenge.

When Beckett walks into the jungle under a burned cross with Mai at the end of the episode, his decision to stay in Vietnam is apparent. The audience is left to assume why he is staying. Does he love Mai, or is he avoiding the motherland that awaits him? Beckett's boots are free for anyone who wants to try them on and take a walk.

So far, *China Beach* has meticulously crafted a small universe that exists in a tight nook of Vietnam, with McMurphy, and now Beckett, making the conscious choice to stay in this realm. "Promised Land" is the first episode that allows the aftershocks of events back home to unequivocally shake the foundation of *China Beach*, and sooner or later someone will have to go back home and confront the changes that have happened in their absence.

IN MY ROOM

"To understand and to be understood is to be free."
-Daniel Johnston, "Go"

Colleen McMurphy is the center of the *China Beach* galaxy throughout the second season, the eternal flame that flickers from a blowtorch to a Bic lighter. One moment, she is the tenacious catcher in the rye. The next, she is despondent, looking at the bottom of an empty liquor glass. The planets that revolve around our nurse terraform accordingly. Dr. Richard isn't so much of a schmuck, and K.C. Koloski is no longer a perfect stranger. Beckett is forming lasting bonds among the living, and Wayloo has wizened up to the propaganda machine. Boonie has become more than the life of the party, and a tiny, fragile orb of ice—Cherry White—is extinct.

The war continues its excavation of McMurphy, telling us more about her than anyone else.

Natch Austin is MIA, an afterthought until he emerges from captivity in "Afterburner" with a beard and long hair. McMurphy submits to this lease on lust, able to connect with his body, if not the soul—then absolves her sin in a dark confessional booth. The priest doesn't understand English, so she resorts to hand gestures in desperation. Natch conveniently forgets to tell her that his wife is expecting a baby back home, and it's the final straw. McMurphy isn't mad. She's over it. Dana Delany reclaims the icy certitude of the woman we first met on the beach, and sends Natch home on the helipad without flinching.

Elements of *China Beach* are continually chipped away in the second season, finally exposing the real woman inhabiting the molten core of the show in the two-part finale, "The World." It isn't McMurphy. It's Colleen.

Wayloo Marie Holmes is headed back to the States, parachuting into a new life and a new job at ABC news, which demands a going-away party. The drinks flow and "Time Has Come Today" by the Chambers Brothers feeds the buzz. McMurphy is summoned for a phone call, and as the chanted refrain of "time!" slows to a crawl, Delany's face contorts along with the beat. It's a moment of holy matrimony, marrying another scene of *China Beach* to its source music, for better or worse.

McMurphy packs her bags and joins Wayloo on the helipad for the next lift out of China Beach, Dr. Richard visibly pained by the thought of losing them both. Director John Sacret Young recalled filming this scene during a "magic hour" of daylight where the sun softened toward gold—a coveted window of time in the desert that was his favorite to roll camera. After the doctor bids Wayloo goodbye with an "I love you," she responds with a passionate kiss. He successfully repeats the gesture with McMurphy in the lone laugh-out-loud moment of the episode.

China Beach is a TV show with few kindred spirits or contemporaries. During two years of conversations with John Young, he hardly mentioned any other television series that had a direct influence over *China Beach*. Feature films, novels, paintings, and photography were all swimming in Young's head as he crafted scenes, and I pressed him to name a television show that might have crept into the proceedings. He squirmed, and reached. *The Fugitive* (1963-67) followed a doctor on the lam, saving lives and proving his medical acumen under extreme, unlikely duress. *Maverick* (1957-62) had quippy frontier humor that leaked into *China Beach*, and *M*A*S*H* (1972-83) successfully brought in visitors to the military like reporters and psychiatrists to shake up the formula.

The creative touchstone of my conversations with Young was William Wyler's 1946 Best Picture post-war film *The Best Years of Our Lives*. To set a tone for "The World," Young reserved an empty screening room on the Warner Bros. lot to view a 35-millimeter print of the film with Delany and writer John Wells. (In the 2016 documentary *Five Came Back*, Steven Spielberg revealed he screens Wyler's film on an annual basis for his uninitiated collaborators.) Young was ready to break the mold of *China Beach* with an entirely different method from "Vets." The Vietnam War and the supporting cast would recede, and Colleen must confront the friends, family, and homeland she has been divorced from.

McMurphy's temporary vacation from war mimics three World War II veterans who return home together in *The Best Years of Our Lives*. Fredric March, Dana Andrews, and Harold Russell play vets bringing their own private struggles home from the war, unable to identify with anyone but each other. While they were saving the world, it continued turning on without them. Spouses, jobs, politics. Nothing is the same.

Wyler had shot footage of World War II from planes during air raids in Germany, suffering hearing damage and losing one of his cameramen during battle. Wyler came home, fully able to harness the veteran experience of service and sacrifice into his storytelling. *The Best Years* is informed by personal points of view similar to those in *China Beach*: characters dealing with an individual crisis magnifying bigger issues within the world at large. The struggle isn't unique, but it is lonely.

In the only screen performance to ever win two Academy Awards, Harold Russell portrays Homer, a buoyant sailor whose hands were replaced by hooks after a submarine accident. He strikes matches, opens beer bottles, and channels the sanguine mood of Boonie Lanier. In reality, Russell had lost both hands in a military training accident and wasn't an actor by trade.

Young took drastic, maybe absurd measures in crafting "The World" in the image of *The Best Years of Our Lives*, coaxing Russell out of retirement to play McMurphy's uncle Conal, and licensing Hugo Friedhofer's original score to be used in the episode. Young was determined to include an airplane in a scene akin to the film, and paid twenty-thousand dollars out of his own pocket when Warner Bros. refused to cover the bill.

> ***John Sacret Young:* I've worked on a lot of shows. I liked some of them, I loved some of them, but this was it, folks. This was the one I loved with an ongoing passion that just took me off of the normal, rational, everyday world and into its world for four-and-a-half years.**

McMurphy and Wayloo arrive in the States, greeted by anti-war protestors throwing eggs and insults at them. The two hide away in a bathroom where military uniforms fill the trash can. They wait for their connecting flights and spray warm Vietnamese beer at each other, shriek at the sound of indoor plumbing, and own up to their mutual dislike. The laughs, and then the uncomfortable silence between them, cements an understanding, if not friendship.

"The World" removes the fisheye lens of *China Beach* that has distorted the Vietnam War so far and places McMurphy under a microscope in America, with Delany holding the focus of each and every scene in an Emmy-award-winning performance. Instead of digging her toes into the sand of China Beach, McMurphy indulges in first-world customs—indoor carpeting and the snap, crackle, and pop from a bowl of Rice Krispies. All along, a high-pitched hum of unrest runs through each scene, emitting from new, alien satellites. McMurphy's mother (Penny Fuller) criticizes her haircut, her drinking, and then trashes McMurphy's bloody clothes, right before Colleen loses her temper and digs them out of the garbage.

They don't smell like Vietnam, they smell like *her*.

The McMurphy household is full of passive-aggression. There are hints of dad's alcoholism and mom's enablement—all trampled eggshells quickly brushed under the rug. McMurphy is removed from the war and her vocation, yet behaves more like a nurse than a daughter when she visits her ailing father (Donald Moffat), inspecting his vitals and IV. McMurphy is treading in a gulf between Vietnam and Kansas, unable to decide which direction to swim.

Delany reflected on "The World" as a proud moment, relishing in the opportunity to work with her co-stars, Fuller, Moffat, and Russell. The end of "The World, Part 1" holds one of Delany's favorite scenes in all of *China Beach*, where McMurphy finds her father drunk and confused at an abandoned train station. Her father manages a moment of coherence to tell her how proud he is of her, right before he calls her by the wrong name. McMurphy stands on his toes, and they slow dance together into the credits.

John Sacret Young: **[Dana's] dad died when she was sixteen years old. Her parents broke up and she (for a while) was sort of a mother to her father. He moved out, and she took care of him, and she carried the loss of him with some size, and understandably so. She talked about her memory of taking off her shoes to stand on his feet, and I don't remember her saying much more than that, but it was absolutely an inspiration, or a creative nugget that led to that sequence.**

Dana Delany: That came from my life because I told John that I used to do that with my father, so he put that in, so that meant a lot to me. I get emotional thinking about this stuff. It is so very, very deep inside me and sometimes I don't know whether it's conflated with remembering my youth or remembering the show, you know? [_laughs_] I'm not sure which, but they're both mixed in there together.

John Wells: There was nothing you could write that you didn't think Dana could do. She has one of those abilities to be still and calm, and as a viewer, you can put your emotions into what she's doing. I used to joke with her and ask her about it—what she was thinking about—and she would say things like, "Well, I was thinking about what I was going to have for dinner," but I think truthfully she was able to internalize these emotions. You could write scenes that would be melodramatic, and the way in which she would play them was anything but melodramatic.

She refused to play the obvious and that's very liberating for writers, because you feel increasingly that there's nothing you couldn't write that she couldn't do. There are a number of things we did over the years on the series, and bits and pieces of it came from stories she told me about her relationship with her own father, and all of those things kind of become part of the fabric that makes the character feel real because the actor is drawing upon some of their own experiences.

"The World, Part 2" begins in tragedy with the funeral of McMurphy's father. As she mourns the man who reared her, the Vietnam War taps her on the shoulder when an honor guard fires three volleys. A neighboring military funeral buries one more American casualty, and the nurse can only salute. McMurphy holds it together for her family, then returns later in the evening, drunk with her brother, Brendan (John Laughlin). Kansas has rejected her, and she reacts in grand fashion, crying, digging her hands into the fresh soil atop her father's grave.

Within the pages of Bill Broyles's *Brothers in Arms*, Broyles recalls standing on the tarmac of the Travis Air Force base in San Francisco, California, waiting in line to board a plane to Vietnam. He loses his nerve and flees to the city with second thoughts. McMurphy traces Broyles's steps in the second half of "The World," in search of an old friend from the Five and Dime. Someone who will understand.

On the verge of superstardom in *Misery* (1990), Kathy Bates guest stars as Jan, a no-nonsense nurse and Five and Dime vet. McMurphy finds her working at a rowdy veteran hospital, a building full of people who share McMurphy's trauma. It feels more like home than Kansas ever did. McMurphy later hits the town with Jan and her bohemian friends who are obsessed with picking up men and their folk-singing act. Once, McMurphy was onstage rocking out with Laurette. Now she's in the crowd, unable to understand how her contemporaries can lose themselves in flower-powered frivolity.

China Beach is as much about the Vietnam War as it is matchmaking strange bedfellows: people, emotions, even music. In a device John Young fondly referred to as "scorce," orchestrations bleed into source music and create a moment for characters and their feelings to transform along with the soundtrack.

Later that night, McMurphy defends her sacrifice and service to a couple of naysayers, and a veteran in a wheelchair (Grand Bush) asks her to dance. She laughs, before realizing he is serious. Orchestral strings begin fading into Procul Harum's "A Whiter Shade of Pale," to create a "scorce," and McMurphy and the vet twirl around a platform. The music forms a metaphysical wall, and anything outside this bubble is secondary. McMurphy's despair disappears into the music, and she straddles the vet and throws her head back, entirely lost in the moment. The moving picture slows to a passionate crawl, and the vet smiles as if his ability to walk has been restored. McMurphy's dance with her father was an act of holding onto the past. This dance affirms the identity she has forged outside of Kansas.

***John Sacret Young:* It was something we could sort of rehearse, but not really. We could set up marks on boards, and then you really had to let it happen. I was so affected by the dancing in *The Grapes of Wrath* and in *My Darling Clementine* that John Ford did with Henry Fonda. Both of those sequences were powerful, but they both were awkward because Henry Fonda was awkward. "Well, is there a way to do something that we would not expect to happen?" Then, in**

a way, Grand Bush in the wheelchair is going to lead her in the dance. I don't think I've ever seen this before, and that's often a measure of what we were trying to do.

Dana Delany: **It was sad and it was sensual; I remember when we shot it, it was another twenty-four hour day of shooting. As we were wrapping that scene, the sun was coming up and we'd been shooting all night. I just remember feeling, as the sun came up, "Wow. I am so lucky." I just appreciated the moment, I appreciated that scene, and then I appreciated the fact we went out for breakfast. [*laughs*] It was one of those magical moments.**

On November 11,1989, Delany penned an op-ed in the pages of *USA Today*, claiming, "Growing up, I never quite believed in altruism." She had approached every scene of her career so far with four basic elements. Anger, fear, sadness, and happiness. Former army nurse Nellie Coakley suggested she add a fifth—compassion. The wheelchair ballet is McMurphy's superlative act of altruism, and it's never seen in the "Reflections" credit sequence, remaining tucked away in its own corner of "The World." Of all the brilliant scenes carried by Delany in this two-part episode, this one likely clinched her the 1989 Prime Time Emmy for Best Actress in a Drama Series.

Dana Delany: **I was so wrapped up in the work, I wasn't even aware of awards. I'm not just saying that, I really wasn't. Also, that's not something I grew up thinking, "One day I'll win an award." I never thought about that; it was always about the work. So, when it happened, I was kind of like, "What?" It was very different back then, too, you didn't have any campaigns. I went and bought my own dress at the store. It was not what it is now—the industry of the Emmys. I felt a little weird about it, and I get embarrassed by stuff like that and I remember I was against Angela Lansbury, which is absurd. [*laughs*] I felt almost guilty. I felt I didn't deserve this yet, but, once you get it, it's a fun party. It's true what they say.**

Once you get it, then you want it: "Oh, there's these *things* called awards."

McMurphy bids goodbye to Jan at the hospital the next day, and encounters a soldier (James Marshall) who was medevacked from China Beach. He recognizes her: "That's my nurse!" and leads the room in a round of applause for her. This moment reaches back into the pilot when she stands on stage in another moment of "scorce," where she allows herself to feel love, to feel appreciated. She once found a reason to stay in Vietnam, and here, she sees why she must go back. Renewed and repurposed, McMurphy returns to the Five and Dime, the same as it ever was.

"The World" is a premier chapter in the *China Beach* odyssey, taking the nurse out of McMurphy and the story out of Vietnam for the first time. Delany's masterful performance completes a story that once more redefines what the series is capable of. "The World" also prompts revisiting Young's early notes that sired McMurphy.

Her inside is her outside except for that way deep down wall where she has learned almost perfectly to hide behind.

The end of season two reveals that the Vietnam War is McMurphy's wall, and one day, it must come crashing down.

Dana Delany at the 1989 Prime Time Emmy Awards

III

The overnight sleeper train rocked back and forth like a crooked cradle, all the way south from Hanoi to the former ancient capital of Vietnam, Hue. Morning light overtook the cabin, and I craned my neck from the top bunk to peer out the window. Rice fields stretched as far as I could see, carved into massive squares outlined by canals. The countryside was dotted with dilapidated shacks and farmers in canonical hats. I couldn't tell if they were children, adults, or the elderly. They were all the same height, moving at a snail's pace.

The pastoral vista looked like a scene from the Stone Age. My imagination painted in American GIs trudging through the paddies with their M16s, praying they didn't step on a bouncing betty, wondering whether their unimposing hosts were the enemy in disguise. It was one of the few moments of my trip that I felt right there with the vets. Two days in Hue flew by before heading to Danang—home of the real China Beach.

Danang is the third-largest metropolitan area in Vietnam behind Saigon and Hanoi, not to mention cleaner, quieter, and much more relaxed. The motorbikes are fewer and travel faster, making the pedestrian experience all the more dire. The Zone 5 Military Museum was deserted—just me, my wife, the staff, and some repairmen. Inches of dust covered the floor in front of every exhibit. An old motorbike was displayed for its service of delivering bombs during the Tet Offensive, finally offering some physical evidence connecting the Vietnamese of today to those of the past.

In our instantaneous, on-demand world of 2018, it's a chore to find the actual China Beach grounds. The Five and Dime never existed in reality, but pieces of it did, and I was determined to see some of it with my own eyes. These days, China Beach is a blanket pseudonym for My Khe Beach, stretching for miles of white sand and huge waves amid booming resort development. American GIs landed on the shores of Danang in 1965 and gave their oceanside dwelling an imperialist name that has come and gone, now championed by a hotel community that is happy with any brand name to bring in paying tourists.

Googling the coordinates of former US installations in the area was fruitless, resulting in a few faded photos of old USO offices and barracks. I wouldn't track Ziggy down for another few months, and my only option was to ask the hotel manager for help. A proper young lady in a pressed blazer grinned at my inquiry, shrugging her shoulders: "The Vietnamese learn history in school and move on." A couple of days later, a local tour guide knew where to go. Across the street catty-corner from Marble Mountain and still in sight of the tall, skinny, shining Lady Buddha statue that watches on from the Son Tra peninsula, the ruins of an old American evac hospital laid before me.

Piles of broken bricks, mangled rebar, and trash sat in a sandy field of dunes. Any thought of a television show was remote, while all the people who had led me to that particular spot at that particular moment were right there with me. I closed my eyes and tried to put myself in Bill Broyles's shoes, with rows of broken teenaged boys writhing in a massive sheet metal bivouac before me.

I took in a breath and opened my eyes. I felt so close, but I couldn't see them. I couldn't touch them or hear them. I wish I could have.

EVERYWHERE
AND NOWHERE

SUBTERRANEAN HOMESICK BLUES

The third season of *China Beach* is the best of times and the worst of times. One minute can feel like watching an IV drip, waiting for appetite and vigor to return. The next may feel like somersaulting into another plane of existence. It is the inverse of television that is now packaged for binge consumption; certain episodes reach their conclusion and the last thing one may want to do is press play on another episode. This titanic, twenty-two-episode volume ranges from exhausting to exhilarating, and is perhaps best enjoyed weekly over the course of eight months—as first intended.

After two seasons of eight and sixteen hours, *China Beach* arrived in the fall of 1989 as a full-sized, deluxe network television series, and renowned photographer Annie Liebovitz was brought in to capture the moment. A smiling, sizzling, swelling cast of ten holding up a surfboard. *China Beach* had forged its identity on the tenants of "less and less," "dig deeper," and here began searching for its soul amidst *more.* A whole lot more.

The world of *China Beach* proliferates throughout season three, and two combustible personalities ride through and through the storm. Colleen McMurphy has a firm grip on the throttle. Riding sidesaddle behind her is K.C. Koloski in a kimono blouse, coolly dragging on a cigarette. Both women leering, hair blowing in the wind, not taking shit from anyone—least of all each other. The McMurphy and K.C. dynamic is more than another odd coupling in the show; it is emblematic of the timeless American divide in Mayberry and on Capitol Hill. Helping others vs. helping yourself.

Pride comes before every fall, and any act of diplomacy.

The comparisons and contradictions never end: A brunette and a ginger. One born Catholic and compassionate, the other born secular and agitated. Both self-aware, cornfed girls who came to Vietnam looking for what they couldn't get in the heartland. One is addicted to smack, the other to drink. Both are talented healers of the human anatomy, overly dedicated to their work. One worships the almighty dollar, the other agnostic to it. Both hold disproportionate values of themselves. Not their inalienable, American rights.

K.C. began season two as an outsider, then McMurphy makes a familiar out of her. Attrition also helped. Laurette and Natch were stripped away from McMurphy, then Cherry White was wiped from the chessboard, leaving McMurphy and K.C. to face off during Tet. When the Vietnam War finally cracks McMurphy in "Psywars," she climbs to the top of the water tower, despondent. Catatonic. K.C. returns from Cherry's funeral in Iowa, and is the only person who can talk the nurse down. The two women trade war stories, and there are no hugs, smiles, or music to curb the trauma.

Just the morning breeze whistles beneath their words.

McMurphy describes her recurring dream of seeing Natch disappear in the sky, and K.C. derides the feeling of sleeping in Cherry's bed, listening to the White family's unending stories, and enduring a sub-zero funeral. McMurphy and K.C. typically communicate with flurries of verbal jabs and roundhouses, and for once, they shut up and listen to each other. Director Fred Gerber places both women side by side to study their faces concurrently, exposing what the proud words of the characters won't. They need each other. Now, more than ever.

The dysfunctional sorority of McMurphy and K.C. is royally sealed in "Afterburner." Carol Flint's script and Christopher Leitch's direction strike flint in a dry forest. A campfire lights up the night on China Beach, and McMurphy and K.C. are getting lit with the help of Jack Daniels. Natch is on his way home for good, and K.C. casts a spell over her new friend, instructing McMurphy to destroy any remaining horcrux of romance. Kleenex and aviators are tossed into the fire, and the women cackle like witches. K.C. is bringing something foreign out of McMurphy that Laurette never did. Something selfish. Sadistic.

Instead of McMurphy walking stark naked into the ocean, alone, like in "Chao Ong," she now has a turbulent tag team partner. The third season premiere, "The Unquiet Earth" presents their first opponents. The Vietcong.

McMurphy and K.C. begin the season as they always do, in the shower stalls, drinking beer, arguing over who owes who. The angle of the plywood humorously, hardly covers the slope of McMurphy's bare breast. Delany is a method actor and customarily did these scenes in the buck, living up to her character's nickname in the writers' room, "nipples to the world." Nothing will ever stop the eternal argument between McMurphy and K.C., and it continues when both women are kidnapped by the VC and held captive in a cave later in the episode.

The further they recede from the surface, the dirtier, sweatier, and panickier they get. Paul Chihara's ominous score blends with echoes of incantations, helicopters, and rickety railroads to compound the terror. A communist commander is suffering from a sucking chest wound, and the enemy knows McMurphy can save him.

The origins of "The Unquiet Earth" can be traced to the 1986 book, *The Tunnels of Cu Chi*, by Tom Mangold and John Penycate. Researcher Toni Graphia knew she had found the ideal setting for an episode upon reading the book, a document of underground warfare that was prevalent in Vietnam throughout the decades. A vast, hidden honeycomb of caves was an ever-present thorn in the side of any foreigners who came looking for a fight. The US brought state-of-the-art aircraft, artillery, and gung-ho attitude.

In return, the Vietcong went medieval on our ass.

Dug by hand, a network of tunnels stretched underneath the country, deep into South Vietnam past Saigon. The caves were a vital component of the kamikaze Tet attack, far more than any underground railroad. As the book accounts, the tunnels were boobytrapped and camouflaged to house hidden hospitals, workshops, performance halls, and barracks. The Vietnamese had their own version of *China Beach* dug into the soil—out of American sight, right beneath their feet.

***Alan Brennert** (writer, "The Unquiet Earth")*: **What impressed me from the research was the sheer perseverance of the Vietcong, and the lengths to which they would go in their struggle: living in damp tunnels, barely subsisting on rations, moving from place to place to avoid getting caught. A sympathetic view of a onetime enemy was hardly a new theme—it goes back, at least, to *All Quiet on the Western Front.* But I for one had never seen this particular backdrop—cramped tunnels filled with tripwires and poisonous snakes—and**

> **that's in large part what made the episode so memorable. The set design was brilliant, as was Mike Rhodes's direction; the viewer really feels like they're down in those tunnels. And the decision not to cut away to any action at China Beach—I assume it was John Young's—was spot-on. It really added to the tension, the claustrophobia.**

The tunnels of Cu Chi are memorialized in Vietnam with an educational center thirty-five miles northwest of Saigon, a popular destination for day-tripping tourists. The Vietnamese are more than happy to show off this archaic method of warfare—a fucked-up version of *Home Alone* come to life, starring Vietnam as the tiny youngster luring big, bad, foreign intruders into a den of torture. Marg Helgenberger counted "The Unquiet Earth" as one of her favorite episodes, and visited the tunnels in late-2016 during her long-awaited trip to Vietnam. I followed in her footsteps to see the caves for myself.

A guide led my tour group to a shady grove and asked if we could spot the hidden entrance to a cave. A dozen of us peered around, muttering among one another, until a Vietnamese man's head popped out of a tiny rectangular hole in the ground. A few of us took the bait for a photo op before proceeding to a number of exhibits and in-ground hamlets showing off an array of hidden traps and primitive weapons that plagued visiting forces.

Mannequins sat in assembly lines making rubber sandals from discarded tires, a show of solidarity with Uncle Ho who sported the same footwear in Hanoi every day. M16's and AK-47's could be fired for a few dollars, right before the grand finale: crawling through a black underground tunnel. The caves aren't quite authentic, widened for the above-average-sized visitor, yet still tight, hot, and uncomfortable. A few minutes down there left me drenched in sweat with achy hamstrings, thinking about those who spent years in the same void.

A typical episode of *China Beach* was filmed on a familiar set under the sun-kissed sky of California, and "The Unquiet Earth" presented the challenge of executing an episode in the restrictions of a cave. A would-be bottle episode turned total pain-in-the-ass. John Sacret Young got ahold of Alan Brennert's script and threw in another curveball, adding a scene where McMurphy performs surgery while dozens of Vietcong hold a candlelit vigil so she can see. Young had already fired the first director, helmed a few scenes himself, then hired Michael Rhodes to finish the job. The end of filming approached, and Rhodes was out of ideas to make the scene happen.

> ***Michael Rhodes*** *(director, "The Unquiet Earth"):* **At lunchtime I had been up at the screening room to look at dailies and John was there. He was finished with the dailies and he didn't say anything, which I figured was a good thing. I said, "John, this is going to be really tough to shoot. Maybe we could simplify it." He asked me, "Why would I want to do that?" I said, "It's not the best, but it'll work and we'll get on schedule again." He says, "Look, if we're going to do stuff like that, I could go home and write a book back in Maine. I'm not going to do that."**

Rhodes rose to the occasion and delivered a memorable scene that lived on in the "Reflections" sequence throughout the third season. The sight of McMurphy sweating, siphoning, saving a life, surrounded by the enemy reaches past the art of war. Past logic. Past words. For a second, it doesn't matter which team the catcher in the rye is playing for. K.C. balances out McMurphy's good deed with a selfish, failed escape.

McMurphy and K.C.'s lives flash before their eyes as they await execution. A basic instinct of survival is surpassed by paternal shame when imminent death presents itself. Writer Alan Brennert's father had died years before he wrote the script, and he channeled his own experiences into the dialogue. He recalled Dana Delany telling him she "didn't need to act" during much of this scene. McMurphy reflects on the events of "The World" and wishes she had been in Kansas when her father needed her. K.C. had other wishes. To die every single afternoon before her abusive father came home from work. Marg Helgenberger reaches deeper into the pit of K.C. than she ever has, shedding tears with every syllable. Another dire situation K.C. can't buy her way out of, and that scares her more than anything.

The conversational topic of death reverts to a classic McMurphy and K.C. debate of supply and demand when the VC chief needs a blood transfusion. McMurphy cradles the old man while K.C. looks away, refusing to engage, pumping her type-O blood into his veins. The commander reminds them that the Vietnamese will do what they have to do to win this war, and that Ho Chi Minh's declaration of

Vietnamese independence was copped straight from the words of Thomas Jefferson. "The Unquiet Earth" skates close to the theme of Bill Broyles's script for "Home," taking a short walk in the enemy's rubber sandals. Instead of McMurphy bringing a little Vietnamese life into the world, she saves an old one from the brink. The opposition prays and takes care of each other, and defends their mother land from alien invaders at all costs.

Would McMurphy, K.C., or any red-blooded American do otherwise?

McMurphy and K.C. rise to their feet, ready to take a bullet, and the VC soldier loses his nerve, right as bombs rock the compound from overhead. They escape through a water trap, meeting oxygen, freedom, and daylight, and walk arm-in-arm back to *China Beach.* A swooping crane shot pulls up and out into the sky, and the two women shrink down to stick figures while the earth unfolds around them. The opening hour of the third season is a confined look at a crisis for McMurphy and K.C. that masks a growing world above them. Vietnam will keep expanding and enveloping them, and they will have to continue holding on to each other to survive, whether they like it or not.

Geno Escarrega, John Wells, Toni Graphia, Mimi Leder, Lydia Woodward, Josef Anderson, Carol Flint, Fred Gerber, Georgia Jeffries, and John Sacret Young dressed up as the China Beach cast

HARD TO HANDLE

In the opening moments of "The Unquiet Earth," Dr. Dick Richard stands opposite Dr. Gerard Bernard (Derek de Lint) at an operating table. They trade asides, swiping at each other's home countries. America. France. Both hexed in Vietnam. McMurphy bounces between them, and Dick sighs and rolls his eyes when she flirts with the *other* guy. Dick's first impression of their liaison never goes away, and it sticks for a total of nine. never. ending. episodes.

China Beach places McMurphy on a pedestal, and any interested suitor is justly met with skepticism. Who is worthy of her love and affection? Natch broke her heart and drove her deeper into addiction. Away from her patients and away from the viewer. McMurphy is never better than when she's on her own, fighting the good fight, but a case study backed by ABC demanded a new romantic appendage along with several other creative change-ups.

The French doctor's look is distinguished by a chocolate sweep of hair, a dash of salt and pepper, a bandana around his neck, and a dress shirt with one too many buttons undone. Things begin sufficiently in "Independence Day," when McMurphy shares with him a loot of American junk food. Bernard takes her and her country's good Samaritan plight to task, and parlays his condescensions into the heat of passion. By the end of the episode, McMurphy is held hostage at a French plantation by Bernard, his homicidal ex-wife, and his adorable kids. Everyone else is back at China Beach, having the time of their life, populating one of the more ardent spectacles of the series—a rainy, slow-motion baseball game lit by fireworks.

McMurphy and Bernard continue fussing, fornicating, and faltering for over a third of the season, and it stalls much of the show's forward momentum.

Delany and Derek de Lint

More than fascinating individuals, *China Beach* coasts upon the ties that bind. In McMurphy's case, she is never more insecure, jealous, or distracted than when she is occupied with Dr. Bernard. Precious time that could be spent with K.C. and Dr. Richard spoils, along with McMurphy's dedication to the betterment of the human race. I took all the principal writers to task on the plot of Dr. Bernard, and each digressed. It was a mandate from the powers that be. Dana Delany was the sole defender of the plot, justifying, "Well, you know, all women go through that phase [*laughs*] of thinking they need the exotic foreigner when there's somebody right at home. It did bring a certain exotic element."

The second network directive "by popular demand" was to lift the collective mood of the show. The doom and gloom stemming from Tet, the death of MLK, and existential displacement in the prior season was met with a number of gleeful gimmicks, varying in success. Unyielding patriotism is on display during "Independence Day," a battle of the bands follows in "With a Little Help from My Friends," and then a visiting circus comes to town in "Magic."

"Skin Deep" follows after "The Unquiet Earth" with the inaugural attempt at instilling a more perky air with a Miss China Beach pageant. Each woman and their individual femininity is celebrated via conveyor belt onstage, reintroducing and reacquainting each character with the audience. McMurphy loosens up and acts like a *Price is Right* model, displaying IVs and bedpans, and Lila Garreau lets her hair down and bares "the best arms in the world," according to Dana Delany. A glorified extra takes the crown and sash, and we never see her again. Frankie Bunsen shows up late, covered in grease from a shift in the motor pool, and ends the showcase with a stand-up roast of her new boss, Sgt. Bub Pepper (Troy Evans).

The third season receives another modular lift with the season's mantle guest star, Ricki Lake, portraying the new Red Cross donut dolly, Holly Pelegrino (named in honor of Linda Pelegrino, one of the show's technical advisors). Holly is the white-bread babyface answer to Cherry White. Full-figured, loud, and cheerful, the one major chord in a depressing ballad. Literally everything Nan Woods was not. Holly turns lemons to lemonade like Laurette and relaxes everyone with more immediacy than Wayloo—all while instilling a jovial, boisterous spirit with every appearance.

Ricki Lake as the new donut dolly, Holly Pelegrino

***Ricki Lake** (Holly Pelegrino):* **I knew of *China Beach*, but I wasn't a fervent watcher. I wish I could say, "Oh, I consciously chose this show." Basically when you're an actor, you think your last job is going to be your last job. This was the next job that came along, I didn't see myself as this serious actress at the time, so to be asked to be a main character in an already-successful drama series — it felt like an amazing opportunity. I lost my virginity during that time, so it was a turning point.**

I didn't know if I had the chops for it, but I feel like I did a good job. I just remember being nervous. Like, I was in really good company, they upped my game. The cast was amazing. I really felt intimidated a little bit because I was so obsessed with Dana Delany and Marg Helgenberger — all of them, really. Brian Wimmer was a great friend of mine. He took me to the Emmys as his date. I remember my twenty-first birthday party; the whole cast of *China Beach* came and all of them sang karaoke!

Another onscreen addition to the show was Jeff Hyers, played by Ned Vaughn, upped to a full-timer based on the strength of his turn in "Where the Boys Are" in the prior season. Hyers is a friendly, Southern, amiable medic, and like Holly, is not a complicated character that needs to be unpacked. Boonie is already the resident nice guy, and Hyers is quickly lost in the ongoing shuffle of the season.

Many enticing threads from season two remain unaccounted for. Boonie Lanier is paired up with Holly for comic relief, and the bartender loses his edge. His identity crisis putters, along with the aftershocks of combat. Less of a Brian Wilson, more of a Davy Jones. Samuel Beckett also suffers throughout the third season. Michael Boatman hardly carries a plot on his own, and his character's promising relationship with Mai dissipates without a satisfying conclusion.

More experiments in the third season bring wild, unexpected success. Bub Pepper is introduced as a gruff, middle-aged, stout, bigoted redneck with a buzzcut. Within a few episodes, he is outed as a charmer, combing his hair in a mirror before asking Lila Garreau for a dance. The unlikely lovers eat post-coital fried chicken in "Who's Happy Now?" and stress over the dichotomy of coming home to parades in World War II and hosting their own return parties from Vietnam. Lila finally feels available, susceptible to love, thanks to Bub.

Concetta Tomei: **Bub Pepper made Lila Garreau a woman. That was an amazing transformation for Lila, and for me. It was really quite wonderful because I wanted to be able to show a range for that character, but you can't necessarily show it if it's written in a certain direction. I was so happy and grateful that they thought of my character in that way, to bring in someone as sensitive as Troy, and what a fine actor! I feel like my wings were literally clipped until he came on to the show.**

Troy Evans *(Sgt. Bub Pepper)***:** **Concetta is a marvelous person. She's incredibly high-strung. I don't mean that in any negative way, but from the time she hits the studio gate in the morning until she drives away, her mind never, ever stops. I'm not the kind of actor who gets romantic parts. That sort of forbidden romance—it usually happens the other way—some non-commissioned, attractive young woman messing around with an officer, or an enlisted person that has power over her. That's the common way it comes about, but to have this major, this ball-busting, powerful figure fall for Bub Pepper—that was really a leap for the writers to take. They took a guy who appeared to be an obstreperous buffoon and they allowed him to improve. They allowed him to change, and I believe that people can become better if they want to become better. That was important to me, to not just be: "Oh yeah, you were the asshole on *China Beach*!" They allowed that character to become something.**

Holly, Hyers, and Sgt. Pepper are the first of countless new faces that flood the third season of *China Beach*. Recurring guest stars, cameos, and a couple of one-and-done directors infiltrate these early hours, all topped off by McMurphy's relationship with Dr. Bernard. A silver lining of that arc comes with the recurring guest appearance of Tom Sizemore in one of his first screen roles as Vinnie Ventresca, a scrappy GI who is smitten with McMurphy. Vinnie's boyish disposition can't match McMurphy's depth and sophistication, yet still usurps the Casanova as a more likable suitor.

John Levey *(series casting director)*: **My assistant at the time was allergic to cigarette smoke, and Tom Sizemore came in and sat on the corner of her desk. He had just arrived in LA from Michigan and he lit up a cigarette and was kind of teasing her and blowing it around her office. He just took over the space and there was something horrifying. You wanted to punch him in the mouth, but at the same time you couldn't stop watching him.**

By the time Dr. Bernard exits the show in "Magic" and reveals himself as a two-timing philanderer, Vinnie is still hanging around and hits his highest notes in "Warriors," when he and McMurphy euthanize his braindead friend who was wounded in action. Sizemore shatters Vinnie's glass house of bluster and mourns his fallen friend with McMurphy at his side. This strained, overwhelming mix of sorrow and attraction feels more alive and more *China Beach* than any moment with Dr. Bernard.

All while McMurphy is tending to Dr. Bernard and Vinnie, her workplace relationship with Dr. Richard cools. They are still contentious coworkers, but their suppressed attraction isn't as playful or promising. Pressing pause on McMurphy and Richard at this juncture feels like a misfire, and even worse, a prolonged waiting game to just get back to that delicious pairing. With Dr. Richard left to his own devices, Robert Picardo turns in a couple of dynamite arcs in his character's quest to become a new man in "Ghosts."

Toni Graphia's first script for *China Beach* strips Dick of more humility and self-sanctity upon the receipt of a wedding invitation from his ex-wife Beth Ann, spawned by a true story seen in "Vets." The invitation compels him to exorcise the trappings of his former life through an elaborate weekend of black wedding festivities. Graphia channeled her Louisiana Bayou upbringing into the voodoo processional, anointing Dick Richard as the emcee. Picardo is on point, capturing Dr. Richard's longing to let go of the past while tempting manic depression.

Director Michael Fresco set a tone by playing Mozart's Requiem aloud while filming a candlelit parade through the Five and Dime. It is a ludicrous sight, held together by a straight-faced, tuxedo-clad Picardo. Effigies of a groom and a bride are hoisted and carried to the nearby river, New Orleans-cum-Vietnam. The macabre bride even has a picture of Picardo's then-wife stapled to her face. As Dr. Richard sets the couple ablaze, the fire is the sole source of light illuminating his face as he howls into the evening. The crowd roars along with him. Richard brought false ideals of life and happiness to Vietnam, and will be going home without them.

Dr. Dick has another standout turn in "Who's Happy Now?" when he befriends a brain-damaged GI after a failed craniotomy. The boy is beyond saving, just like the little girl with a heart murmur in "Crossing the Great Water." The doctor slumps down on a wall, losing it again over one more young life he is beyond helping. Picardo takes the composure and poise of his character and tears it to shreds. Dick sees himself, his sons, and everyone else he has lost in this young man, resent pouring from every outlet. The doctor swindled the audience into empathy at some unidentifiable point, and we are now more than willing to climb down in the trenches with him and mourn.

"Who's Happy Now?" is another prime example of *China Beach* attempting a lighter tone, presenting the most preposterous thread of the show slipped between Picardo's operatic arias. I indicted all the principal players about a storyline where Col. Buster Darling (R. Lee Ermey) dies in K.C. Koloski's bed, handcuffed to the headboard. For the rest of the episode, Boonie and Hyers shuttle his disguised corpse around the Five and Dime in attempts to hide it, a la *Weekend at Bernie's*. It first felt irreverent, out of place, and even offensive to the show's standards. John Young, director Fred Gerber, and writer Lydia Woodward brushed it off their shoulders during interviews. Ned Vaughn paused, and searched his thirty-year-old memories. I thought he had hung up the phone until he cried out, "Oh my God! Lee Ermey!" I was never in on the joke, until Vaughn explained further.

Ermey was not only a Vietnam veteran, he was two years removed from his unforgettable role as Gunnery Sergeant Hartman in Stanley Kubrick's *Full Metal Jacket* when he was cast in "Who's Happy Now?" Ermey's signature performance as Hartman is notorious for throwing teakettle tirades and threatening to tear the heads off of soldiers and shit down their necks if they didn't un-fuck themselves. In the world of *China Beach*, Hartman is reincarnated as a hapless putz, respected by no one.

> ***Marg Helgenberger:* I love black comedy, and the episode in which R. Lee Ermey dies while handcuffed to K.C.'s bed was right up my alley. R. Lee was such a gentleman and a sport during the shooting of that episode. He made what could have been an awkward situation a fun and breezy one.**

I ridiculed and debased the Buster Darling arc in "Who's Happy Now?" until realizing it was one huge prank that took a lot of gall to do. Woodward claimed she did not write the episode with Ermey in mind, but someone knew what they were doing when Ermey was cast. With the episode title, Woodward was poking fun at the longtime suspicions of former Vice President Nelson Rockefeller dying in bed with an aide during an extramarital affair. His wife was named Happy. The third season of *China Beach* feels very much like *The White Album*—an indispensable, Homeric tome comprising greatest hits, deep cuts, and the kind of punchlines that only find a home on a double LP.

A DAY IN THE LIFE

There are astounding moments in *China Beach* where the thin lubricant between lived history and the screen product runs dry. Both sides begin to chafe the other, swapping their flesh and blood to form a substance in the middle all its own. "Vets" was obvious in its approach, and Georgia Jeffries's two-part script for "How to Stay Alive in Vietnam" was entirely oblique.

Jeffries envisioned an episode that would offer a glimpse of in-country combat and continue brightening up the proceedings. Dodger, Beckett, the Answer Man (Robert Lasordo), and a photojournalist, Cat Von Seeger (Lisa Baines), trek into the bush in search of Vietcong, while denizens of the Five and Dime tell stories of war at the Jet Set, in a send-up of the comedic variety show *Laugh-In* (1967-73). The concept morphed during production into something closer to the interview format from "Vets," with each character in a dark room, lit by spotlight.

One after another, the characters recount their in-country experiences: McMurphy describes her desire to fit in with the guys, Lila reflects on her third war, and K.C. even tells a joke. Sgt. Bub Pepper outshines them all with his list of darkly comic rules of warfare. The episode's dueling concepts march together in lockstep. The moment Cat's reflection of her camera draws the squad into a firefight, Sgt. Pepper's fifth rule reminds us "all your equipment was made by the lowest bidder."

Sarge diverges from his rules of surviving guerrilla warfare and offers a terrifying tale, right as Beckett stabs a VC to death and Hyers is sprayed with a hail of bullets. Troy Evans sheds Sarge's thick skin and downshifts his timbre from a brash tone to a near tremble. Bub Pepper's platoon included the dog man, who always led the patrol thirty feet out with his trusted canine companion. With five days left on his tour, the dog man and his companion took enemy fire ahead of the platoon, diving into an enemy bunker for shelter. An enemy machine gunner sat atop it, opening fire at Sarge and his men. Sarge could hear the dog howling, and the dog man screaming in pain: "I'm hit, but I'm alright!" Sarge was the custodian of an M-72 bazooka, saving the weapon of destruction for a rainy day or an enemy tank. It was a catch-22 of either the dog man and his dog, or Sarge and all his men. Bub fired the bazooka at the bunker.

The dog man went home early in a casket. Sarge got a Bronze Star.

The episode ends on rule number eleven: "Do what you have to do. Those are the jokes, folks." Evans stares a hole through the camera as a crocodile tear runs down his cheek. It's a stunning monologue that pushes the episode into the credits. The raw conviction within Evans's performance might make one believe it all really happened.

> ***Troy Evans:*** **That is an actual, true story of mine from Vietnam. Everything that I tell in that story is gospel. I didn't think about this when I got the job, but now in retrospect, I think *China Beach* really sort of saved my life in a way. *China Beach* was really my therapy. It wasn't the first day on *China Beach*, but it was early. I got called to the set and it was rainy and muddy and dark, and I was running, and I tripped on something and fell. I stopped to see what I tripped over and it was a bodybag [*pause*] and, oh. Jesus Christ. That blew me out of the water, man. That was a harsh moment to come back to reality and realize it is TV, but it actually gave me a safe place to kind of work through a lot of that survivor's guilt and that stuff that soldiers have.**

A viewer at home in 1989 wouldn't know any better without a smartphone, but long before Evans was an actor in Hollywood, he was drafted in late-1967 to serve in Vietnam after dropping out of college. The Montana native spent a year in-country, coming home in July of 1969 and getting shot with rock salt by a police officer two days later. Evans was still in formal military dress. The dominoes began falling from there. Evans entered the bar business in Montana, fist-fighting with drunk patrons, police, and anyone else who looked at him the wrong way. After serving time in the Montana State Prison, Evans relocated to Southern California with hopes that a criminal record wouldn't hinder his prospects in the acting profession.

Opposite page: Troy Evans in-country, 1969

Nancy Giles: Troy is soulful, and he was *there*, so just getting a taste of what it was like from somebody who was there was awesome. He's the real deal. Those big, beautiful, droopy, dreamy eyes of his—they could flick from being really mean to soulful. I loved his voice, I loved how we looked together; we were like this mismatched couple. I loved how snide he was to me, and that helped give Frankie some backbone because she started out a little unsure of herself with him. Eventually, she got to give back as much as she got from him. There seemed to be a grudging respect that I got from him. He's just a masterful actor and he makes it look easy.**

Evans spent much of the eighties splitting time between stage work, film, and television, including guest appearances on *Cheers* and *Night Court.* Evans also performed a one-man stage show, *Troy Evans' Montana Tales and Other Bad Ass Business*, full of his frank humor and stories from Vietnam. Evans's theater work soon crossed paths with John Wells and led to a guest-starring appearance in "The World," waywardly resulting in the recurring role of Sgt. Bub Pepper in the following season.

***Troy Evans:* I worked the second season, one day. It's the episode where Dana Delany is called back to the US for something and they are treated horribly by the army stateside. I was a sergeant running a decontamination center where they get off the plane. I made them run through this shower of pesticides and stuff to kill any Southeast-Asian cooties they had on them, you know, just ranting and raving, "Move it! Move it!" and being a general non-commissioned asshole. Back then in television, you could appear one season and then next season you are someone else. Today, they just don't allow that any more. If you go on a TV show as the cab driver, they're not going to let you come back next year and read for the lawyer. But they did, and they created that role of Bub Pepper for me, and I was appreciative.**

After Wells invited the writing staff to Evans's stage show, Georgia Jeffries knew that she had to incorporate the story of the dog man into her script. It was an unprecedented plot device, surpassing any conventional term of surrealism. Director Fred Gerber said he called

"Action!" and turned Evans loose to do his thing. The lens of distorted reality shatters in the moment, and Evans picks up the shards with his bare hands, putting it all back together for the audience to peer through.

The successes of "How to Stay Alive in Vietnam, Part 1" are as striking as its shortcomings, with the magnitude of Evans's performance minimizing the death of Hyers. Even with McMurphy's presence curtailed in the episode, too much is happening too quickly, and the proven, labored pace of *China Beach* is ignored. The end of "Part 1" is a microcosm of the third season—sheer brilliance piercing through excess and reckless zeal.

> ***Ned Vaughn (Jeff Hyers):*** **I had a mixed reaction when I found out they were going to kill Hyers. On one hand, I thought, "Hey, it's a war show, you can get that bullet any old time, so no huge surprise, it could make for something dramatic," and I think they made a lot of how Hyers died, which I was grateful for. Also, I was aware that the cast had grown quite a lot and frankly I don't think they quite knew what to do with everybody.**
>
> **I was loving being on the show, but I also had some episodes where I would basically walk through the background and ask what time it was or hang that bottle of plasma on the side of the bed, so I felt a little bit like, "Hey, maybe I can go on and find something where I'm more needed." So it was a bit of an ambivalent reaction. I wish I could have hung out there a little bit longer.**

For "Part 2" of her script, Jeffries enlisted another individual to beam their nightmares from Southeast Asia through the prism of *China Beach*, casting Haing S. Ngor as a Cambodian POW, Seak Yin. Ngor was five years removed from winning the Academy Award for Best Supporting Actor in *The Killing Fields*, joining Harold Russel as the only other amateur actor to win an Oscar.

As detailed in his vivid, remarkable memoir, *A Cambodian Odyssey* (1989), Ngor was not a classically trained actor, having no choice but to learn how to pretend he was someone else during years of captivity in 1970s' communist Cambodia. The fascist Khmer Rouge regime would have killed Ngor had they discovered he was a physician. After watching his wife die during childbirth, Ngor escaped the country and ended up a refugee in Los Angeles. Ngor was later cast in *The Killing Fields* and reenacted many of the same terrors he had already endured. The morning after winning his Oscar, Ngor was back at his day job, helping fellow Cambodian refugees.

> ***Dana Delany:*** **When [Haing Ngor] came to the States, he was not allowed to practice medicine because he didn't have a Western degree, but he devoted his life to helping refugees from Cambodia, especially the children. [*sigh*] God. These memories are killing me! I remember sitting with him on the set and saying to him, "You are *so* positive. How can you be so positive after everything you have witnessed in your life?" I'll never forget this, and I think about it all the time. He said, "We must never forget to dance," and he really believed that.**
>
> **"We must never forget to dance."**

The first half of "How to Stay Alive in Vietnam" took the life of Hyers and offered Seak in his place as a suspected Vietcong. McMurphy nurses Seak back to health, and with no evidence, proclaims his innocence to every doubter. Ngor's screen presence as Seak falls somewhere between Master Yoda and Fred Rogers. Lovable, unimposing, and inviting. McMurphy knows her patient is not guilty, and so does the viewer—and this episode gifts the audience the first notable chance since "The Unquiet Earth" to rally behind McMurphy, pump their fists, and rage against systematic odds. The plot of a friendly native suspected of treachery bears a striking resemblance to *Good Morning, Vietnam!* (1986) and is an authentic dilemma that many Americans faced during the war. *China Beach* ran with this story thread on two other separate occasions in the third season with different characters, and the performances from Delany and Ngor deem those instances unnecessary in comparison.

This episode is fully loaded with several other guest stars, including a visiting Commander Otis (Dorian Harewood) who arrives to micromanage Lila Garreau and ravish K.C. Koloski. A head scratcher of a scene is when Otis and K.C. spend the night together and wake up in each other's arms. A fully satisfied interracial couple, still clothed.

Opposite page: Delany and Haing S. Ngor

Dr. Bernard is still loitering, and Cat Von Seeger hangs around to finish her story about Seak Yin. Haing S. Ngor rises above all of these exotic flavors and brings gravity to the center of a busy episode.

Seak disappears from China Beach, and McMurphy traces him to a Vietcong prison at the exact moment he is executed. The scene is inspired by the famous 1968 Eddie Adams photograph of a South Vietnamese police chief shooting a Vietcong suspect on a Saigon sidewalk. The gun is at point-blank range, firing straight into the skull of the accused. The image makes one forget about good or evil, and abhor the brutality of it all.

> ***Steve Dubin*** *(director, "How to Stay Alive in Vietnam, Part 2"):* **I said, "Listen Dr. Ngor, we're going to recreate this moment, so we're going to pretend we are shooting a bullet in your head and you're going to react to it." We're standing there and I go, "Action!" He had seen a thousand people shot to death, so he knew what to do. He fell, I said, "Cut!" Chip Vucelich was my AD on that. We looked at each other and said, "Holy shit, that was incredible," because it just seemed so damn *real.* Just being around Haing Ngor was an inspiration.**

Ngor was unable to outrun violence onscreen and off. Five years after his appearance in *China Beach*, Ngor was shot and killed outside his apartment in Los Angeles Chinatown. An anonymous friend of Ngor's claimed it was not a robbery as reported, but political revenge for his work with Cambodian refugees.

At the end of "How to Stay Alive in Vietnam, Part 2," McMurphy returns to the Jet Set to drink down her most recent defeat. For the first time in too long, we've seen her fight something, anyone other than the French doctor. It's a pivotal victory for *China Beach.* An augury of the series restoring its former glory, preparing to surpass it.

LET'S GET IT ON

When Dana Delany won the Emmy for Best Actress in a Drama Series for her performance in "The World," the cast and crew of *China Beach* partied all night in celebration. John Young remembers the sun coming up, and Delany standing in an open sunroof, Emmy in hand, claiming to Marg Helgenberger, "Next year, it's your turn." Delany's words were prophetic. Helgenberger made damn sure of it.

K.C. Koloski was a mystifying delight through seasons one and two, and the first opportune moment to let K.C. steer the ship was withheld. At the end of the second-season highlight "Cherry," K.C. boards a cargo plane headed for the States. She is ensconced by caskets, one holding the remains of Cherry White. The camera draws in on K.C., and John Rubenstein's theme hits a note of suspended agony, darkness swallowing the hustler.

Accompanying K.C. back to Iowa for Cherry's funeral held every explosive promise of following McMurphy home in "The World." K.C. never volunteers for anything, let alone an unpaid vacation. Why is she going? To score drugs? To cut a business deal? Out of the goodness of her heart? K.C. is still that woman in the doorway, and still has the audience asking questions that will never be answered. Helgenberger's shot at headlining an episode grows long overdue, into arrears in the third season, and then paid in full with "Nightfall."

Something must have happened midway through the third season of *China Beach* that scared the writers' room straight. "Nightfall" marks the beginning of a walkabout where the show is hellbent on finding a new spirit to inhabit its body. From the count-off, everything is different. Boonie finds a dead woman in a cocktail dress washed up on the shore, and Paul Chihara's spy-hunter theme instills the air of an erotic noir thriller. Beckett examines the corpse in the GRU, and McMurphy spots an earring once owned by K.C., who must know *something*. The mood continues shifting toward late-night Cinemax schlock from the days of Bush 41. A smooth saxophone soundtracks Beckett interring the body, while K.C. bathes with a customer in slo-mo.

It's highly stylized, cheeky in taste, and exists nowhere else in *China Beach*.

McMurphy and K.C. playing Sherlock and Holmes sounds like a fool-proof plot; instead, K.C. takes the reins as a naughty and nefarious Nancy Drew. Someone killed her employee, and by defending her storefront, K.C. begins to reclaim her humanity. K.C.'s part-time lover, Commander Otis, attempts to quash any investigation, and K.C. begins tearing apart the Five and Dime in search of the murderer. Along with Dana Delany, Helgenberger was regarded by the cast and crew as a patient, dedicated leader without ego. During "Nightfall," the taxing conditions in the desert finally got the better of Helgenberger, for one fleeting moment.

> ***Marg Helgenberger:*** **We did work hard. I remember blowing up one time because I was tired, I was cold. It was at night, of course, out at Indian Dunes, and it was described as this *light mist*, and it wasn't a *light mist*, I'm talking about *rain*. It doesn't read on camera, so it has to be a pretty substantial rain to visually see it, especially at night. It was coming down so hard to the point where my contact lenses were swimming around in my eyeballs. I just blew up, and I don't do that often. I'm really not one of those diva types. Dorian Harewood was in the scene with me and he was pretty cool. He had much more class than I did. That's the only time I remember losing it.**

> ***Chip Vucelich*** *(series assistant director):* ***China Beach*** **was supposed to be tropical. It is winter, and it was cold out at Indian Dunes. We had a rain scene where Marg was in shorts and a t-shirt in the rain. I've got the parka on from *Lost in Space* with the fur collar. It was cold, and she was doing this. [*laughs*] I'm not laughing at Marg, I'm laughing at the absurdity of it. I remember Marg said, "I need a minute." She stepped out of the rain about twenty feet away and just went [*yells*] "Fuuucckk!!! [*pause*] Okay, I'm ready." And that was it.**

***Dana Delany:* Listen, Marg deserved to have a diva fit. I usually had long sleeves and long underwear on, and she was always in some skimpy outfit. [*laughs*]**

K.C.'s moral code is exposed in "Nightfall" without any help from McMurphy when the murdered prostitute's daughter comes looking for her mother. The girl doesn't know her mother is dead and tries to land steady employment from Ms. Koloski. K.C's conscience can't handle that burden, and the internal dialogue reads as a novel on Helgenberger's face. The soul of K.C. begins to stir from a coma. K.C.'s money can't solve the crime, but it ensures the girl doesn't live her life in the sex trade when K.C. later frees her from another madam.

In one long, unbroken, four-minute take, K.C. sits in the cathedral among dozens of lit candles for a make-believe confessional, bearing herself like never before to an audience of none. K.C. reminisces back to her first job at a meatpacking plant, sneaking to the slaughter room to watch the cows meet their death. The camera creeps in a slow spiral around her, and when K.C.'s face meets the light, tears cascade down her cheeks. The constant sight of the butchery induced emotional atrophy, in the same way that selling her body now does. K.C. strikes a deal with herself to allow love in if it comes. Director Christopher Leitch recalled fourteen takes over two days to get the scene and lighting and camera work just right. Helgenberger's performance in "Nightfall" later secured a Prime Time Emmy for Best Supporting Actress.

***Marg Helgenberger:* The episode that concludes with K.C.'s meatpacking monologue all began with writer Lydia Woodward reaching out to me to pick my brain, and spitball ideas. Over a meal of burgers and fries at Canter's Deli, I shared with Lydia my experiences of working at a meatpacking plant, while a teenager in Nebraska. I had no idea, until reading the final draft of Lydia's script, that my real-life experience as a meatpacker would become a metaphor for K.C.'s detachment to her own emotions. I'll always be grateful to Lydia for crafting such a beautiful and haunting story for K.C./me.**

***Lydia Woodward** (writer, "Nightfall"):* **I felt there were parallels between [a job in a meatpacking plant] and the experience of being a prostitute—the kind of emotional numbness that is essential to survive in certain circumstances. That notion became the central question of the scene and the episode: what happens if/when we lose the defenses which have sustained us? How will we survive if we begin to feel the things we have always blocked out?**

China Beach continues doubling down on a new identity in the latter half of season three, willing to discard its essential opening sequence in a one-time Pavlovian fake-out. The opening seconds of "Phoenix" are jarring every time—the sight of the *China Beach* title card and a walking bass line that isn't "Reflections," but a specially commissioned cover of The Animals' 1965 classic "We Gotta Get Out of This Place."

William Broyles Jr.: **That was our anthem in Vietnam. That's what we would sing. We would all go out and put a position up on the ridge line right in the jungle, and we would cut bamboo to make our little hooches and keep the monsoon rains out. We'd all be singing: "We gotta get out of this place, if it's the only thing we ever do." We had Eric Burdon and Katrina and the Waves come and record a new version for us. He was the lead singer of the Animals, who'd done the original, and that was really fun.**

China Beach reached the upper echelon of pop art status in 1990 and released a soundtrack, *China Beach: Music and Memories*. The collection is comprised of Motown songs, "We Gotta Get Out of This Place," audio dispatches from "Vets," and a few original cuts, with one track sung by Dana Delany. John Young claimed the LP topped out at the sixth bullet on the Australian Billboard chart. The substitution of "Reflections" was audibly booed at a 1990 Paley Center for Media panel. The cast and crew shifted in their seats, and "Reflections" was promptly returned to its place in the show.

"Phoenix" also poses the end of another hallowed *China Beach* institution—the dysfunctional sorority of McMurphy and K.C. Toni Graphia was intent on writing a script that could split up the two unwilling sisters who were never really sold on each other in the first place. This is not the typical *China Beach* script that lets silence do all the talking—it is full of meme-ready, flip-of-the-hair dialogue and 100 mph plot turns, feeling more like a Quentin Tarantino script than any previous yarn from the Five and Dime.

McMurphy and K.C. begin the episode with a petty exchange. Koloski, LLC is liquidating, purging earthly goods that are no longer of use, including a crucifix that was a gift from McMurphy: "It's a crucifix, for God's sake." McMurphy enters a bidding war with a GI, until K.C. puts on the necklace and vows to never take it off. A few scenes later, it shows up in the triage unit as evidence in the killing of a local VC chief.

***Toni Graphia** (writer, "Phoenix"):* **We would interview people in the CIA who did Black Ops on secret stuff in Vietnam. A bizarre rule of war is that you can go shoot at each other in a field and kill hundreds of people at one time, but if you go and put a gun to someone's head in the middle of the night in their bed, that's a murder. The question always fascinated me, "How do you have a murder in the middle of a war?" K.C. is a shady operator and she's the type that would get mixed up with these CIA types who might use her for this assassination. If something happened where she needed McMurphy to lie for her, would McMurphy cross her own principles and lie for a friend in the middle of this war? I wanted to throw that dilemma at these two women.**

***Mimi Leder** (director, "Phoenix"):* **Together, Dana Delany and Marg Helgenberger were magic. Dana in her greens and her uniform, and Marg in a very tight, short dress. I would do these long tracking shots of them walking and fighting and bickering and the imagery just always spoke a thousand words. It was like doing a comedy in the midst of the horror of war with this prostitute business woman with this nurse who saves lives. They were probably the two most diverse, most opposite characters on the planet thrown together into this place that both serviced soldiers in life-saving ways. [*laughs*] The characters were incredible individually and together, explosive.**

McMurphy's Girl Scout honor is pitted against K.C.'s unlikely innocence, and the episode worms its way through espionage, slam-dunk one-liners, and K.C.'s arrest. By the time McMurphy discovers K.C. is innocent, it's too late. K.C. bailed herself out and is back at the Jet Set, awaiting her former best friend. Leder visualizes a moment, a feeling between the two women that can't ever be forgotten: K.C. rolling her eyes, lighting a cigarette, and McMurphy clutching a bottle of booze, expecting a "thank you." Two nuclear cooling towers ready to blow.

McMurphy and K.C. take it outside, and a shattered bourbon bottle signals the start of round 1. Insults over their respective shortcomings in life, love, and the American way project like shrapnel, while Delany and Helgenberger display absolute mastery of their characters' toxic, rhythmic codependency. K.C. attempts to take McMurphy down into the gutter with her: "We're not that different. Both at our best with men on their backs." Graphia choreographs this duel so that neither woman is right or wrong, and the audience doesn't know who to cheer for. K.C. tests the point of no-return, declaring herself as the sister McMurphy never had and never wanted. McMurphy is unable to hit the unfriend button, and unwilling to admit K.C. is worth anything to her.

"And there you are."

"Phoenix" ends on the flushed face of K.C., out of words. Out of gas. This no-holds-barred brawl ends in a split decision and marks the final exercise of pragmatism in *China Beach*. Surrounding episodes shake the fault line of the show, and when the McMurphy and K.C. bond threatens to splinter in "Phoenix," the tectonic plates of the Five and Dime shift into unabashed Dadaism.

This is the end of *China Beach* as we know it.

BEYOND THE SEA

The last half of *China Beach*'s third season is intent on dismantling any preconceived notion of the show. Tales of morality retract into a world that seems more and more unsure, unsound, unwelcome. This edition of the Vietnam War is turning into a different kind of hell. One with no end and no beginning, stretching time, characters, emotions, and patience like Silly Putty. Most of these creative approaches are elaborate, ignoring the rules of physics, logic, and Father Time. Another succeeds in creating an alternate reality with something that all of us in 2018 can relate to.

Fake news, folks.

Without psychedelics, screenwriter Josef Anderson alters the minds of everyone at the Five and Dime in his script for "A Rumor of Peace," offering a false hope of the Vietnam War coming to an end in 1968. As Anderson wrote the script, he clung to the idea of how endings loosen lips and inhibitions, particularly in the workplace. Frankie's DJ shift ends with the news that the Cowsills and Rolling Stones are banned by the Armed Forces Network. The censorship enrages her, so she and Beckett start their own bandit radio station to play whatever they want and mock the establishment. Michael Boatman impersonates a Frenchman, Walter Cronkite, and a velveteen-voiced DJ known as Dr. Dark within a span of seconds. Then, we all wonder why Boatman didn't get more juicy material to sink his teeth into this season. Beckett's practical joke convinces the listening audience that the war is over. Before he delivers the punchline, the circuit board crashes and China Beach is cut off from the outside world.

For an entire episode, there is no tomorrow, at least in Vietnam.

Lila beams with joy, getting more blasted than anyone and offering free champagne to all in the Jet Set. The major beds Bub Pepper while soldiers drive in donuts on the helipad. Frankie and Beckett grimace, too ashamed, too afraid to stop the party. K.C. and Boonie share a genuine kiss, imagining a possible life together after the war. The excitement is palpable. We're all going home in one piece. Everyone soon wakes up from this wet dream that one day must come true, and that day comes early for Dodger.

Jeff Kober's character is often out of sight for long stretches of episodes and yet always in mind, creeping through a rice paddy to the tune of "Reflections" during the opening of each episode. Like the Vietcong, he's hardly seen or heard from, but his presence is felt. The character was always with Kober, who drew from his own misspent youth each time he inhabited Dodger.

> ***Jeff Kober:*** **I'll just be honest, I had tragedy in my own adolescence which perfectly matched [Dodger]. Today I recognize that I was suffering from my own form of PTSD, and the kind of acting that I learned was all based upon living truthfully under imaginary circumstances. You use your own inner life, but you put different pictures, different images on it. In your imagination, if you put yourself through situations, your emotional life doesn't know the difference. I took that well of grief and sorrow and rage that was within me and put the pictures of Vietnam on it. And voila, you have Dodger.**

Kober is articulate and soft-spoken, owning a zen-like presence of calm, thorough insightfulness. Kober has been a gainfully employed actor since long before *China Beach*, and fills up his downtime with tintype photography and teaching Vedic meditation. Dana Delany and Chloe Webb are two of his students.

Dodger is MIA in the third season until "Dear China Beach." A side-scrolling panorama of smoke rising and GIs beating up Vietcong leads to a small hill, topped by Dodger, draping his arms around a machine gun. A Christ-like image. The minister of destruction, staring up and out into the beyond. He looks indestructible, until the next scene when he isn't.

Jeff Kober on the set of China Beach

Dodger and Boonie are the only lasting male-male relationship in the series, both shell-shocked by the war into more extreme versions of themselves. Boonie goes out, Dodger goes in. When the pair sits down for a few beers, the limits of their brotherhood are exposed when they forge their Christian names. Dodger claims "Delbert" and Boonie owns up to "Shirley," both knowing the other is full of shit. Their shared experience of trauma is still partitioned by their own insecurities.

William Broyles, Jr: **I had such a kick working with Brian and Jeff because they were, like, *my guys.* They were truly based upon the guys in my platoon that I had known, so I got to really just say, "Here's how you would be thinking, here's what you would be feeling. Between the two of you, you would never say what you really meant, but you would understand each other. One of you could never be at home back in the rear, and the other one of you could never be at home back in the bush."**

A Vietnamese boy won't leave Dodger and Boonie alone until they figure out he is trying to tell them that Dodger is the father of a baby at the nearby orphanage. No one has had the power to alter Dodger's coordinates, until now. Dodger's unlikely fatherhood feels dangerously close to a dropped plot when he heads back into combat in "Ghosts" and "How to Stay Alive in Vietnam," then roars back with a vengeance in the third season stand-out "Souvenirs." *China Beach* couldn't reinvent itself on a perpetual basis, but the show did find ways to stretch its own innovations as far as possible. Plenty of interviews were left over from "Vets" and later put to use in "Souvenirs," interwoven with Dodger's transfiguration.

Jeff Kober in Vietnam, 1988

***Jeff Kober:* The thing about Dodger—the way he was written and the way he ended up being presented—he is someone who had done so much destruction and was so good at it. He had no other skill set that he could discern, so that when the baby arrived it forced him to access another aspect of himself and allowed him to see a way of giving back. It felt like his bridge back to being a human.**

***Michael Rhodes** (director, "Dear China Beach"):* **You got a feeling that Jeff's a method actor. He would kind of stay away until he got ready to work, and it felt like he really was [in Vietnam]. I kinda feel beneath that was probably a teddy bear, but I never saw it. I never joked around with Jeff; I figured he's got something rolling and I didn't want to mess with it. It's interesting because I went to a play where he played it very light and he was a teddy bear. When the episode ended with him hugging his baby, he came to life for the first time.**

A buzzing chainsaw is taken to the trunk of *China Beach* in "Souvenirs" when McMurphy tries to help Dodger and his baby go home to the States. K.C. asks for top dollar to cut through the red tape. It's a strange act of cannibalism: everyone working together to exile a founding character. As Dodger and Boonie embrace, they study each other's faces, unable to voice their feelings out loud.

In Dodger's silence, he has harbored his own secret all along. Cradling his baby and bidding goodbye to McMurphy, Dodger professes that he loves her. He refuses to let her respond, and asks that she not track him down back in the world. Dodger's revelation seems stunning at first. In his muted state, his capability of love and affection has suffered. Now, it is coming back to life through fatherhood. It was McMurphy, and Dodger's longing to connect with her, that brought him out of the bush and back to China Beach, time and again.

"Souvenirs" taps into the harsh reality of goodbye when the actual China Beach bartender Bill "Ziggy" Siegesmund chokes back memories and describes his promises to stay in touch with fellow soldiers, sending Christmas cards that were never answered. McMurphy watches Dodger chopper out of 'Nam in a grand exit full of uncertainty. Unlike the departure of Laurette Barber or Wayloo Marie Holmes, we tag along with Dodger to his destination, riding a train into Montana cheek-to-cheek with his baby. Director John Sacret Young peers at father and son through the window of the passenger car as they gawk at the Big Sky Country awaiting them. There are no words, just Paul Chihara's orchestral take on "Hush Little Baby." The lullaby trails off with a suspended note offering no comfort. Kober received an engraved lighter as a farewell gift from a crew member, and assumed his time with the show had come to an end.

Dodger is MIA for the next few episodes until "The Thanks of a Grateful Nation." McMurphy writes Dodger a letter from 'Nam, and sends the story through the sidewalks of Red Lodge, Montana, and into the Winslow family mailbox. Dodger has moved in with his mom and dad, bringing domestic disarray with him. Dodger's baby boy sits alone, crying at news coverage of the 1968 election, while Dodger hides away in his old treehouse, clinging to the past. Like "Souvenirs" pushed the concept of "Vets" further, "The Thanks of a Grateful Nation" adds permanence to the prior themes of "The World" that Colleen McMurphy experienced.

> ***Jeff Kober:*** **That was a dream job. They set it in Red Lodge, Montana, which was like fifty miles from where I grew up. It was so close to my own experience, I was able to play where I had really come from. I'd had the experience of being a bit outcasted in my own hometown and feeling like I didn't belong. I definitely felt that Dodger's story wanted to be told and every time I got to work, I had a feeling of gratitude and a feeling of wanting to take it as far as I could take it.**

Director Mimi Leder crafts a singular episode with fluid camera movement and simmering emotion, cramming Dodger into the center of a universe he doesn't fit into. He is no longer dispatching the enemy with extreme prejudice, he is just Evan Winslow, a dish-washing dad making minimum wage. His prior identity and vocation have been repossessed, replaced with a son he doesn't know how to love.

Helen Hunt guest stars in an all-too-brief appearance as Sissy, a former high school classmate of Dodger's. They hit it off over a game of pool and end up sleeping together. Sissy wakes up after their tryst to see Dodger watching the rain. Leder's camera does all the talking, pulling Dodger's face into focus and obscuring Sissy in the background. He's not thinking about his son or the woman he just slept with, rather the place where he belongs and the people who understand him. And McMurphy.

The treehouse seems to be the one place Dodger feels safe. Sporting his old letter jacket and Converse high tops, there is a screaming, unspoken desire to reclaim his former identity and forget the war. His dad (Tom Bower) climbs up to join him and find some way to connect, sharing his own story of getting wounded in World War II. For over three minutes, Leder gradually draws in on the pair with one lingering take. Dodger doesn't blink, but his jaws twitch at his dad's words, realizing he is not alone as he thinks. The scene is a crack in the dam of Dodger's inability to identify with anyone who wasn't in Vietnam.

Leder filmed over a dozen takes of the scene with a crane on a dolly, outdoors. "Something you just don't do," added Kober with a laugh. I asked him if he ever lost his patience or composure deep into a string of takes, and he replied, "No, man. I love, love to work. I love to act. If you're really in it, it's different every time, so you're having an experience every time, and it's your job to be present and full and real as if it were the first time. I didn't really allow myself to get frustrated."

"The Thanks of a Grateful Nation" hits its crescendo in the final act when Dodger's soul-searching crosses paths with Sweetness Elroy (Bobby Hosea), last seen in handcuffs in the second season episode "Twilight." Sweetness is a rare and precious element throughout the series, gone but never forgotten with the recurring vision of Boonie throwing his arm around him during every instance of "Reflections." Drinking Budweiser on a rooftop and baring their souls, Dodger and Sweetness burst every capillary of post-war strife. Black or white—they are vets who feel left behind.

They laugh, they cry, they consider ending it all right there.

Sweetness stands on the ledge, pulling Dodger up to lock arms and form a suicide pact. A shot of passing cars below presents an easy way out. Any thought of Dodger's son is distant. They glance at each other and take a deep breath. After a beat, they fall backwards, howling at a joke only they are allowed to laugh at. It's a disturbing sequence that unleashes Kober's versatility, and questions why Hosea's character was relegated to the outer limits of the series.

"The Thanks of a Grateful Nation" is a testament to the depths of Kober's talents, his character's complexities, and the show's dexterity—transcending its fundamental concept while remaining faithful to its identity. *China Beach* no longer requires Colleen McMurphy or K.C. Koloski to carry an episode, nor does the story have to begin and end

in Vietnam. John Wells's script and Leder's directorial work merge for a game-changing triumph, all led by a performance from a supporting cast member who has hardly spoken so far.

Dodger's time with Sweetness proves to be therapeutic. He later dusts off his formal military dress for church and visits a local cemetery in search of casualties from Vietnam. Leder's camera strolls along with Dodger through the graveyard just as it did through the streets of Red Lodge. A groundskeeper points him to the fresh arrivals from Vietnam, remarking how no one else comes through but the lawnmowers.

The third season introduced Dodger as an indestructible idol of war, looking up to the Gods in defiance. Here, he is brought to his knees in mourning at an unmarked grave. Before Dodger can love his son or anyone else, he must save himself. Dodger presents an offering of tears and an oath to not forget his fallen brothers, screaming out, "Please, no one forget *us*." Dodger is one with the lost and forgotten, dead or alive. Director Mimi Leder crafts one final, desolate shot by drawing her camera up and out into the sky of Montana, abandoning Dodger among a boundless labyrinth of headstones.

Opposite page: Bobby Hosea, Brian Wimmer, and Jeff Kober

IN DREAMS, I WALK WITH YOU

It couldn't have been easy in the writers' room of *China Beach* to get an episode to the screen as fully intended in the script. Screenwriter Josef Anderson mailed me an old Christmas gift he received from the show's producers in 1989, a compilation of all the material he wrote that had been, as described on the cover page, as either:

"Misinterpreted by the director

or: Censored by ABC Standards and Practices

or: Designated Unproducible by Fred Gerber

or: Sacrificed in Editing by Chris [Nelson], Randy [Morgan] et al.

or: Rewritten until Unrecognizable by The Writer's Better Instincts

or: Rendered Deeper, Darker, Fuller by John Sacret Young"

After reviewing a number of scripts as they are on the page, it's a clever joke underlined by the truth. Anderson's original script for "China Men" was returned by ABC censors with a memo curtly stating: "This script is unacceptable." Boonie Lanier's unwitting attraction to a transgender woman and his subsequent, episode-long erection were deemed especially offensive. A discussion of McMurphy's birth control pills had to be stricken from the record. References to condoms, *Playboy* magazines, and soldiers spying on showering nurses also received complaints. Boonie's erection turned into a "hernia," and much of Anderson's draft hit the waste bin.

That said, it could be considered an act of God Herself that "Holly's Choice" ever made it to air.

After Ricki Lake's breakout role in John Waters's *Hairspray* (1988), *China Beach* had its eyes on Lake to join the show in season two and lift the collective mood. Timing wasn't right, and a year later, Lake didn't even have to audition when she signed on to play Holly Pellegrino.

Holly doesn't own the surliness of McMurphy and K.C., nor does she own the displacement of Frankie—she is a pastel kite ever climbing into the sky. Holly mostly pals around with Boonie, and while that is a fun pairing, she doesn't draw out the compelling sides of him like Laurette and K.C.

Not until "Ghosts" does Holly alter the narrative, forcing K.C. to confront a box of her dead father's personal effects that is sent to Vietnam. K.C. wants to literally bury it, and Holly steps in for McMurphy, refusing to let K.C. keep running from what she fears most. The ugliest parts of her past. Holly returns to mostly comic relief afterwards, hamming it up side stage, until "Holly's Choice." Much like "Promised Land," Holly's defining moment dials directly into the rousing, divisive spirit of today's political conversation. A perplexing, amazing, and somehow sad feat for a TV show three decades old.

(left to right) Carol Flint, Lydia Woodward, and Josef Anderson in Hanoi

"Holly's Choice" may as well have nothing to do with the Vietnam War. It has everything to do with the female experience of the late-sixties. At the spine of the episode is Holly and a political lightning rod striking through the last fifty years and beyond: the woman's right to choose. Today, the mere mention of abortion remains capable of dividing a household, a classroom, a church, and the United States of America—and *China Beach* ran with it. In 1990.

Backwards.

Written by Carol Flint and directed by Christopher Leitch, "Holly's Choice" begins with a false front of R&R, with Holly and a fellow Red Cross volunteer laughing and joking with the soldiers. Holly hands one of them the Cincinnati Reds cap she is wearing and boards a helicopter back to China Beach, then weeps uncontrollably. There is no context, until a title card reads "Earlier…"

As more and more scenes continue backpedaling, the viewer is left to piece together a story on their own accord. Holly and McMurphy sort of make amends over a disagreement, Boonie visits a sick Holly, and as the clues pile up, an argument between Dr. Richard and K.C. drives it home. Holly had an abortion.

Upon the airing of "Holly's Choice," the woman's right to choose had only been legal for seventeen years, when Roe v. Wade, 410 U.S. 113 was decided by the Supreme Court on January 22, 1973, deeming Holly's decision in 1968 illegal. In 2018, this fragile law might sail on the next breath of a Supreme Court Justice and erase the episode's status as a history lesson. It remains unclear whether a veteran interview spawned the plot of this episode, and either way, it doesn't matter. For the thousands of American males and females who served together, it's perverse to think no woman ever faced the same circumstances as Holly. Women with unwanted pregnancies were undoubtedly in Vietnam and on the home front in 1968. Abortion or not, the personal, legal, and private fallouts were inescapable.

"Holly's Choice" presents just one way it could have gone.

Ricki Lake: **I just remember there being so much backlash, you know? And feeling like I didn't understand. Still, *now*, abortion is such a hot topic and it's so ridiculous, that like, this reproductive right —the fact it's a controversy and being**

threatened is so crazy. I think in some ways, that episode is as timely as ever. The issue is still at the mercy of these men, you know? It's crazy. Looking back on it, ["Holly's Choice"] is one of the achievements I'm most proud of. There's a number of them, but it is up there.

Concetta Tomei: **That episode, when I read it as a Roman Catholic, you know…** [***laughs***] **Enough said! That just really blew me out of the water. I learn a lot from watching other actors work, and I certainly learned a lot from my cast. I would often be off to the side and watch them work. It wasn't a job for me, it was a great passion. Then I thought, "Oh my God, these decisions are hard." Even though I'm not for it, but to know what a woman goes through with that, everything was so real that I was always pulled in. It shook me up—me, Concetta—to look at things in a completely different way than I had looked at them before. That was a very sensitive episode and it was so brave. At that time, no one talked about it, much less put it on national television, especially with the choice that she did make.**

The ABC brass went berserk when they caught wind of the concept. An episode running in reverse while hurling a hand grenade toward the conservative audience was the network's anti-Christ of clean, old-fashioned entertainment. Controversy typically helps ratings, yet scares off fearful advertisers. John Young recalled the network "hated everything about it" and made a "struggled concession" to air the episode without a re-run after Young threatened to not produce a replacement. Young concluded, "I think [president of ABC Entertainment] Bob Iger relented because he was new and he respected the show, and perhaps me…and, of course, his mother loved the show."

Flint did not reinvent the wheel with her backwards narrative. Harold Pinter's play *Betrayal* (1978) had brought the plot device to the mainstream with a feature film in 1983, yet this approach allowed Flint to stifle the shock of Holly's decision and offer a complete emotional arc in place of a polemic. An offended viewer could turn off the episode in protest, but they did have the law-abiding Colleen McMurphy on their side advocating Holly to keep her baby and put it up for adoption.

Dana Delany: **Politically, I had a problem with the episode, but I loved working with Ricki. I am Catholic, but I'm a strong believer in abortion rights and the fact that my character was against it, I said, "But, that's not good, I don't want McMurphy to be that person because she should be a modern woman who stands up for women." And [the writers] were saying, "No, we need this point of view. It was before Roe v. Wade, and she would have stuck to the law," and I thought, "I don't know if I agree with that." I lost that argument because they needed that point of view, which is good. I mean, dramatically, it's more interesting, but to me, the aftermath is what's interesting—the fact that we aired the episode and it was never aired again, because of advertisers putting pressure on ABC.**

"Holly's Choice" reinstalls each character on their axis, exploring each viewpoint and persuasion with nuance. Boonie is back to being the devoted fixer—he isn't the father, but he will gladly marry Holly to keep her out of trouble. She only asks him for two-hundred bucks, and then Holly takes that money to K.C., who is happy to help Holly terminate the pregnancy by any available means. K.C. takes her to the most frightening, filthy doctor's office in town, before Holly opts for one of K.C.'s homemade concoctions to induce a miscarriage. Holly begins hemorrhaging, and Dr. Richard must begrudgingly finish the termination to save Holly's life. Dr. Richard is now incriminated, and threatens to turn them in to avoid culpability. The story, the economics, and the characters could be plucked out of the Five and Dime and set on Main Street, USA, and likely, nothing would change.

Holly is in the center of a different storm in every scene, and each one strikes hidden layers of her struggle, and the so-far-obscured dramatic depths of Ricki Lake. Holly came to Vietnam to serve her country and the men fighting. She merely wants to continue doing just that. Lake's performance proves her character can be much more than just the cheerleader on the sidelines. And what invested onlooker doesn't want to know the pregnant cheerleader's story?

Director Christopher Leitch fondly reflected on working with Lake, with her youth and innocence informing each scene of "Holly's Choice." One morning he came to the set and was informed Lake was in her trailer, uncharacteristically crying and refusing to come out. Leitch pleaded for a chance to talk to her and discovered she had merely skinned her knee while jumping over a chain-link fence that morning. Lake was terrified her wound would affect filming, and Leitch was relieved and amused it was nothing worse.

> ***Brian Wimmer:*** **Oh, man. [Ricki and I] got in so much trouble because we were like brother and sister. We would get kicked off the set almost every day, because they were like: "Hey, you two! Shut up! That's it. Go back to your trailer!" It was so much fun working with her.**

> ***Michael Boatman:*** **When I saw Ricki years later, after all her later success with *The Ricki Lake Show* and all the things she had done, there was a moment before we encountered each other where I thought, "Oh wow, that's Ricki Lake! But she's 'Ricki Lake' now, she's not like the Ricki I knew. She's this star and she's done all this stuff and so much time has gone by, is she even going to speak to me?" She turned and she was like, "Booaatmaan!" and I was like "Riickiii!" and nothing had changed.**

Ricki Lake and cast

In a weird way, I think of Ricki as the female Boonie because she was the donut dolly and she loved to dance. The girl could dance and sing, obviously. Sweet, and this crazy smile, and you can't believe when this girl walks into a room that she could possibly be this bright and joyful. I don't remember her ever complaining. One of the best dancers I've ever seen, by the way.

***Ricki Lake:* That's not true! [*laughs*] Oh my God. I'm not a trained dancer at all, although I did do *Dancing With the Stars* a few years ago and became a ballroom dancer. I was, I guess, light on my feet and have rhythm. I didn't take myself too seriously, but I'm not a trained dancer at all. At all. I guess I just have this naivety and sense that I can do anything.**

***China Beach* was a blessing and a curse for me in that I was only on for one season, and I made some financial decisions based on the fact I was going to be on the show for its run. It ended up being a huge lesson in life. I bought a house because of that job and I kind of lost that job. They didn't pick up my option the last year of the show, so I couldn't afford my house, and it was foreclosed by the bank. I was homeless for a little while, so a lot of amazing stuff happened and then the shit hit the fan.**

I was so insecure, in a way, about my body during *China Beach*. I was more than two-hundred and fifty pounds. I was enormous at such a young age and it was after that job I ended up losing a hundred pounds and starting my talk show. *China Beach* was a real springboard for me, even though it was a disappointment I didn't continue the show.

If there are any shortcomings of "Holly's Choice," it is that the episode could have served as a cruel and unforgiving exit for Holly—a rite of passage for most every other character during the show. Holly remains in the background for the remainder of the season after "Holly's Choice," mostly unseen and out of action, and never receives a proper farewell by the time Lake left the cast at season's end. A prominent departure loaded with import could have elevated "Holly's Choice" from a standout episode to even higher ground.

Christopher Leitch *(director, "Holly's Choice")***: That was a very bold piece of work. I look back at certain things and the only regret I have is that I wasn't nominated for an Emmy for that episode. [*laughs*] I'm being incredibly selfish and egotistic about it. I look at it and I go, "Not only is there nothing wrong with it, it was a brilliant episode."**

"Holly's Choice" carries the pioneering spirit of *China Beach* and remains one of the most memorable hours of the show, bound with Ricki Lake's supreme performance as Holly. Flint's script is like no other in the *China Beach* pantheon, and Leitch solidifies his place in the upper echelon of the show's directors with his efforts. The episode is also notable for beginning to manipulate the time continuum, a device that soon upends the show and strip-mines the characters in unthinkable ways.

For Holly, the clock keeps winding back, and her story finds its genesis. In the final scene, she visits with a married GI who has just lost his best friend in combat. As he cries on her shoulder, they find laughter, and soon begin to kiss. At this moment in time, Holly finds herself somewhere between the polar methods of healing between McMurphy and K.C., lost in a heated moment of young passion and vulnerability.

Somewhere we've all been.

CAMELOT

The jukebox sits mute and neglected under the neon lights of the Jet Set during the opening moments of "Dear China Beach." We join a high-stakes prizefight already in progress, where an electric company has gathered to place their bets on a winner. In the middle of this horde, Colleen McMurphy trades drinks instead of punches with a young GI. A cigarette dangles from K.C.'s lip as she collects wagers and sponges water on McMurphy's forehead. K.C. wants the money. McMurphy wants the pride. Dr. Richard is officiating, checking pupils and filling each shot glass to the rim with liquid courage. Director Michael Rhodes puts the camera and the audience at home on the front row, careful to not break the tension in the room with any sudden movement. *China Beach* has plenty of other quiet moments, but none like this.

Wet, empty glasses clink on the table. Oohs and ahhs. Sudden death.

McMurphy and the unknown soldier must now eat their choice of a native critter. McMurphy chokes down something disgusting, and the GI slinks under the table. The crowd roars, and the fools learn to never bet against McMurphy. And still the undisputed champ, our nurse staggers out of the drinking hole, refusing any assistance, looking like shit. K.C., Dr. Richard, Frankie, Beckett, and Holly stare in slack-jawed astonishment. McMurphy sleeps through a rocket attack later that night and ends up hospitalized with dysentery, wearing a diaper.

The next point plotted on McMurphy's path to oblivion is in "Magic" when she ends up drunk in the Jet Set after catching Dr. Bernard in a lie. In her belligerence is an off-putting confidence that she uses to pick up Vinnie, and they end up sleeping together on the beach. McMurphy is sinking further into substance abuse and sexual gluttony, her body fading further into an apparition. McMurphy even admits to Beckett, "I'd like to just disappear. Poof."

Drinking is engrained in McMurphy's Irish-Catholic guilt, and the audience is unable to fully gauge the extent of McMurphy's emotional, chemical, and psychological damage until the paramount hour of *China Beach*, "F.N.G." (Military slang for new guy or new gal. Insert your own f-word). The episode does not sift through the dregs of McMurphy's rock bottom—it re-gifts her the hope, idealism, and sobriety she once possessed. When we see the nurse at her zenith, we can then start to comprehend how far she has fallen.

And then wince at that time we cheered her through a drinking contest.

Screenwriter Carol Flint recalled a desire in the writers' room to approach an episode through a fresh pair of eyes, weighing a pitch for an episode told through the stationary viewpoint of a visiting patient. *M*A*S*H* had already done that, and further discussions led to exploring McMurphy's first few days in-country, winding the clock back to a simpler time and a simpler woman.

"F.N.G." embraces the mad science storytelling methods of the late-third season, further pureeing continuity and gravity. McMurphy and company are losing touch with reality. So are we. 20/20 hindsight introduces the viewer to a McMurphy we never knew, and in turn, claims her as a martyr for the American optimism of the early nineteen-sixties that met crushing disappointment.

As the arbiter of that decade's hope, President John F. Kennedy's inaugural address in January of 1961 invited Americans to serve their country in the new decade. To be the change they wished to see in the world. At the time of JFK's milestone speech, 900 Americans were stationed in South Vietnam, advising the government in efforts to thwart the spread of communism from the North. Kennedy was a stately, fashionable, forty-three-year-old Democrat replacing the grandfatherly Republican, Dwight D. Eisenhower, in an emblematic changing of the guard.

His first night in office, Kennedy was lying naked in an ice bath called the Cold War. The Berlin Wall would soon be complete, the US was racing the Soviets to the moon, and the Cuban Missile Crisis flirted with nuclear holocaust. Fighting communism needed little justification on the president's part, and Vietnam was dubbed the first of many dominoes that could fall and trigger a new world order. By the time Kennedy was assassinated in November of 1963, American military presence in Vietnam had crept up to 16,000, tiptoeing toward a splendid little war in 1965.

Carol Flint in the office

McMurphy epitomizes the Kennedy paradigm throughout *China Beach*, enlisting for a year in Vietnam in the name of patriotism and service, and getting more than she asked for.

Written by Flint and directed by John Sacret Young, "F.N.G." strands the show's trajectory in 1968 to encounter McMurphy two years earlier in 1966 as a civilian nurse in Kansas. She's an excitable girl with long hair and wide eyes. A far cry from the long, cool woman in a red one-piece reading *The End of the Affair*. McMurphy and her friend Nellie (Kerry Noonan) share a morbid crush on Kennedy and a dream of jet setting across exotic cultures as army nurses. Hawaii, Japan, or Germany will suffice for Nellie, and a trip through basic training convinces McMurphy to go where America's boys are dying—where she is needed most—Vietnam.

> ***Dana Delany:*** **Oh, I loved "F.N.G." To think back to that innocent, Catholic girl who really believed it when President Kennedy said, "Ask not what your country can do for you," and she really answered that call. I relate to it because I grew up in that era, I was raised Catholic, and there's a part of me that easily could have been a nun. [*laughs*] That was so enjoyable to go back and find the innocence there—and the hopefulness, the optimism—and then the tragedy of that all being squashed.**

> **["F.N.G."] was fun because before *China Beach*, I usually played that innocent girl, so it was more just going back to what people had asked me to do before. So, I had it in me. I had talked to a lot of women vets at that point and I had inside me what they had told me—especially Jan Wyatt, our tech person. These girls, and they were girls, really, went to Vietnam with the best intentions. Innocent and hopeful. That was kind of moving for me, to think about what they were like when they just got there.**

McMurphy's preternatural independence is on display from day one, retracing a familiar story of Diane Carlson Evans. She doesn't tell her parents before she volunteers for service, and bites her lip when her last call home is cut off before a proper goodbye with her father. She climbs off the helicopter, planting two feet in Vietnam on a freshly painted helipad. Delany reverse-engineers McMurphy in real time, replacing the role she has refined for three seasons with a timid and beguiling rookie.

The Five and Dime is still under construction while McMurphy learns the ropes from Jan Wyatt (Debra Stricklin), an adept nurse who gets by with a little help from alcohol and an affair with the married Dr. Singer (Scott Jaeck). McMurphy's long brunette locks prompt multiple orders to get her "hair off the collar." Dr. Dick Richard enters stage left with a helmet and golf clubs, a first-day draftee more concerned with his own survival than crafting a witty insult. He recoils at the notion McMurphy would choose to be in Vietnam. The opening gavel of their Kennedy-meets-Eisenhower divide.

A surprise party for the FNGs is quickly interrupted by a chopper full of casualties, and McMurphy's first day on the job takes off. Bodies are everywhere, smothered in agony, carrying the kind of puncture wounds never seen in a suburban emergency room. The nurse's eyes meet the doctor's. They aren't so different anymore. With the flip of a switch, Delany razes the nurse we know with unsure hands and fumbling words. Her first patient dies on the table before she can give him a morphine shot. Dodger and Sweetness Elroy carry a bloodied Boonie Lanier into the triage unit. He's not the carefree bartender yet, just another walking wounded who will have to wait. K.C. Koloski is an entirely different woman. "Charlene" answers to a blowhard boyfriend (Wings Hauser) and a Colonel Broyles (ha!) who may as well be her pimps. Vietnam will change her into K.C.. But how?

After a harrowing first day, McMurphy begins to assemble her emotional mail of armor from a junkyard. The sound of music and laughter lures her to the Jet Set for recovery. Jan offers her a drink, and McMurphy's cherry ghost of Vietnam past claims she has never cared for the taste. Someday, she will drink the joint dry. McMurphy's uneventful first hello with "Charlene" is followed by another order to get her hair off the collar. Like the tumultuous decade that McMurphy reflects, she makes a conscious decision to evolve her appearance. She retreats to the medical hut and shears her hair with surgical scissors that are caked in dried blood.

A sacrifice as much of a statement.

"F.N.G." toys with the idea of beginnings, dialing into the pilot episode's themes when a short-haired McMurphy finds Jan sitting on the beach. A year later in the same spot, McMurphy will close this ellipse with Laurette. Jan is the ghost of Vietnam Yet to Come; her lover is leaving in a few days, and she has six more months left of sitting on the beach alone. Debra Stricklin effortlessly owns the residual trauma and heartbreak of a grizzled vet who has seen it all, warning McMurphy to not get involved with geographic bachelors. McMurphy nods, not knowing Natch and Dr. Bernard will betray her, nor how she will waterboard herself in an eighty-proof fountain of youth to numb the pain. Neither McMurphy, nor JFK, paid enough attention to sound advice. In 1961, French President Charles de Gaulle foretold Kennedy of an endless entanglement in Vietnam. 55,000 French troops and civilians had died fighting there, and the United States set about trumping that number.

McMurphy meets a wounded soldier named Tommy on day one. He recognizes her scent of Chantilly, the same perfume his girlfriend wears. He dies on day two. McMurphy had him in her grasp, and he still slipped through the rye. McMurphy sits on the beach, speaking into a tape recorder, conceding to Nellie that she may not be cut out for all this. The blind determination of McMurphy, whether she is trying to save someone's life or swallow one more drink, is non-existent. Something distracts her in the distance, and she stops the tape. Suddenly, healing begins when she stops doubting herself and joins her comrades in a game of volleyball.

"F.N.G." is primarily devoid of an oldies soundtrack until John Lennon's take on Ben E. King's hit "Stand by Me" provides catharsis for all, marrying to the picture of McMurphy and company diving for balls and missing spikes. Lennon's voice is a signature sound of the sixties and a rare accoutrement in *China Beach*—a significant coup for the show when Yoko Ono personally authorized Lennon's spin on the 1960 classic. The famous bass line and string section of the original is minimized in favor of a strumming acoustic guitar, a thumping beat, and wailing saxophone. Lennon sings of undying devotion in the face of the sky and the mountains falling into the sea, right as mutually assured destruction sinks into the flirtations between Jan and Dr. Singer. The frames per second begin to drawl, emphasizing how each second away from the blood and guts is invaluable and must be squeezed dry. As Lennon's voice fades out, a helicopter appears in the sky, and McMurphy applies Chantilly before another shift.

This peerless episode in the *China Beach* canon authors a new beginning and reaches far past the virgin image of McMurphy on a beach, rewriting the rules of the show all over again. Delany exhibits commanding virtuosity of her character and earned a 1990 Emmy nomination for Best Actress in a Drama Series for her performance.

No episode should have to follow "F.N.G.," but *China Beach* returns to 1968 in the next episode, "The Gift," where McMurphy is accused of life insurance fraud with her departed patients. Delany continues cementing the McMurphy legacy during a four-minute take, with a camera closing in on her face in an empty Quonset hut. The bells and whistles of the third season are muzzled, and our nurse stares down the barrel of the Vietnam War, defending her honor to a pair of investigators.

***Josef Anderson** (writer, "The Gift"):* **I had looked all season for a place to write a monologue for Dana. Some of this was my writer's ego, but it also was the challenge of creating something for one of the best actresses I ever worked with. I was sure I had found the right spot when in her defense she would simply recall a day in her life. It would turn out to be the longest speech she would have in the series.**

Normally directors and producers and especially network executives will object when they see a full page of dialogue.

It's just not done in television, they will say. But this was Dana, and some of these words came from interviews with veteran nurses at the start of the season. The term "crispy critters" and "cleaning the jungle out of them" came from those talks.

On the day we filmed the scene, [director] Michael [Katleman], myself, and the camera operator squeezed together in a corner of the Quonset hut set, with Dana all the way at the other end. We all knew it had to be a oner, an uninterrupted shot with no cuts.

Michael told Dana he was going to roll film and for her to start whenever she was ready. It was the end of a long day and he had not rehearsed her doing the monologue because he didn't want to use up any of her emotional reserve. He did two takes. Remember, this was film and he needed a second one for protection. You had no idea what you had until you looked at dailies the following day. But I knew as soon as she began speaking that this was something special. And it's not only for her remarkable and moving performance, but I think it captures the toll on the lives of those nurses and doctors who were there.

When Dana finished the second take, there was a long beat before Michael very quietly said "cut." And for the longest time nobody moved. It was as if we all wanted to acknowledge what just happened. Dana still had tears in her eyes when I crossed the room to give her a hug and thank her. I couldn't have been more proud of what we did that day.

These four minutes comprise Delany's cardinal one-take performance of the series, drawing from a deeper well of remorse that reaches a new bottom struck by "F.N.G." That one hour descrambles all the words and behaviors of our nurse into something more haunting, more troubling upon revisitation. What was once a shortwave radio signal is crystal clear. It is now Orson Welles narrating a different, more distressing rendition of *The War of The Worlds,* raging on within the confines of Colleen McMurphy.

SUPERSTITION

The third season of *China Beach* ends in "Strange Brew," just as it began in "The Unquiet Earth," with Colleen McMurphy in a cave, wrestling with the ghost of her father. McMurphy's mom (Penny Fuller) is there too, wearing a field jacket, performing CPR on Pa McMurphy in a casket. Dead on arrival. McMurphy has become the by-product of her parents—an enabler and an alcoholic—entirely unable to redeem herself or the family sigil. Our nurse closes the casket and hugs her mom in efforts to end the nightmare.

It is only beginning.

A chain of events first grounded the narrative of *China Beach*, beginning with McMurphy crossing off the remaining days of her first tour in November, 1967. Christmas came, then Tet, then MLK's death. July 4th was a certainty. Sometime after, the calendar stopped turning. Went back in time. Maybe it returned to the present in "The Gift." The only certainty of *China Beach* at this point is a fugue state in late-1968, and the third season attempts to trap McMurphy there forever.

China Beach was never meant to be an almanac of the Vietnam War. The story exists in its own time and space, within a Vietnam and a war that did and didn't quite exist. To quote John Young, "If you write about Vietnam, you have to spin the dial from reality." Young further cited the seminal Vietnam memoir *Dispatches* by Michael Herr as an inspiration long before *China Beach*. At my entreat, Young was digging through his archives for filming documents and found a putrefied copy of Herr's tome. Page 103 fell to the ground, titled, "Postscript, China Beach."

> ***John Sacret Young:*** **And there is no doubt the book was tremendously important to me as far back as *A Rumor of War*. It effected tone and dialogue, not to imitate—an impossibility—but confirmed for me, as well as the**

extensive interviews with veterans, that there had to be a tone beyond straight old-fashioned realism in scene and setting in revisiting and in any way attempting to elucidate truths about the Vietnam War.

A sense that surreality was reality—a combination of time, that hallucinating decade, the 1960s, the overwhelming music, the landscape and culture of Vietnam, how distant from ours, and that war and war itself.

I didn't remember now, and maybe not even then, how the several pages speak, again not literally, to the template of where we set the show. A real place, accurately described, but then the tweaks begin and began like our own unique and calibrated occupation of that territory.

The dial of reality has been spinning since we first saw McMurphy in a red swimsuit, and it began to malfunction during "Skin Deep." Frankie Bunsen is stuck on motor pool duty, unable to rehearse for the Miss China Beach pageant. She begins humming the Dionne Warwick standard, "Don't Make Me Over," and builds to a Broadway-worthy performance as she mounts the vehicles and sprays water from the hose in rhythm with the beat.

A delirium, maybe a suggestion: Vietnam is exactly what you make of it.

Nancy Giles was a capable performer, up to the task, and faced the daunting challenge of filming the sequence without a backing track. The scene kept getting delayed to the last day of filming, and a sound assistant had to play a penny keyboard off-camera while Giles mouthed the words to the chords. The seams don't show in the final product, nor expose the fact Giles recorded the master track with an orchestra during post-production—the exact opposite of how such a performance is typically crafted.

Nancy Giles: **It was exhilarating and frustrating but ultimately very triumphant for me, because I felt like things just didn't happen the way I wanted them to. I really wanted to get up there and have the song recorded and really be able to relax with it and know my moves and none of that really happened until the last friggin' minute. I still watch it and I'm like, "Go girl! Good for you!" [*laughs*]**

"Vets" removed the fourth wall of the show, and "Don't Make Me Over" opens the third eye. Many moments follow in this vein, and the viewer has no choice but to go along with it. And believe. Surrealism falls on its face midway through the season in "Magic" when a visiting circus amounts to a sideshow distraction from much more intriguing affairs. Boonie slow dances with Holly to "You've Really Got a Hold on Me" and K.C. gives McMurphy a tarot reading, advising her to drop her guilt over sleeping with Dr. Bernard and Vinnie during a two-night span. The river of *China Beach* is flowing fine on its own here. No smoke or mirrors needed.

Later in the season, "Skylark" drubs "Magic" by allowing fantasia to consume the show entirely. Lydia Woodward had already invented a number of provocative approaches to *China Beach* through her scripts, and "Skylark" sits in its own enchanted snow globe. The story begins without auspice—Dr. Richard and McMurphy bickering in the medical ward until the trilling of flutes reaches their ears. A beat.

The doctor and the nurse follow the music outside to the helipad and find Ruby and Ernie (Ruby Dee and Joe Seneca) waltzing the day away to Ella Fitzgerald's "Skylark." McMurphy and Dr. Richard look like kids at Disneyland with dumbstruck smiles, minus the mouse ears. Ruby and Ernie notice their stalkers and strike up a conversation, claiming they are members of a dance troop in need of a place to stay. Soon enough, every actor and extra is out on the helipad doing the cha-cha.

> ***Lydia Woodward** (writer, "Skylark"):* **One thing about working on a show like *China Beach* is that you were relatively limited in terms of the age group you could write for. There's a natural population in a war zone of people from eighteen to maybe thirty years old and that's about it. There isn't much of an opportunity to write about older people. I did have some kind of a vision in my head of this older couple dancing on the helipad, and that's sort of where it started. It was more just the image and an interest in finding, in this case, a bizarro entrance. How can you possibly get two sixty-five-year-old characters into a war zone? It's not that easy to do. [*laughs*]**

> ***Robert Picardo:*** **The writers continued to mix it up and challenge themselves and thereby gave us new challenges, and**

I think the dedicated audience members really liked that. I think if you were a Vietnam veteran who never saw *China Beach* and the first episode you turned on was "Skylark," you might understandably be a little bewildered and possibly even angry that this was the portrayal of Vietnam. It felt like we were making a little movie.

Ruby and Ernie carry a cheerfulness bordering on menace: cartoonish characters come to life, energy radiating out of their eyes. They materialize in the motor pool and bring harmony to the racial tension between Sarge, Frankie, and Answer Man, and later show up in K.C.'s heart-shaped bed—the only one on the base that fits more than one person. K.C. climbs right in between them without hesitation and falls asleep during a bedtime story. Unlike "Magic," these shifts and moods feel like they wouldn't exist without extraterrestrials infiltrating the base. McMurphy doesn't even sniff a glass of the hard stuff.

Behind the scenes of the "Skylark" dance contest

The Christmas spirit first drew McMurphy and Dr. Richard to the precipice of romance, and Ruby and Ernie's presence summons that missing element from the show's past. Ruby and Ernie are dancing on the bridge, and Dr. Richard nudges McMurphy, declaring that he wants what they have. If he never gets it, it won't be for lack of trying. Ruby and Ernie cease to be abnormal visitors in the moment and stand for something unheard of in *China Beach*. Everlasting love.

Later that night, a dance contest is held at the Jet Set. Boonie and Holly break it down to Sam the Sham and the Pharaohs' "Wooly Bully," and K.C. and Beckett do the disco a few years early. Director Fred Gerber delivers a quintessential moment of *China Beach* by cutting to the medical ward and letting silence speak in tongues. McMurphy and Dr. Richard are on a graveyard shift, tending to their duties in solemn diligence as the party pulses through the wall next door. Their paces and glances around the room confirm a telepathic frustration and ineffable desire to cut loose and join the fun. Maybe just give love a goddamn try.

K.C.'s pessimism has rubbed off on McMurphy, who thinks that Ruby and Ernie are not who they say they are. Beckett comes across

Giles, Helgenberger, Boatman, and Tomei

evidence that Ruby and Ernie died years ago, and that their grandson was a dead GI who passed through *China Beach*. At the episode's end, Ruby and Ernie run down the beach, cackling, never to be seen again. McMurphy and Dr. Richard are left dancing on the helipad, rubbing noses, and ready to kiss before the credits kick in.

Surely, stranger things happened in 'Nam.

> ***Fred Gerber*** *(director, "Skylark")***: Lydia is an amazing writer and we knew when she wrote it what her intentions were, that these were apparitions. So we had to toy with the idea of who saw them and who didn't see them, who they affected, and who they didn't affect. I think typically you do that show and you would then identify who these people were actually visible to, and then you'd probably play a little vignette at some point where they were in a room and nobody noticed them. We actually had a meeting, myself, the actors, Lydia, and just spoke about how the conceit of doing that would have made it a different episode, it would have signaled to the audience that this is a fantasy. So it was one of those opportunities where we just didn't do anything, we just played them straight.**

Unlike a few attempts at mitigating the mood of *China Beach* in this season, "Skylark" doesn't feel forced, resurrecting the very hope that was birthed in "F.N.G." *China Beach* is a reflection of the American songbook, and in that, there is ample room for myth. Scholars still debate whether the Godfather of Blues, Robert Johnson, sold his soul to the devil or if he existed at all. Ruby and Ernie join the club.

The pixie dust and chamber harps of "Skylark" melt into an ego-slaying rampage in "Strange Brew." Angels scatter and dead men rise from their graves to walk the earth with McMurphy and K.C. Only in dreams are the women prepared to confront their insecurities, failures, and personal ghosts that await them back home in the world.

Before departing the show, supervising producer Georgia Jeffries handed in her final script titled "Sex, Drugs, and Rock 'n' Roll," to be directed by Mimi Leder. Jeffries happened upon a rumor that the rock supergroup Cream had toured Vietnam in the sixties, and wanted to explore the cost of McMurphy ditching the imaginary concert to nurture everyone but herself. Jeffries was never happy with the final onscreen result, and sent me her final draft for reference. Eventual director Michael Fresco recalled showing up for filming with the script in turmoil, unsure of how the episode was going to end. Jeffries's name was taken off the re-titled script, and each day was mostly improvised on the spot with the assistance of John Young.

Dreams come and go during the episode, forming one big requiem: sharp, vivid images submerged in an empty expanse. The Five and Dime never feels so lonely, so unreal. Late-night drinking commences on the helipad as Beckett stresses over a wedding ring that was lost from a corpse's finger he severed. He scurries away to find it, leaving McMurphy and K.C. alone to drift into slumber. A Salvador Dali dystopia of Vietnam comes to life, and McMurphy and K.C. sift through the debris. Plumes of Crayola colors puff like chimneys. Everyone who went to the concert is MIA. McMurphy and K.C. call out for Boonie, Holly, and Frankie, only to revisit unresolved conversations and relationships stuck in their subconscious.

K.C. encounters Joey (Clancy Brown), her high school sweetheart from Missouri. One man in a long line of them that has let her down. The reason K.C. flinched at McMurphy broaching the subject of senior prom earlier in the episode. K.C. lays out the hard truth for Joey, and anyone else who missed the memo: Her dad made a wife out of her. She cooked and cleaned and warmed his bed starting at the age of ten. It's Joey's fault for not saving her. Marg Helgenberger opens the veins of K.C., crying, quaking, bleeding out every bad break that has come her way. It's a coarse and jagged performance that would have won Helgenberger an Emmy had "Nightfall" not.

McMurphy lurches in the shortcomings of a hard day's night, communing with the Dream Walker (Gary Farmer), one of her patients who lost both of his legs. She sits with him in a sweat lodge, defending her alcoholic tendencies and her selfless behavior. Except for that time she bit a childhood bully when he made fun of her father's drinking. The more McMurphy sinks into denial, the faster the room spins. A glass-bottom boat ride to hell hits full speed, without Willy Wonka or anyone else at the wheel.

> ***Michael Fresco** (director, "Strange Brew"):* **I got this idea to have a big turntable in the middle of the hut and put Dana on one side at twelve o'clock and put the other cast member at six o'clock and have a fire between them. As the scene progressed,**

> **this turntable would begin to spin, so in my mind it felt like they would begin to spin as she was coming on to this drug.**
>
> **I started looking at the scene as it was cut together (well after shooting it) and the effect was not that they began to spin, but that the shack that they were in began to spin around them. You couldn't see that they were spinning, because the camera didn't move in relation to them. It was startling. That was a really fun scene to shoot, and really wonderfully surprising in the best ways, editorially, to cut together. That episode was fun to shoot because there were no holds barred.**

Both Georgia Jeffries and John Young experienced alcoholism in their family trees, and both seemed intent on exhuming the root of McMurphy's addiction in this episode. The final screen product takes that initiative on literally, while Jeffries's original script uses a softer tone in act 4. On the page, McMurphy finds herself on a playground instead of in a cave with her mom and dad. Children are playing in the mud, swinging on jungle gyms and monkey bars, and McMurphy realizes it is K.C., Holly, Beckett, Boonie, and Frankie in child form, Dr. Richard conspicuous in his absence. They all board a carousel, and before the merry-go-round can begin, McMurphy spots her own self as a young girl watching on. She walks over and embraces who she used to be.

This deleted fantasy of McMurphy finds her yearning to reclaim a carefree existence, and another interpretation begs the desire for a child of her own to care for. It is apparent that Young and Fresco preferred to end the season as it began—wallowing in the bowels of fatherly shame. McMurphy and K.C. have been seeking out a surrogate soul sister in each other to replace their fathers this whole time, and they've been too proud to admit it. Even in their wildest dreams.

"Strange Brew" ends the third season with an unscripted deus ex machina from Young that shows McMurphy waking up once more in crisp white sheets. The sound of helicopters chop in her head, spinning into the credits. The open wounds of 1968 left to fester with infection and eternity. Young makes us question just how many windows we were looking through, right before nailing the last one shut. *China Beach* surrenders to the unknown at the end of "Strange Brew," and again beckons the audience to keep following Colleen McMurphy deeper into the darkness.

IV

After twelve days in Vietnam, I was down to two days left in-country. Waking up in Danang, flying to Saigon for one last day touring the Mekong Delta, and then headed back home to Nashville. I looked out my hotel window at the rolling waves, the sand, and the vacationers. Somewhere in time and space, the nurses and soldiers from my country were right there on China Beach, taking a break from the war. Hueys buzzing around them, kicking up sand and ocean spray.

My eyes were misty because I didn't want to leave Vietnam. I wanted to keep learning from these people and their culture. The faces of cab drivers, waitresses, tour guides, and hotel managers ran through my mind. I can still see them. I wanted to ask them all how the American War had impacted them and their bloodline. I wanted to hear every single story. I wanted to continue building my own private bridge back to my country's thirty-year mistake that was never designed to be understood, explained, or justified.

Easier to do in Vietnam than Tennessee. Easier if I spoke some Vietnamese.

On the way out of Danang, the cab driver turned off the main drag and I watched the Lady Buddha statue at the end of the northern cape slip out of sight, the way lovers do at airports. I wondered when I would see her again. I knew I would think of her every time I see McMurphy staring out at the sea, the same way I think of Bill Broyles passing out at the sight of so much horror in one Quonset hut.

The plane out of Danang taxied by old hangars full of ancient military aircraft, piquing my curiosity of their past as we took off. *The Very Best of The Righteous Brothers* was pounding through my earbuds during the ascent, the way it did for much of this creative chapter of my life. Bill Medley and Bobby Hatfield's voices were dipping and diving out of the other in stereo, and I looked down to find Lady Buddha and pinpoint China Beach from above, just one more time. My eyes darted desperately, and the coast gave way to the sea. The tears came, the tears that I wasn't ready to give up at the Wall that one summer day. For all the soldiers who watched Vietnam disappear beneath the clouds and cheered with joy, here I was, dying to stay in my own private episode of "The World."

It was time to go home and get real.

TUNNEL VISION

THE MIDNIGHT HOUR

"...And destruction after all is a form of creation."
- Graham Greene, "The Destructors"

"If I can leave my emotions a little bit like blood on the wall in something, and it works, that's the excitement for me."
- John Sacret Young

Colleen McMurphy used to be the center of the universe, sharing an inherent character trait with everyone around her. She carried the patriotism and protocol of Lila Garreau. The intimate relationship with death known to Samuel Beckett. She could match Dr. Richard and K.C. Koloski in the verbal contests of linguistics and forensics. There is a silence in her that only Dodger understood. McMurphy was the glue that held everybody together, anteing up every self-sacrifice of Boonie Lanier. Not anymore. Not in the fourth season. McMurphy is now a dying star, sucking everyone and everything with her toward a neighboring black hole.

The first, lasting image of our nurse sitting on the beach in a red one-piece meets its match at the end of the fourth season's first hour, "The Big Bang." It's a hollow reverberation from the end of "Strange Brew"—McMurphy lying in bed, a dead china doll, unable to sleep. She has a head full of grey hairs, wrinkles in her face, and a stranger lying at her side. It is now 1985, seventeen years from when the third season's stylus began skipping in the groove of 1968. We don't know where McMurphy is, and we will wait for most of the season to catch up to her and this moment. It won't make us feel any better.

Reflecting on the creative process of co-writing and directing "The Big Bang," John Young said, "*China Beach* was sort of haunting. It was haunting to us who made it, it was haunting to the actors, and often haunting for the audience. Part of the haunting-ness was 'how can we haunt *you*, you poor victims, you audience anew?'" Young decided to terrorize the audience by any anachronistic and iconoclastic means necessary.

Colleen McMurphy, we hardly knew you.

***William Broyles Jr.:* I think at the very center of *China Beach* is not only Dana and her performance, but John Young's just incredibly stubborn, obstinate determination to make it real and honest and deep and good. You have all those stars aligned. Believe me, he was constantly under fire: "Do we really have to show this burned person? Does K.C. really have to be a prostitute? Why does Boonie have to lose his leg? Why does McMurphy have to get drunk? Why?" In the end, he carried the day and he got supported. There are lots of wars about making *China Beach*, aside from the war it was about. John was like the general that led everybody through the rice paddies and jungles and got them home again.**

***Toni Graphia* *(series writer and researcher)*: I was in my twenties, so to me, my whole life was that show. For many of us, we would stay there all night. I literally had a sleeping bag under my desk and would actually sleep there sometimes. John Young tells a story of: "Yeah, I used to stay at work till 3 AM and when I would go walking down the halls, I would see a light on and it would be Toni." No one had to make us stay. We wanted to be there, and we put 100 percent into it. We ate, slept, and breathed *China Beach*.**

***Troy Evans:* It's very difficult to get a television show produced. By extension, any venture of theater—a musical venue, a saloon—there's a certain amount of single-minded, obsessive insanity that's required to find your way through, to get that kind of thing done. John Sacret Young feared no one. He, at all times, wanted to do it his way and that's whether he's talking to me, or the head of the network. So, the episodes he directed were frequently difficult. They were always the worst hours.**

Concetta Tomei remarked that Bill Broyles was obsessed with the Vietnam War in the best and worst of ways, and I believe the same sentiment holds true with John Young and *China Beach*. Making a golf analogy, Young said, "I think I went into *China Beach* having not won the US Open, but wanting to, if you will. I had that edge. I think eventually I came out the other side [*pause*] I would say exhausted." The opportunity to tell a story of his generation and pay tribute to his cousin, Doug, amounted to a personal Bermuda Triangle for Young—creatively, professionally, and emotionally. Young's maniacal, maybe unreasonable dedication to the series was contagious, and I believe it is why staff writers slept in their offices, editors slept in their trucks, and crew members drove home from Indian Dunes at the break of dawn, falling asleep at the wheel, getting pulled over by the police.

Before production on the fourth season commenced, Young recalled the feeling of a casket opening. *China Beach* was supplanted in its Wednesday time slot by a new police musical, *Cop Rock*, and moved to the 1990 ratings graveyard of Saturday night. ABC insisted that more people were staying home on the weekends, backed by research that home video was growing exponentially and that cult audiences could be nurtured in that time slot, a la *Saturday Night Live*. This justification didn't cover a reduced order of thirteen episodes (which grew to seventeen) and didn't blunt a dive in confidence from the network brass.

ABC didn't care that *China Beach* was churning out its most innovative material as the third season wound to an end, nor did it care about the multiple Emmy nominations that followed. 14.4 million people watched "The Unquiet Earth," and viewership dwindled throughout the season to an audience of 8.6 million for "Strange Brew." It made no difference that *China Beach* was aging like wine, because what really mattered in the corporate bottom line was rotting away.

If *China Beach* was to die, it was going to die by John Young's mercurial hand.

John Sacret Young: **We knew that the move to Saturday night was a death threat. We thought it sounds like, in a way, they're picking us up but moving us without a lot of faith. What does that mean? Well, let's project. Because it gives you a freedom in a way, what could we do that would be interesting and new?**

> **I remember [John Wells] would come into my office to try to incite me to do something crazy. Maybe so that he could go home, and I would sit there and wonder what that crazy thing is. But in terms of that, it was from talking to veterans, because they talk about the war alright, but at some point, it got to coming home, which was as traumatic as the war. Whether it was literally getting off the plane and being given the finger, or being yelled at. Some of them couldn't talk about it, so they were carrying it with them, and the explosiveness of it. If you look at nurses' lives after they came back, it's not pretty stuff, but it seemed important.**

The passage of time brings people together for a precious moment and then splits them apart, shooting them down their own paths that might or might not cross again. There is the luxury of looking back, and the illusion that the past was more simple, less complicated, even if it was none of those things. Not in life. Not in *China Beach*.

Sixteen years after I graduated high school, I was back in my hometown for a wedding, walking down a city street. Something caught the corner of my eye. A presence. It was someone I grew up with and hadn't seen since I went to college. When we were young, there were sleepovers, ninja costumes, and living rooms turned into wrestling rings. Prank calls were made, videos were rented, and pizzas were scarfed down. Jeff had none of these comforts anymore. Just long, dirty hair and a tin cup in front of him. I walked up to him and couldn't believe it. We studied each other's faces and embraced. I will never shake the disbelief, or the questions.

Why him?

Why not me?

I hear the same questions asked in the opening moments of "The Big Bang."

Dick Richard hasn't seen Boonie Lanier in sixteen years, until the former lifeguard shows up at his front door in 1985. The changes are drastic. A long ponytail and a Fu Manchu obfuscate Boonie's face, and one leg is missing. Boonie writes off his disability as an excuse to never drive a stick shift and get double his money for a pair of socks. The war took his leg, not his joy. Dick has changed too. His hairline has crept back toward a crown, and his biting sarcasm has dispersed. Their conversation is a meager trail of breadcrumbs: both are family men with wives and kids, Dick was there whenever Boonie lost his leg, and McMurphy's Christmas cards stopped coming years ago.

1968 becomes an afterthought. More pressing, underlying questions are posed with a pantomimed Wilhelm scream.

Later that night, Boonie drives home in silence. He didn't get whatever it was he wanted from his visit. Dick is troubled too. He can't sleep, and retreats to his office where he looks at old photos from 'Nam. His eyes twinkle at the image: a short-haired McMurphy standing on the Five and Dime helipad, sticking out her tongue. Dick's fading pictures come to life.

The pre-pilot entrails of "F.N.G." spread right into "The Big Bang" and follow the early in-country days of McMurphy and Dr. Richard. The contentious co-workers get to know each other while staring into a black mirror, where Dr. Singer (Scott Jaeck) and Jan Wyatt (Debra Stricklin) carry out a reckless affair. They make it look easy, drunkenly slow dancing on the helipad to the tune of Bobby Moore and the Rhythm Aces. Colleen and Dick ridicule them, just as they realize how easy it would be to give in and indulge one another. A Vietcong attack later breaks their will. They kiss, almost fuck, and suddenly realize they will need much more from each other than a platonic orgasm.

For all this time, for both of their towering flaws, they knew better.

> ***Robert Picardo:*** **Dana and I were, and still are, very great friends. We could talk about anything. Onscreen, even though our relationship was very comfortable and kind of like brother and sister, when we actually had to make out on the show, which we did very rarely, that was always funny because it seemed odd. We had such a close friendship that the moments where we actually had to kiss were kind of strange; however, the moments where I kind of had to pine for her and really care deeply for her—that was all totally easy to do because I had really great feelings for her.**
>
> **I got that the rest of America was in love with her. Our working relationship was great and very clear and well defined and never slipped. It was never misunderstood that we were really good friends who loved working together and**

absolutely nothing more than that. I think that made it easier in a way. My guess is that if you were working opposite Dana, she is the kind of actress someone could easily fall in love with and that would probably make things a lot harder. I could make her laugh and she could certainly make me laugh and that was the antidote that you desperately need when you're dealing with that kind of heavy material.

"The Big Bang" takes abrasive measures in sacrificing the show's established trajectory in 1968, denying the bread and butter of McMurphy and K.C. from all, and hiding away Beckett, Frankie Bunsen, Sergeant Pepper, and Lila Garreau for a number of episodes. Motown music recedes in favor of more silence, classic rock, and Paul Chihara's score. The ensuing episodes are a leap of faith and an incomplete jigsaw puzzle, masterminded by Young, John Wells, Lydia Woodward, and Carol Flint, all sharing story credits for the first seven hours.

Lydia Woodward: **It was done a little bit differently than the previous years because we had a bigger map in mind in terms of going back and forth in time, but I think that we did do the weird thing of having four names on the story credits because we really all were throwing out stuff. I would feel dishonest laying claim to "this was my idea or Carol's idea or Wells's idea." It really wasn't as straightforward as that. We threw a lot of stuff out and at some point, things landed in this episode or that episode.**

John Wells: **One of the things we were all fascinated with was the idea of "Who are these characters years later? How did the experience of being in Vietnam and in these jobs change them? Are they going to be who we thought or who we would guess they were going to be later on?" And that led to sort of the framing device of the season and it was a very liberating and kind of fabulous thing to be able to do as writers to kind of use a very novelistic approach, but actually put it on screen. It was certainly an adventurous thing for that time and one of the reasons why we were very appreciative, ultimately, that ABC gave us that opportunity to just do it.**

The last season of *China Beach* ignores much of what came before, approaching each character as both an FNG and a weathered soul who bleed into one another. The season continually mirrors the human memory by clinging to beginnings and endings, and the faulty, selective fragments scattered between. In "Escape," an old man Beckett in 1985 is at odds with a hotheaded joker named Sammy B in 1967. One minute, the elder is quoting 1 Corinthians 15:35 in a wooden pew with a rich, mahogany baritone. The next, eighteen years in the past, a man-child is stealing the corpse of an escape artist to stage an elaborate prank. Both incarnations of Beckett have been living within Michael Boatman's portrayal for the prior three seasons, and we are never told how or why until this far into the game. "Escape" breaks Beckett's split personality in two, then fuses them back together before our eyes.

The final seventeen hours of *China Beach* are as challenging as they are rewarding and uncompromising. Maybe maddening. The first season of *China Beach* felt like a cozy, fragrant foyer with skylights and a fetching hostess. Now we have made it down into the dank, neglected basement where secrets lie within Polaroids, journals, and moldy LPs. The memories held within are violently shaken to life, awakening fantasies and furies that span two decades.

The successes and failures of the fourth season can only be gauged against what has preceded in *China Beach*, and in that regard, it's a discombobulating triumph. Each chapter poses provocative, unprecedented viewpoints of the characters. Struggles that weren't so evident before are now transparent. The show is turned upside down, inside-out, and then pureed for the viewer to digest. This creative approach kowtowed to no one. Certain actors and their agents took umbrage with decreased screen time, one writer walked out mid-season in protest, and the 1990 audience had to take copious notes to keep up. The new Saturday night time slot didn't help. Upon its premiere, "The Big Bang" was the victim of *China Beach*'s smallest viewing audience to date, and the series struck a number of false bottoms in the ratings throughout the fall.

Wherever and whenever *China Beac*h goes in the fourth season, we are reminded of what once was. As McMurphy's identity drifts further away from her and from us, the "Reflections" opening sequence remains unchanged. Everything that is now gone forever is running in an infinite loop. K.C. is convincing McMurphy to wear the skimpier dress for a date, Dr. Richard is offering a toast, and Dodger is still dashing through falling mortars. These pictures are how we will remember everyone from the Five and Dime, right before they fight an entirely different war waiting on them at home.

HEY, BABY

K.C. Koloski is capable of love, or so we were told once upon a time in "F.N.G." More shocking than the sight of a sober Colleen McMurphy was the artist formerly known as Charlene. She rescues Boonie from drowning himself, then they make love, soaked in sweat and salvation. K.C. is never so generous, pulling strings to get Boonie a job at the Jet Set to keep him out of the bush. She gifts him a harmonica, and he merely gifts her a nickname. *K.C. from K.C.* It's not the sort of equitable exchange expected from Ms. Koloski.

K.C.'s good mood continues into the new season in its second hour, "She Sells More Than Sea Shells," which is basically part 2 of "The Big Bang." Dr. Richard has set out to find McMurphy in the eighties, and here, someone else is tearing through the past and present looking for K.C. According to John Young, Marg Helgenberger's performance is "more luxurious, more delicious" in these early fourth season hours, and K.C. is glowing with good reason. Helgenberger was pregnant, entering her third trimester as filming on the season began.

Helgenberger's upcoming delivery presented its own strain of creative and logistical obstacles. Time was limited with the actress before she went on maternity leave, and there was no way to pull off a season with K.C. as a constant presence. The writers' room didn't hide Helgenberger's swelling belly behind shower fences and flowing tops—they impregnated K.C. as well—birthing a new, central character for the season, Karen Lanier.

"She Sells More Than Sea Shells" commences in 1967 with the fresh pairing of Dr. Dick Richard and K.C. The doctor puts his OBGYN degree to use, confirming K.C.'s pregnancy. Pink light beams through the stained glass of K.C.'s dwelling, foreshadowing the arrival of a baby girl. The two resident wise asses of the show have hardly crossed paths aside from "Holly's Choice," and their dialogue volleys back and forth like a ping pong championship throughout the episode. McMurphy is off to the side for much of the hour, allowing a fresh war of words.

K.C. lounges by the Five and Dime fountain to soak her feet in the water and tan her outie as the Shangri-Las' "Remember (Walkin' in the Sand)" soundtracks a breezy afternoon. Director Mimi Leder's camera tells us everything we need to know, panning down K.C.'s legs and to her toes. The chorus of the song hits, and an invisible umbilical cord leads to 1985, where her daughter, Karen, is sunbathing in a bikini.

Christine Elise first appears as Karen in "The Big Bang." She hardly utters a word, and then commands much of the following hour. The second coming of Koloski inherited the take-no-prisoners tenacity of her mother and the good will of the man who raised her, Boonie. The mere existence of Karen creates dark avenues to address, like where she has been during the preceding three seasons, and who her biological father is. Elise takes on the mantle of Chloe Webb, Megan Gallagher, and Ricki Lake as the visiting guest star of the season, and more importantly, a proxy detective for the audience to piece the broken past together.

> ***Christine Elise** (Karen Lanier):* **I cite that job as the best job of my career, partly because everybody was so talented and so nice to me, and the writing was so amazing. If I just knew my dialogue and paid attention to the people acting opposite me, my job was done for me. You do a scene with Marg Helgenberger or Dana, and if you just focus enough to connect with them, then your job is halfway done. I'm not a trained actor. I sort of decided to become an actor on a whim when I was twenty-one, and they had me doing emotional stuff I was I worried I couldn't pull off. I was worried I wouldn't be able to do it, and I think I was only able to do it because everyone around me was so good.**

Karen finds a stream of checks coming from a woman named K.C., and when Boonie won't explain the situation, she tracks down Dr. Richard for answers. Robert Picardo's character is once again a begrudging link to the past, lured into a meaningful conversation when Karen asks for advice about contraception. Dick laughs at the traits her mother did—and didn't—pass on to her young. The painful past untangles.

It turns out Karen was not conceived in love between Boonie and K.C.—the loudmouth Col. Mac Miller (Wings Hauser) from "F.N.G." is her father. K.C. dreams of better days ahead, plotting to run away with her baby daddy to Manila, while the audience waits for her well laid plans to implode. Mac's genitals are then blown to bits during an attack on his helicopter, sending him home to his family, and leaving K.C. behind as an expectant, single, working woman.

The Vietnam War is again a background setting for another timeless, female-specific dilemma in the vein of "Holly's Choice." The power of hindsight tells us K.C. will go through with the delivery, yet keeps us guessing as to what happened to her daughter. All along, Boonie is at K.C.'s side, pining to be the man in her and her child's life. Brian Wimmer recovers all the momentous potential Boonie carried during the first season, wanting to be all he can be for everyone around him. K.C.'s husband in the sixties, and Karen's father in the eighties. It's the one solace Karen can take away from memory lane. A father figure who has loved her no matter what. Like McMurphy, K.C. is somewhere out there in 1985, hiding.

> ***Marg Helgenberger:*** **K.C. definitely was terrified of becoming too vulnerable with anyone because she didn't like to relinquish any kind of control. I think she knew if she had ever fully opened up to anybody, I think she would have, in her view, fallen apart and lost her way. And her way was "I need to get out of this situation." I think mostly she was terrified of allowing herself to really feel and to really fall in love, or be committed to somebody. It would have taken her off the rails. She was not going to have any of that. She was always editing herself, for sure. She really was pretty brave, certainly she was selfish, and she didn't want to be bothered with that child. It was going to drag her down. It was going to stop her from getting to where she really wanted to be.**

It was a fearless move for *China Beach* to mostly ignore the McMurphy and K.C. dynamic throughout the fourth season. Time between them is scarce in these final hours, and while both are continually crucified throughout the season, "You, Babe" blesses their sisterhood with a new beginning, along with their sweetest joy. And they still can't quite get along.

At the beginning of "You, Babe," McMurphy is feeling herself, strutting out of the triage unit after a long shift. It's still 1967, and she's still got her bobbed hairdo. Director Mimi Leder stages a powerful static shot, capturing McMurphy from head-to-toe on the helipad. The edges of the 4:3 frame cry out, demanding 70-millimeter glory. McMurphy is singing Sonny and Cher's "I Got You, Babe," and performing a striptease, slinging her bloody scrubs to the ground one garment at a time. For a moment, it feels like dozens of extras will cartwheel into the scene and perform an epic musical number with her.

China Beach opts for something else: a comedy of errors revealing whether it is McMurphy or K.C. who has been truly indebted to the other all along.

"You, Babe" is the black sheep of the fourth season—a freewheeling, funny, and sentimental backstory that *doesn't* hopscotch across the time continuum, joining "The Big Bang" and "She Sells More Than Sea Shells" as the underpinning of the season. "You, Babe" is in the vein of "F.N.G.," adding another prologue to *China Beach* that never existed prior, re-questioning every move K.C. has made. For an entire episode, McMurphy and K.C. get acquainted during one calamity after another in Saigon. Cockfighting, hemorrhoids, and mistaken identities abound. Military Police later chase McMurphy and K.C. through the urban blight of Vietnam to the tune of "I Got You, Babe" in one of the few whimsical moments of the season.

McMurphy and K.C. end up in a church, hiding in a confessional booth where a friendship fails to launch. But it's trying. Sort of. K.C. has lied to McMurphy at every turn so far in vain efforts to steal her identity and finalize an adoption, and in this holiest of holes, continues her long con. McMurphy's evangelism is resolute, compelling K.C. to keep the child and raise it on her own. Both of their faces and their hushed voices hold desperation in this place neither wants to be. Sisterhood is an afterthought. Salvation would suffice. K.C. finally offers a truth: "I would raise this child in a second if I knew it would turn out better than me."

After catching K.C. in every single one of her lies, McMurphy handcuffs K.C. to a pole in the middle of Saigon squalor. Beggars, sewer rats, and street walkers bear witness to the first ever McMurphy and K.C. catfight. They scream, hiss, and call each other bitches. Then, K.C.'s water breaks. Neither she nor McMurphy are ever happier than the moment baby Karen enters the world. She isn't a clean stage baby, she's a screaming little human covered in plasma. *China Beach* had found another unexplored method of slamming life and art together, not quite knowing the outcome. Instead of actual Vietnam veterans re-creating their experiences, an actual pregnant woman was feigning birth.

Dana Delany: **I was supposed to be delivering K.C.'s baby, [*laughs*] and you can't get much more intimate than that. We're on the set, and poor Marg, it was such an act of trust. She really was pregnant, and she was pretty far along, and for her to have to pant and breathe deeply and fake delivering a baby—it's risky, you know? I had this fear that the baby was really going to come out, and I was going to be delivering it! I really appreciated how much she gave over to that moment.**

Mimi Leder *(director, "You, Babe"):* **I think Marg was in her ninth month. The trick is when pretending to give birth, the actual actions of the breathing and the pushing can put you into labor. I was terrified that she would go into labor, and there we were recreating a birth. That was my first Emmy nomination as a director. I don't mean to brag, but anyway, we were in this alley on a set and she goes into labor and all these beautiful Vietnamese women bring candles singing "I Got You, Babe" to hold her down and help her through the birth. It was one of my most favorite scenes that I was privileged to have directed.**

Susan Rhinehart *(teleplay, "You, Babe"):* **Oh my God, Marg was so pregnant. I was sitting off to the side thinking, "Don't make her push, don't make her grunt, don't make her do any of that stuff! She's gonna have the baby!" She was like, within two or three weeks of delivery—humongous—doing this very active birthing scene.**

Marg Helgenberger: **I actually was a little nervous about it because to make it seem real, to like, push and push out this baby, I had to make it seem somewhat real, but I remember having a conversation with my OBGYN about it and he said, "Oh, everything should be fine, don't worry about it."**

Mimi Leder: One of the funniest things about that episode is when her water breaks. We had a little water going down and then when we edited it and showed it to the network, Standards and Practices, and they said, "No bodily fluids coming from the hidden place was allowed," and we said, "but it's the most beautiful fluid in the world, this is the water of life," and literally fought with them for how many seconds the water would be breaking.

Marg Helgenberger: Mimi was awesome, _is_ awesome. You just always felt like you were in good hands with her. She never raised her voice, she never lost her cool, she always came up with interesting shots. She knew how to direct the actors, she was a mother, she was very much family-oriented. Her mother was a Holocaust survivor and I got to know all of her family. We laughed a lot and she was always cool as a cucumber, but also very maternal.

K.C. never feels more human, more complete than when she shares a hospital room with her baby. She struggles to breastfeed the child, and it's a revelation to see K.C. submit to a situation bigger than she is. She holds the miracle of life, and her ball and chain. Leder frames a portrait from overhead of K.C. slumbering with the baby at her side. Both souls are at peace, and the heartbreak is that it won't last. K.C. is a dedicated workaholic, after all, and Karen is shipped off to live with a nanny in Bangkok. For as long as we have known her, K.C. has been working for a family of two.

Susan Rhinehart: The baby they were using as the newborn was probably two months old, and was still breastfeeding. So Mimi was with the woman who had the baby, and she was breastfeeding her. She said, "Would you mind if I did a very tight close-up of you breastfeeding the baby? All they'll see is the baby and sort of the swell of the breast. We won't show the nipple or anything, but I would really like to insert that for the first time K.C. sees her baby." The woman was like, "Sure." It was the tightest shot in the world _because it is TV._

Honest to God, ABC went nuts when they saw it in the dailies. They said the most horrible things: "Oh my God! No one wants to see that horrific, swollen, grotesque mammary gland!" They were so awful. The whole place went crazy. This whole notion, that every episode where Marg Helgenberger could wear anything she wanted low cut, her perky little boobs could hang out, but the minute a boob was there for the express reason of feeding an infant, it became this horrific thing. John Young said, "Fine, we just won't do an episode this week. We're not cutting it." [ABC] eventually backed off.

McMurphy and K.C. return to China Beach and hit the shower stalls. Karen is out of sight, out of mind, and yet K.C. can't get rid of the midwife—the woman who holds her secret, who knows exactly how full of shit she is, and who won't give up on her. From the depths of a VC cave to the middle of the Tet Offensive and back to a Saigon ghetto, misery has never loved company more.

THE WANDERER

Every time I dug into my pockets to pay for something in Vietnam, I thought about Ho Chi Minh. The man's face is inescapable in Vietnam—on every piece of currency, looking down on every other city block from a mural. After I got home I kept thinking about him. Who was he? What made him so damn special? What does he mean to today's Vietnamese millennials?

I started reading one of the few biographies of Ho, *Ho Chi Minh: A Life*, by William J. Duiker. It quickly became apparent that much of the man's life is a mystery. He spent three decades of exile away from Vietnam, bouncing around Europe, the Soviet Union, China, and allegedly the United States of America. Rumors of wives, children, and menial jobs all feel hazy and suspect. It wasn't until the early 1940s that he returned to his country as the face of Vietnamese independence. A rare consensus is that he championed nationalism and embraced communist ideals early in his life, searching for a way to harness both outlooks and liberate Vietnam from French occupation.

The image of a frazzled Colleen McMurphy in "The Big Bang" is akin to a city mural of Uncle Ho. A captivating portrait hanging on a wall that hides a locked safe full of stories untold.

Like Ho, McMurphy left Vietnam and lived a life in the shadows. "The World" first set this arc in motion when an army nurse went back to Vietnam and a lost woman was left waiting in Kansas. Both have been speeding toward the other, on a collision course ever since.

"Fever" is an intimate view of the wreckage.

Time swings like a pendulum between 1967 and 1970, glamorizing McMurphy's good ole days in Vietnam and magnifying her existential dread at home. The episode begins with a short-haired McMurphy laughing in slo-mo and getting tossed into the ocean by Boonie and Dodger. The opening credits tick by, and the last one causes a tilt of the head: *Directed by Diane Keaton.*

Dana Delany: **Diane likes to shake things up. She likes things to be *messy*. She would say, "Just go for it!" and shout out things. *China Beach* was very controlled at times, and very minimal. That was John Young's big thing: "Do less. Do less," and Diane is not that. [*laughs*] It was fun to go the opposite direction.**

Jeff Kober: **We were lying in the sand, Dana and I, with our heads close to each other and the camera was looking down on us. Diane said, "Okay, I want this scene to be like a Hallmark card." We did the scene and she came back over and I said, "Diane, I'm sorry. The Hallmark card thing is not working for me." She said, [*excited*] "Oh I know! That was such a stupid thing to say! Oh, I'm sorry!" I said, "No, it wasn't stupid! Let's just talk about it a little bit." She totally did that Diane Keaton thing. [*laughs*]**

Brian Wimmer: **We had Al Pacino standing off to the side of the set watching while Diane was directing. I was like, "Who's the guy in the long black coat on the beach over there?"**

"Oh, that's Al Pacino."

"Oh, I've heard of him. What's he doing?"

This dude comes and shows up, this iconic figure off to the side, in all black. It was like this weird, ghostly apparition—and he was on the beach! [*laughs*] That kind of stuff was happening all over the place and we just thought that was normal. Diane was so intent on directing a great episode, and I think it was important for her to set a mark as a director.

In 1990, the legendary *Annie Hall* actress was feeling out a short-lived directorial career and infused her signature nervous charm and skittish energy into the camera lens of *China Beach*. For all the surrounding death, Vietnam never feels so alive. Dodger runs around in a gorilla costume, McMurphy and Dr. Richard are covered in blood and screaming over the thunder of the helicopter. After work, it's time for drunken sing-a-longs on the beach. Three years later, McMurphy is in a starched white uniform sitting at a desk, organizing medication for geriatric patients. Paint can be heard drying.

McMurphy is bored in the USA, and so are we.

Keaton is as much a fashion and style influencer as she is a world-renowned actress. "Fever" resembles her Instagram account and her coffee table books that are full of sleek architecture and lucid contrasts. Her visual choices are deliberate and unapologetic. Whether it is a hat and gloves Keaton is wearing on the town or a room she is decorating, her presentation carries a cerebral intent and a devout artistic statement. Everything means a little more than we think.

Keaton's episode of *China Beach* is but another worthy, fitting entry in her oeuvre.

Throughout "Fever," Keaton places McMurphy within parallel lines and right angles in America, cornering her into solitary confinement. Our nurse is transferred to the maternity ward and walks the aisles of cribs, accompanied by crying babies with their proud grandparents on the other side of the looking glass. Later in the episode, the rows of cribs resemble church pews when McMurphy is brought to her knees in desperate prayer. There is no urgency in Kansas, no crisis for McMurphy to manage, except for the trappings of her inescapable, mundane suburban existence.

Chip Vucelich and Diane Keaton

"Fever" allows Delany to derange McMurphy like never before in an Emmy-nominated performance. Penny Fuller returns to *China Beach* as Colleen's mother, Mary Margaret McMurphy, and delivers her own Emmy-nominated turn as well, pushing every button of Colleen along the way. Mother and daughter are now contentious roommates, and each scene between the two is a round of boxing in the ultimate grudge match. Drinking, passive-aggression, and rancor escalates, questioning which woman will melt down first.

***Dana Delany:* I saw Penny on Broadway in *Applause* with Lauren Bacall. I think it was my eleventh birthday, and I remembered her. When she came to play my mom on the show, it was great. She was *strong*. She had no fear in playing the mother. She didn't worry about being liked, which I always appreciate in an actor. She was very complex in that role. You saw the mixture of feelings that she had about McMurphy. I loved working with her, she could go toe-to-toe—she does not back off! Then to have Diane Keaton direct us was even better.**

Scenes between Vietnam and Kansas tick-tock back and forth, breaking off in 1970 when McMurphy loses her temper at Nellie's baby shower. A couple of snide remarks from her mom send her to the bar for more self-destruction. She slurs and slow dances with a stranger, they make out, and end up on the floor. Keaton cuts the screen in half with a pool table, trapping McMurphy into one more rectangle for a conjugal visit.

McMurphy later reports for a night shift, where Keaton parks four ambulances in perpendicular rows outside. Our nurse shatters this geometric harmony and reclaims her role of catcher in the rye, darting into the busy emergency room to diagnose injuries, check IVs, and save some lives. McMurphy reaches her nadir, performing CPR on a dead man. She pulls herself out of the moment and backs away into the wall, covered in blood. Hueys whomping in her head. Delany's empty face brings us one step closer to that woman we saw at the end of "The Big Bang."

***William Broyles Jr.:* There's Chekhov's gun, where you dramatically put a gun on the wall in act 1, and you better fire it in act 3. Part of the amazing thing to me about writing**

for film and drama that is so true, is sometimes you don't know that you put a gun on the wall, or you don't know what the gun is. That whole last season, the gun on the wall was Colleen McMurphy wanted to go home in act 1, scene 1, episode 1, and realizing that she would never go home again. Her home was in the war.

McMurphy returns to her house in a frenzy, pulling mom out of bed to play charades in the pouring rain. Keaton rubs out every line in Kansas, and turns mother and daughter loose with hysteria. The blood begins to wash out of McMurphy's white uniform, and she can't fake it anymore. The mad laughter turns to tears, and McMurphy announces that she must take the next bus out of Kansas.

Dana Delany: **I had some scene in that episode where I was on a bus, and I start to cry or something like that. [Diane] said, "I don't know what to tell you. I don't know how you do what you do." [*laughs*] That was her direction to me! She said, "I don't do what you do. When I was in *The Godfather*, I had to cry, and I just listened to music." Music helps her, so she would have a Walkman in her ear back then when we had Walkmans. She said, "You just do it. I'll be here." It was so her.**

Colleen McMurphy was designed as the all-American girl-next-door to guide an audience through Vietnam, and *China Beach* tests the audience's relationship with the nurse by ripping away her identity, her appearance, and any remaining geniality in the following episode, "Juice." Written and directed by John Sacret Young, the episode picks up over two years after "Fever," leaving the audience blank pages to dream up their own version of McMurphy's lost years.

John Sacret Young: **We had so many stories of women really falling out of their lives. That's sort of what happened to many veterans. They came back and they couldn't stand to be where they grew up, and they went on a journey. Some coming back, some not. Whether it was to the woods or wherever, they went to get lost in hoping to get found, and that was certainly the metaphor or the symbol of ["Juice."] She was trying to get as far away from Vietnam and from her life as possible. And of course, she can't.**

From 1969 to 1970, *Then Came Bronson* aired on NBC for twenty-six episodes. A reticent biker named Jim Bronson (Michael Parks) has quit journalism and hit the road, searching for the meaning of life, helping whoever he comes across. At the beginning of each episode, someone asks him, "Where ya headed?" and he replies, "Wherever I end up, I guess." This same sentiment breathes through every episode of *China Beach*'s final season, and more specifically, Colleen McMurphy's circuitous road trip through 1970s' America. On a Harley Davidson. In leathers.

In a just and perfect world, Dana Delany would have starred in *Then Came McMurphy* to account for her misadventures between "Fever" and "Juice." Instead, we'll never know how McMurphy ends up in Miami, Florida, over two years later, working in an orange juice factory and living with an alligator-wrestling boyfriend (Gavan O'Herlihy). Young recalled a big fan of the show—also a Catholic priest—who watched "Juice" and protested, "That's not *my* McMurphy."

"Juice" is one gaudy, billboard-sized postcard from Miami. Piles of fresh oranges, glowing fish tanks, and Florida sunshine clash with McMurphy's new look. She's the one black orb left in a gumball machine. Her aviators reflect and reject the hues, and her leather jacket absorbs them. Beneath a mustache and fedora is a balding Dick Richard, visiting Miami for a getaway with his girlfriend and future wife, Colleen (Colleen Flynn). When he sees McMurphy on the other side of an orange juice rack, he drops a bottle of champagne in shock.

Robert Picardo: **I kidded John Young that he based the entire season on taking my hairpiece off. [*laughs*] Dick is so gobsmacked when he runs into [McMurphy] and she's so damn *different*, her whole biker act and all that. John had a great way of taking his theme and dealing with it smack on. "Juice" is a metaphor for whatever life energy is. If you're running out of juice, you're running out of whatever has propelled you thus far in life...and McMurphy works at an orange juice factory. [*laughs*]**

I think I pitched the idea of Dick having a mustache, and the moment McMurphy comments on it, he shaves it off. John said to me, "Look, he's at a point in his life where he's kind of at sea. He doesn't know what the next thing is.

He's dating a younger woman, he's trying to appear younger and more vital perhaps than he is." I thought it showed her influence over him still, and perhaps at a deeper level of his desire to please her. But mostly it shows that she saw through him, and once she saw through the curtain, you might as well take the curtain off.

Dick and McMurphy's relationship has been a primary color of the show since the pilot—the delineation between man and woman—forged in the fires of crisis and the boredom of the downtime. The two share a bond from Vietnam that is deeper than any act of sex could generate, making for one awkward date when McMurphy joins Dick and Colleen for dinner. It's as if McMurphy has been possessed by the ghost of K.C. Koloski. Long, straightened hair reaches down her back toward the hem of her red leather miniskirt. Shoulders are back, chin is up. She's cocky, self-assured, and pissed off.

McMurphy sums it up for the future Mrs. Colleen Richard, and everyone watching at home: "You don't know anything about me."

Young reflected on the creative process of "Juice" as trying to stuff too many tomatoes into a can, and how eight minutes of deleted footage would have produced a more complete story (some of this cut footage found an outlet in the series finale, "Hello, Goodbye.") A brief Vietnam flashback of a burial at dusk is a bit of a head-scratcher with no context, but a peek at 1969 shows McMurphy and Dr. Richard treating a wounded chaplain who offers to marry them on a lark. He dies before the vows can be completed. The connection between doctor and nurse pings across time and the globe as cursed love, a cruel joke, or whatever else it wants to be in the moment.

Young's episodes are known to linger in moments of silence and stylish camerawork, but "Juice" sails on cutting dialogue throughout, allowing McMurphy and Dick to drudge up their past, unfiltered and inebriated. The evening grows long and drunk, and McMurphy straddles Richard on a hammock. They lock eyes, remembering what once bound them together and whatever is keeping them apart. The still of the night doesn't speak for them this time. Her stone face cracks: "I was valuable. I loved it there. You. Me. It's over. It's gone. I don't want it to be, but it is, Richard. No more jokes." They pass out on the beach together without incident, then McMurphy wakes up alone.

"Juice" joins "X-Mas Chn. Bch. '67," "Skylark," and "The Big Bang" as an essential episode in the saga of Dr. Richard and McMurphy, and continues chasing the white rabbit that holds the secret of their Vietnam farewell. Young steps in at a pivotal moment in the season to begin answering questions instead of asking them. At the end of "Juice," Dr. Richard heads back to New England with his Colleen, and our nurse hops back on her bike, headed for God knows where.

McMurphy descended into the swamps of Florida to get lost in hopes of finding herself. Dick foiled her plan and found her first. "Juice" squeezes every preceding emotion of *China Beach* to a pulp in 1972 and McMurphy nearly drowns trying to swim in it, clad in leather. Richard heads back to New England with his Colleen, and McMurphy hops back on her bike to convince someone, somewhere else, she is bad to the bone.

WIPEOUT

Depending on who I was talking to for this book, I would casually mention I have a black, six-pound poodle named after Cpl. Boonewell G. Lanier. The first time I watched *China Beach*, Boonie connected with me in a way that the other characters didn't. More than anyone, Boonie was who I'd want to hang out with in the middle of the Vietnam War. A fun-loving guy who casts no stone. Brian Wimmer's performance popped off the screen. It was unrefined and infectious, as if Wimmer wasn't really acting. Wimmer was Boonie. Boonie was Wimmer.

> ***Dana Delany:* There's nobody who doesn't like Brian. First of all, he was gorgeous. Perfect body, perfect face, perfect smile, and *the nicest Mormon kid you ever met.* [*laughs*] Just a lovely, lovely person. He did not have a lot of experience acting before then, and he was just eager to jump in and do it. I thought he did a great job with the aging thing, and you just sensed Brian's true goodness coming out. He has a huge heart and I just love that scene in the pilot where he's with Bobby Hosea, where they punch each other in the water. That, to me, is the epitome of Brian and what he was like. Like a big puppy dog. It's fitting you named your dog after him.**

Wimmer was cast in *China Beach* with few screen credits to his name. A couple of years prior, he was briefly seen running from Freddie Krueger in *A Nightmare on Elm Street 2*, and *China Beach* was his first chance to sink his teeth into a role and grow with a character. Wimmer was very much learning on the fly, with a string of great sparring partners.

An offstage friendship with Chloe Webb informed moments of passion and vulnerability that wrapped a live wire around the Vietnam War. Like McMurphy, Laurette's absence sunk Boonie into unease, digging deeper into his mania and tortured love with K.C. Much of Wimmer's potential and Boonie's centricity to the early chapters of the show feel lost during much of the third season; many lighthearted scenes with Holly not scratching at what came before. Boonie returns to form in "F.N.G." when his love with K.C. is born, and it poses a legitimate question: Can Wimmer—and Boonie—hold their own?

The fourth season answers. Hell yeah.

> ***John Sacret Young:* We felt it, both a kind of limitation and yet exactly right. [Brian's] inability to express the ordinary depths an actor trains for. His regular guy-ness. His struggle to reach down to such stuff. It worked for the character, his essence. In the best of senses, you could feel the ordinary guy wanting, reaching down against and beyond his prescribed expectations. A moving dynamic. Good shit.**

Boonie is our usher into the final season, forcing all the stunning questions in the opening moments of "The Big Bang." Before the days of green screens and special effects, Wimmer spent much of the season with his leg bent up behind his body, an uncomfortable and demanding challenge the athletic actor welcomed. For all of the changes that time has brought to the characters, the Boonie of 1985 is very much the same. Full of life, optimism bordering on delusion. Throw in a ponytail, a mustache, and take away a leg, and he's still the same guy lighting up a room. Boonie has a wife, children, and seems fulfilled in the wake of the war that took so much from him. As I wrote this book, I encountered living and breathing incarnations of Boonie who touched me more than any episode of *China Beach*.

Noble Craig is a Vietnam veteran who proclaimed to me, "Vietnam made me a special person." Craig had nothing to do with *China Beach*, but spent time in Hollywood after the war building a small CV of memorable screen credits. Roles in *Big Trouble in Little China* and *Poltergeist II* accompany his brief portrayal of horror icon Freddie Krueger in *Nightmare on Elm Street 5: The Dream Child.*

And yet, Craig's film career is the least interesting thing about him.

Noble Craig, living life

Craig was a US Army Sergeant and specialist in booby traps when he went to Vietnam in 1968. A green captain had led Craig's troop out of country and into the mine fields of Cambodia. Craig watched fifty-eight men die in his first month-and-a-half of service, before one day climbing over a paddy dike and stepping on a mine. He lost an arm, both legs, his right eye, and his right ear. He was medevacked and sent home. Today, there is still shrapnel in one of his eye sockets.

Craig studied psychiatry at UCLA and bought a 1970 Trans Am Cuda AAR that he says brought him back into society. A car to match his attitude. One day at the VA, a casting agent was scouting for a veteran with no limbs. Craig talked the agent into considering him by declaring, "I have one arm, and I can do anything you want me to do."

Craig is full of stories, like the time he beat Robert Blake in an arm-wrestling contest on the set of *Baretta*, and how he built a contraption so he could ski down hills in Lake Tahoe. Talking to Craig, I thought about his outlook on life, and I thought about so many other veterans who came home with their own struggles. I asked him what he would tell someone dealing with a setback.

Without hesitation, he said, "*Live your life*. I've had more fun than four people put together."

When I see Brian Wimmer bring Boonie Lanier to life in the fourth season, I can't help but think about the past fifty years of Noble Craig refusing to let one fateful day in Vietnam define the rest of his life. I see Boonie's spirit in others, like Bill "Ziggy" Siegesmund and Tom Coakley.

Tom and his wife, Nellie, are seen during "Vets" and "Souvenirs." The couple sits side by side, talking about what the war experience can do to a man. A story Tom doesn't tell is how he lost his left leg in combat. He came home for rehabilitation and met Nellie, who was a former army nurse in Vietnam working at the Walter Reed hospital. They got married, started a family, and chased the dream. It's a very similar arc to the Boonie Lanier we've seen so far in the *China Beach* of 1985. Nellie doesn't think it's a coincidence that McMurphy's best friend in the States shares her name, either.

***Tom Coakley:* I was an infantry soldier, and I was the radio man. We were ordered to chase North Vietnamese that we had spotted, which you're never supposed to do. Further, I was ordered to put the long-width antennae up by the colonel, who was flying around in the helicopter in the sky. I knew that I should never put that up. When they handed me the stuff, they said, "Never use this." I went back and said, "I hear you loud and clear, can I stay with this antennae?" He got angry and told me it was a direct order to put the antennae up. It was the only time I ever put it up, and I'd say probably within fifteen minutes we had walked close to an enemy bunker and they threw a grenade at the antennae which landed right by my foot.**

Delany with Tom and Nellie Coakley

I never saw it or heard it hit, but the blast blew me up in the air. Fortunately, it was what we call a chi-com grenade, a wooden-handled homemade job rather than an American grenade. It blew me up in the air, and I came down and I reached for my rifle and my arm just flopped in the air. Both bones were broken below the elbow and it just flopped around. I sat up just long enough to notice my left leg; the boot was gone, and the foot was blown apart. It looked like a fan, all the side bones and toes were fanned out and the leg was at a right angle about ten inches below my knee. My right leg also looked pretty well torn up and they later told

me that they thought they would have to take the right leg as well. There was a brief firefight and it subsided. I don't want to diminish it. It was a huge effort on the part of the medic and my folks that cleared a place for a helicopter to come in. I would imagine I got back to the MASH unit within probably forty-five minutes.

Nellie Coakley: **When Tom saw his rifle and his leg, he laid back down and just as he did, a spray of bullets went over his head. Had he remained sitting any longer, it would have gone through his head and chest. He was lucky.**

Tom Coakley: **All three limbs were badly damaged, and I'm so thankful; I could have easily been a triple amputee, or dead.**

China Beach was left thrashing in the muck of 1968 when the third season ended. A hellacious year never got a proper send-off, and the series has been piecing together a torn-up calendar ever since. "One Giant Leap" is the closest addendum to season three and is the only traditional episode of the fourth season—taking place entirely in the late sixties and on the home turf of the Five and Dime.

It is now July 11, 1969. No one and nothing is the same.

Richard Nixon is now president, and troop levels in Vietnam just hit their record high. John Lennon and Yoko Ono are married. The Zodiac Killer is skulking through the neighborhoods of San Francisco. Apollo 11 is launching, destined to put man on the moon. Within the next two months, the Woodstock Music Festival will claim its place in pop culture, and Ho Chi Minh will die. The pages of history are flipping in the wind, and Americans and Vietnamese are still killing each other. Boonie Lanier has a five o'clock shadow and both legs intact. He isn't pouring beers and telling jokes, he is the weed man getting the soldiers high.

After a scolding from McMurphy, Boonie jumps behind the wheel of a jeep, stoned out of his mind. Right as Buzz Aldrin steps foot on the moon, Boonie's vehicle runs over a landmine and flips into a river. The rain pours, and the water rises while everyone works to save his life, in an homage to a similar scene in Paul Newman's *Sometimes a Great Notion* (1970). Filming moved to the Warner Bros. lot to stage one of the most dangerous stunts of the series.

Brian Wimmer: **Everything went off so smoothly, and it could have gone so badly. We really had to do a lot of the things that you saw, like Dana and I were actually exchanging air underwater at times. I felt like this was actually happening; all you had to do was be in the moment. There was no laughing involved. It was so intense, so incredible, it felt like such teamwork, and to me it was one of the biggest scenes that happened with all the characters. I just felt so lucky to have been such a major part of that. When everybody was done with that extraction scene, we were shaking our heads: "That was one of the most amazing, intense things we've ever done."**

John Sacret Young: **The water sequence and rescue was—to call on a bad pun perhaps—a full-boat experience. We had, I believe, three cameras working and walkie talkies and rain birds, and everything and everybody was *wet.* It was exciting, grueling, challenging, satisfying. One big, ambitious night's work. I was on one camera, and it was where I learned out of time's necessity to change lenses or sizes with every take in order to get the work done and have choices.**

Robert Picardo: **It was exciting and probably a little bit dangerous with the helicopter overhead, and then, of course, there was the funny side that I'm working with a toupee glued on to my head. As soon as you take a toupee and put it under water, the glue can dissolve and it can float off next to you like a man o' war [*laughs*] or a jellyfish. I remember telling the hair department, "I'd like to glue my own hairpiece on," because I knew I would like, nail it on so when the helicopter went by or I'm underwater that it would stay there, and it did! So yes, I was underwater wearing a hairpiece and pretending to saw someone's leg at about four or five in the morning as I recall.**

"One Giant Leap" begins a mass purge of characters from Vietnam, regurgitating Boonie back to the States, minus a leg. Boonie's torrid exit goes on without the presence of K.C. Koloski, robbing the characters and the audience of a momentous goodbye. *China Beach* follows Boonie home in the following episode, "One Small Step," and Brian Wimmer cements his finest performance as Boonie Lanier.

The opening moments of "One Small Step" are Boonie in a nutshell. He wakes up in a giant room, surrounded by cots full of broken boys. A gigantic American flag hangs on the back wall. In his hand is a telephone with a long cord stretching offscreen. Boonie is pulling the covers over his head. He doesn't want anyone to see him cry. He doesn't want anyone to hear him break the news to his mom. It isn't out of vanity or shame. Boonie wants to be strong for his men. He shakes and trembles, and all he can really say to his mom is, "I'm okay. I'm a-okay."

John Wells's script for "One Small Step" resembles his prior work in "The World" and "The Thanks of a Grateful Nation" by stripping away the main cast down to one individual who must face the homeland alone. Wells frequented veteran hospitals for research, and drew inspiration from a friend who lost his leg to cancer and later became a rehabilitative physician. John Young suggested further films for Wells to research like *Inside Moves* (1980), *Coming Home* (1978), and the Marlon Brando post-war drama *The Men* (1950) as reference points to capture the rehabilitation process and the dark humor that surrounds it.

Boonie lands in a series of rowdy veteran hospitals where wounded soldiers play cards, smoke dope, and cherish the fact they are no longer in Vietnam. The cuts between Boonie's rehab journey are not fast, they fade to black and fade back in to portray his crawling pace of recovery and growing ponytail. Boonie struggles to sit on a toilet, breaks his nose falling out of a hospital bed, and refuses another operation for his leg to fit a prosthesis. He takes all of his inner pain and projects it, finding redemption through building up others. A bevy of notable guest stars including Michael Bowen, Victor Cruz, and Michael Rappaport flank Boonie as crude company, along with a nurse, Linda (Finn Carter) who also served in Vietnam. Boonie is taken with her, and "The Big Bang" has already revealed he will marry her.

Wimmer's performance and Wells's script are top-tier offerings in the canon of *China Beach*, brilliantly tied together by director Steve Dubin. At the center of Boonie's recovery is the strength he gives to others. A fellow wounded vet from Boonie's hometown of Santa Cruz lies in bed, covered in bandages and missing both legs. Boonie's wheelchair stops in its tracks at this sight. The man doesn't want to speak to anyone, but Boonie's persistent congeniality ekes a laugh from him. Boonie later finds the man in the bathroom attempting to kill himself. Blood is everywhere, and as the man holds a shard of glass to his throat, Boonie sits on the floor with him for a breathless moment and gives him the faith to confront one more day.

> ***Brian Wimmer:*** **I come out of my wheelchair into that mess of a scene, and to me, that was Boonie at his best. Even though he's in the same situation, he finds a way to joke with this guy and bring him back around. That was his job in the war, and that was just one of my favorite scenes of all time. When we were filming that, we had a bunch of veterans in there that had no arms and legs, and they were in wheelchairs and having to go through this role-playing again. That was no light manner.**
>
> **They were fun and gregarious, they played basketball, they did all these kinds of things. [I was] being delicate because they are these handicapped guys who have gone through such an intense thing—and no, no, no—they are so past that. They just do not want that kind of coddling at all, and they taught me that instantly. Like, if I was sitting with my hands on the wheels and not paying attention, they would come in and slam into my hand! [*laughs*] I swear, I broke a finger with those guys.**
>
> **I met my character in several different people; there was one guy in particular. They flew he and I out to *Good Morning America*, no legs, and he was like this great athlete going through some severe post-traumatic stress and having to deal with all this, and he and I connected. They gave you a small Purple Heart pin when they give you your Purple Heart, and he gave me his. It was so intense. He was just like my character.**

"One Small Step" is essentially Boonie Lanier on one leg vs. the world. The moment he hesitates, Dodger appears out of the mist to push him across the finish line and give him the strength to keep going with rehab. What sets this episode apart from almost every episode of *China Beach* is a sense of sweet victory. Insurmountable odds typically chew up characters and spit them into the credits with a sad harmonica playing. Not this time.

Boonie has Dodger drop him off at Linda's house. He has no backup plan, and is doubling down on love. She has a boyfriend and doesn't want anything to do with a damaged vet, and yet Boonie ends up in her bedroom, stripped naked, confronting the bare stump of his leg he has been unable to look at. This moment not only births Boonie's love with Linda, but his fortitude to go through with another operation.

The first two seasons of *China Beach* hint that Boonie is a false idol, overcompensating and in denial, and "One Small Step" affirms his aim was true all along. The audience has been starved for a chance to rush the field of play and carry a character off to the locker room in celebration, and Santa Cruz's favorite son doesn't know how to quit. It's but one apex in the life and times of Boonie Lanier, and a familiar story of courage under fire that Noble Craig, Tom Coakley, and other vets have brought to life—without a camera or script. Without anybody watching.

(THE BEST PART OF) BREAKIN' UP

"One Giant Leap" not only takes a leg from Boonie Lanier, it announces that the Vietnam War is ready to move on without Colleen McMurphy. The Five and Dime has been her home for over three seasons of TV, and now she is the outsider in 1969, snapping at the new nurses to get the hair off their collar. Boonie is toking up with the guys, Dr. Richard has grown close to a new nurse, Gloria (Kathy Molter), and Beckett has signed up for the Free Love movement. Right after Beckett beds the lead singer of the visiting USO act, McMurphy gives him a deep kiss on the mouth to see if she should tag along.

McMurphy's adopted church, the Jet Set, is expelling her too. A wall of marijuana smoke and the stoned groove of the *Hair* anthem "Five Zero Zero" roust her from her dedicated barstool, and she crosses the helipad, where a giant peace sign has been painted. She flees to the triage unit, where Boonie is getting the guys high. One of them pulls out a gun and points it at himself, everyone else, and finally, McMurphy. One more disturbing moment cutting straight into 2018.

Even the soldiers are rejecting our nurse—and her worst, most personal break-up is yet to come.

The Colleen McMurphy of 1969 has much in common with the fourth season of *China Beach*—both entities brought the most dedicated work to the wrong place at the wrong time. McMurphy was more than a nurse in Vietnam, and *China Beach* was more than a TV show in 1990. The engagement and attention at a fine art exhibit was required, then, a week of reflection and meditation. A viewing on DVD now removes the enforced seven days of digestion, along with the possible pitfalls of 1990 consumption: a missed VCR timer or an accidental erasure of "Fever" or "You, Babe" could have tanked much of the experience.

Through the fall of 1990, *China Beach* was a speeding locomotive burning on the coals of its greatest string of episodes to date, and yet, the Saturday night audience kept jumping from the passenger cars. The train ran off a cliff on December 8 when "The Call" aired to 5.5 million viewers, the smallest audience to ever watch a first-run episode of the show.

Nancy Giles headlines another *China Beach* chapter focusing on racial strife, steering Frankie through 1969 Chicago, decked out in bellbottoms and an afro. Frankie bombs an open mic comedy act, then navigates the peer pressure of joining the Black Panther movement, and rejects the perpetuation of racial violence as she did in "Promised Land." The torch of MLK still hoisted in her hand. Witnessing the Chicago Eight trials, Frankie sees the worst of both black and white all over again, and chooses to simply be her own person. A black woman who is a Vietnam veteran. "Isn't that scary?" she asks her audience, and that's when her comedy act begins to connect.

Almost every moment of the fourth season feels like an intricate piece of a master plan, aside from the other 1969 subplot in "The Call." McMurphy discovers Dodger has come back to Vietnam, and he is building a local hospital with nothing but rocks and dirt, hanging out with an eccentric elderly woman who plays an organ. It's an undercooked take on "Skylark," one rare blemish in the final volume of *China Beach*.

McMurphy and Dodger's post-war relationship (and rickety romance) is better explored in a later episode, "Quest," and Dodger's obsession with Vietnam is revisited again when he returns to a desolated China Beach in 1975 during "100 Klicks Out." It is no coincidence that "The Call" is the one episode that isn't a succinct fit in the season—it was the only hour not written or directed by a *China Beach* regular.

After "The Call" aired to poor ratings, *China Beach* disappeared from the ABC schedule for nearly six months. While the show faded from conversation and disengaged from the viewers who remained faithful, John Young and company completed production on the remaining episodes, not knowing if or when they would be aired.

The next six months were unforgiving to the cause of *China Beach*, and according to Young, "full of less than honesty" on the part of ABC. There was also shit luck. Over the holidays, the United States of America edged toward attacking Iraq over its invasion of Saudi Arabia.

The Gulf War was set to be the country's first full-scale military conflict since Vietnam, and no one wanted to be reminded of our last war. One we lost.

To add insult to injury, another Young and Broyles co-creation, *Under Cover*, premiered in *China Beach*'s Saturday time slot and promptly disappeared in January of 1991. March came and ABC head Bob Iger announced the official cancellation of *China Beach*, ending the cast and crew's hopes for a fifth season.

> ***William Broyles Jr.:*** **The sadness to me is that *China Beach* didn't run for ten years. Not only were there other stories to tell, but for me personally, I might have woke up and tried to get a job back writing for it. By then, it was so good I'm not sure they would have hired me. [*laughs*] Sometimes you just don't know when you're experiencing something how amazing it is. It's only when it's gone and done. It was like, "Holy shit, it's not going to be on the air anymore. You can't tell any more of those stories."**

Syndication deals, the handsome royalties they secure, and a number of intriguing ideas weren't meant to be. The great un-produced episode of *China Beach* would have built a trilogy with "Vets" and "Souvenirs" by following the return of eight veterans to Vietnam with their children and exploring their old battlegrounds, harkening back to the premise of Broyles' *Brothers in Arms*. Troy Evans recalled plans for an episode to accompany Sergeant Pepper and Lila Garreau home from their tours, and Jeff Kober was set to direct an episode of his own.

With *China Beach* sitting in its own private purgatory, Young campaigned in the *Los Angeles Times* to drum up interest for the unaired hours, spoiling major plot developments and the final coordinates of the series in mass print.* A faux pas in 2018 terms. A necessity of survival and public relations in 1991. Absence made the heart of the audience grow fonder, and when *China Beach* returned in the summer with "I Could Have Danced All Night...But Didn't," viewership doubled to eleven million viewers, the largest audience of the season.

*(Steven Herbert, "China Beach Wraps Production," *Los Angeles Times*, February 15, 1991)

McMurphy's road trip has landed her in Oregon in 1983 as a bridesmaid at a dysfunctional Jewish wedding. She is not as fierce as she was in "Juice." Her hair is shorter, a few grey hairs are poking through, and she turns down a gin and tonic from the reception drummer, Joe (Adam Arkin). They dance and flirt at arms' length, and the mere mention of a *My Fair Lady* song takes McMurphy back to 1969, where another wedding was taking place at China Beach.

Weddings are a day of celebration for the wife and groom. The witnesses decide their own emotions. Some are reminded of the love they have, the love they don't, or the love they want to escape. Then alcohol is served. *China Beach* sat on this plot device until its final hours, waiting with the patience of the Vietcong. There are no drunken punch-ups, just the ongoing game of musical chairs with the cast. Literally. Robert Picardo remembers reading the script and deriding the entire idea of adapting *My Fair Lady* into an episode. For his trouble, Picardo received the most singing parts.

Dana Delany: **The thing about John Young is if you mention to him (and any actor on the show can tell you this) anything that scares you or is a weak spot or a vulnerable thing, he will make you do it, so you had to be careful what you mentioned to him. I think I mentioned to him that singing scared me, so of course, then we had to do a musical episode! It was fun and scary, and then a lot of people tell me that's one of their favorite episodes. A lot of people love that one, and I love the cheesiness of putting on a show, too. There's something so homemade about it; I kind of love that.**

Carol Flint *(writer, "I Could Have Danced All Night...But Didn't")****:*** **I had this idea of doing a musical. I have no idea why. [*laughs*] From the very beginning, the show had these different layers of reality, like, "Yeah, you're going to have a USO show and then you're going to go blow something up, and then you're going to be amputating somebody's leg." There was also this desire of trying to hold together some normalcy through entertainment. This All-American kind of entertainment was frequently three steps behind what that generation was experiencing. Yes, there was a rock 'n' roll element, but this generation of people also grew up on**

Rodgers and Hammerstein musicals. That was kind of the feeling behind doing the beauty pageant [in "Skin Deep"] and stuff like that. I mean, that was part of the culture in the sixties—this weird hangover.

Music and love are in the air. McMurphy inhales. Lila Garreau is organizing a production of *My Fair Lady* to lift the spirits of everyone, and Bub Pepper is planning on asking the major to marry him. Their matrimonial joy sends McMurphy over the edge. She is now a short-timer with only ninety-nine days left in Vietnam; Boonie has just been torn away from her, and she's not planning on letting go of Dr. Richard. Gloria has become McMurphy's cutthroat competition, stealing her role in the musical, and proposing an open relationship between the two nurses and Dr. Richard.

The walls of jealousy, desperation, and the Vietnam War draw nigh.

After Dr. Richard cuts McMurphy down over how she can drink everyone under the table and then take care of them, she snaps, and for the first time, Dick sees not McMurphy, but Colleen. Delany and Picardo flip the circuit breakers of their characters and surrender any pretense, irony, or wit. They sit by a campfire and pour out their hearts, as if Ruby and Fred are side stage for the sequel to "Skylark." There's kissing, exchanges of "I love you," and a crazy plan of crashing Sarge and Lila's wedding with their own nuptials.

The would-be Dr. and Mrs. Dick Richard call home to tell their families the good news. When things are going smooth in *China Beach*, an unseen villain is waiting to attack. It's not Charlie this time. It's Beth Ann. She is in critical condition after a car wreck, and Dr. Richard's heart and soul are immediately transported to his parent-less children in New England. McMurphy sees it in his face. She will never be his number one.

John Sacret Young makes an onscreen cameo as Sarge and Lila's wedding officiant, holding the honors of asking the witnesses to speak now or forever hold their peace. Both Richard and Colleen keep locked jaws and stare holes through one another. Sarge and Lila become man and wife, and the nurse escorts the doctor to his helicopter headed out of 'Nam. They embrace, realizing this is goodbye, and muster their final words to each other in private, under the rumble of the rotors. McMurphy tells him not to call her when she gets back to the

States. Richard weeps: "You are my best friend." After all this time, it is McMurphy who gets the last word: "You were my best friend here."

Dana Delany: I like unrequited love, I think those are the best love stories. It's more like life. [_laughs_] Getting together is, eh, not as interesting.

William Broyles Jr.: It would have been very easy and "feel good entertainment" to have gone the other way with that scene, but again, that's John Young's dedication to keeping it honest. Even if it breaks your heart, and even if for a moment you think, "How could McMurphy say that to him? After all this?" but it's true. I'm just so proud to have been part of that. That last season, I'm trying to think what credit I could take for it. I'm desperate to take credit for something. [_laughs_]

Robert Picardo: When I first read that script, they had me singing the last lines of "I've Grown Accustomed to Her Face" on a helicopter as it's taking off. I went, "Oh shit, this is ridiculous. This will never work," and I think it's great in the show!

Having to do that was absolutely terrifying. I was on a helicopter only one time when it was taking off. We were playing characters that had to be used to that, it's like another day at the office, but inside, your body is going [_yells_] "hoooollllly ssshhhhiiiit!" when it takes off. The whole scene was about the emotion of leaving McMurphy, not about what was really happening in my body, which was, "I've never felt this feeling before of going straight up in a helicopter."

Believe it or not, I don't really look terrified in the shot, [_laughs_] but it felt very strange to say goodbye. We knew that was going to be our last season, but that early in the season to say goodbye to that relationship and not know where the subsequent scripts were going to jump around, it almost felt a little bit like, "Okay, I'm leaving the show. I don't know how I'll be back."

As a first-time viewer of *China Beach*, I felt steered to root for romance between McMurphy and Dr. Richard. Their spats, debates, and chemistry penned an epic of everlasting love in disappearing ink. I presented this argument to John Young, who replied, "I always thought that these two were wonderfully connected, but it was completely non-sexual, and I don't know if that comes across or not. That was my feeling." I retorted, "In my *China Beach* fan-fiction, they found their happy ever after in New England."

With a laugh, Young ended the debate: "Well, he did marry a Colleen."

The collapse of McMurphy and Dr. Richard's relationship was a given from the beginning of "The Big Bang," yet still manages to infuse "Fever" and "Juice" with even more heartbreak in retrospect. With Dr. Richard removed from the Vietnam chess board, McMurphy uses the last of her money and her R&R to be with the next-best friend she has left in Southeast Asia, K.C. Koloski.

Most farewells are sudden and shocking in *China Beach*, but McMurphy and K.C. get a whole episode to go round and round, drudge up the past, and consider their parting in "The Always Goodbye." Bits of Puccini's *Tosca* weave in and out of the scenes, allowing the fat lady to sing along offscreen to the operatic severing of a sisterhood.

K.C. has quit the hooking life and relocated to Bangkok, Thailand. Better yet, she is giving motherhood a second chance with two-year-old Karen via the help of a live-in nanny. K.C. is making moves into the future, opening a nightclub, and McMurphy is a drunken id—passing out during a toast, puking in the middle of the night, and unable to fathom going home to Kansas in a few weeks.

Screenwriter Lydia Woodward considers this hour more of a "tone poem" than anything. The narrative hardly moves, and I am convinced "The Always Goodbye" is the only episode of *China Beach* void of natural light, taking place entirely within the confines of smoky, softly lit interiors. Each scene resembles a hermetically sealed piece of theater, taking place on a parquet floor under houselights. Each word floating over an orchestra and up to the mezzanine. A bleak aura similar to "Strange Brew" pervades, and anyone not named McMurphy or K.C. feels remote.

Four years before portraying the fiery Vietnam vet Lieutenant Dan Taylor in *Forrest Gump*, Gary Sinise directed his only episode of *China Beach*, delivering an entirely female story built on sheer emotion and mood. K.C. spends much of the episode looking at McMurphy in judgment, turning the tables from Tet when K.C. was the reckless user and McMurphy had her house in order. Woodward's script is busy and full of cracking dialogue throughout. K.C. attacks McMurphy's drinking, and McMurphy is quick to throw up K.C.'s ambivalence over Boonie's accident. K.C. says it was never her job to hold a soldier's hand. McMurphy fires back, "It depends on what you like to hold."

"The Always Goodbye" is a fitting swan song for McMurphy and K.C. that holds the good, the bad, and the ugly that has lingered between them. Delany and Helgenberger hit each note of their characters with aloof precision, reenacting their cheerleading routines from Tet, making fun of the men who have spurned them, and questioning the crooked paths that have led them to always lousy goodbyes. McMurphy and K.C. try their best to pretend they don't give a fuck about the other, and they only fool themselves. There are no sappy Hallmark moments, only pledges to drop what is holding them back. K.C. is shipping Karen and her nanny to Saigon so she can focus on her business, and McMurphy declares her newfound sobriety.

Only one of them is totally full of it.

MAMA SAID

K.C. Koloski receives a third chance at motherhood in "100 Klicks Out," directed by Mimi Leder. It is over before it begins. "I hate you," sneers eight-year-old Karen (Shay Astar). "Get over it," barks mommy dearest. Mother and daughter are reunited after six years apart in Saigon during the last week of April, 1975. In a matter of hours, the capital of South Vietnam will fall to the North Vietnamese Army. K.C. has abandoned the nightclub empire she has built in Thailand—gasp—to save her own flesh and blood. Somewhere in New Mexico, Colleen McMurphy watches the live TV footage at a bar, grinding her teeth. Karen's nanny, Trieu Au (Kieu Chinh), has been imprisoned by the communists, and all that matters now is for K.C. and Karen to get the hell out of 'Nam before it is too late.

Whenever, however they get to the States, K.C. promises Karen all the things she's never had: A pink canopy bed, stuffed animals, Christmases with snow, and ice cream every day. "All this I will give you," also said Satan.

Imitating a pregnancy in "You, Babe," was no big deal for Marg Helgenberger. Aside from crawling under church pews while handcuffed to Dana Delany, filming was relatively easy for the expectant mother. The heartwarming episode sent Helgenberger off to maternity leave, and within a few weeks of delivering a baby boy, she was already back to work. Awaiting Helgenberger was the most demanding moment of her four-year role, with Mimi Leder aiming to "collapse all reality" during a scene on the roof of the downtown Los Angeles post office.

Leder adds another glorious moment to her portfolio by beginning in a dark void and backing the camera out into the blinding California daylight. K.C. and Karen emerge from a door and walk into an infamous moment in American history, reimagined within *China Beach*. Helicopters are swooping up and down from the roof of the US embassy in Saigon, evacuating the last few Americans left in Vietnam. Aircraft carriers await miles offshore, where Hueys are being pushed into the ocean to make room for more bodies.

Tornadic wind from the propellers melds with the screams of a mob fleeing Vietnam. The last chopper is full, and K.C. does the unthinkable. She writes "Boonie Lanier" on Karen's clothing, and wrestles her into the vessel as it takes off. The soldiers scream in K.C.'s face while Karen holds a death grip on K.C., begging her mother not to leave her. Leder's cinematography demands the viewer to look through the eyes of both K.C. and Karen in this moment: A hapless parent and a scared child separating in real time. Karen disappears into the sky, while K.C. shrinks into a rabid crowd.

The viewer must dwell in the moment with K.C. and decide if she is a heel or a hero. K.C. saves her daughter's life while deserting her, acting on the blind faith Boonie will be waiting on the other side of the world to fix it all. Then, we remember the money that Karen found in "She Sells More Than Sea Shells" and realize K.C. was footing the bill for what she just promised. No more and no less. The realization comes: Nothing stops K.C. from getting what she wants, and she wanted free from Karen.

The parting of K.C. and Karen is an ambush in the vein of McMurphy and Dr. Richard in the prior episode, full of its own psychologies. There is no cheeky song to soften the blow. Family ties are perforated. Through bulging eyes and hunched shoulders, Helgenberger offers the possibility of K.C. turning to dust before our eyes at the episode's conclusion. On the surface is an affectation by an Emmy-winning actress. Underneath is something far surpassing any definition of method acting. When Helgenberger described this day of filming, I could feel her pulse rising with each word, tension collecting in her voice with hardly a pause for breath. It isn't K.C. we see ashen, devastated, and weeping at the end of the episode. It is Helgenberger, who wanted nothing more than to just go home and hold her baby boy.

> ***Marg Helgenberger:*** **I have to say, it was much worse coming back. I was just not ready for those hours, because those hours were just monstrous, and I was breastfeeding and just [*pause*] postpartum stuff that you're dealing with. I don't know. I was not happy about having to come back as early as I did. I was an emotional wreck for an episode or two.**

I remember ["100 Klicks Out"]. I got lost on my way to the set; I couldn't follow that map they gave us, so I was forty-five minutes late. I was probably already crying because I was frustrated and flustered or whatever and then it just—I don't know—I was just so *tired*! [*laughs*] You're dealing with all those hormones that are fluctuating and I was missing my kid. He was a baby. It was rough. Somehow, I got through it and I used whatever feelings I was feeling, which were strong, [*laughs*] trying to get her out on this helicopter.

***John Sacret Young:* I got a call saying, "You've got to come down here. Marg can't play this scene." That sequence is primal. Man, she was ripped up. I don't mean a scintilla of negativity about that. Her emotions were not three-sixty or whatever, they were seven-twenty, ten-eighty, pick a number. Pick an over-percentage—300, 400, 500 percent. They were just so ripe, so rich. It was almost about trying to control them rather than let them loose. It is one of the most wrenching scenes I've ever witnessed.**

Sorting through Helgenberger's personal tumult of filming "100 Klicks Out," I encountered a woman whose real life startlingly mirrors the peaks and valleys of K.C. Koloski. She even shares the same initials.

The life of Kieu Chinh is more dramatic than any episode of *China Beach*, deserving of its own big screen portrayal. I called Chinh to discuss her role as Karen's nanny, Trieu Au, and instead heard a stream of stories from the actress's early life in Vietnam. She didn't remember filming the Fall of Saigon in "100 Klicks Out," but she remembered living through the real thing, and the travesties before and after.

During World War II, Chinh's mother was giving birth to her infant brother when Japanese forces bombed the Hanoi hospital, killing them both. Years later in 1954, Chinh was a teenager when her father pushed her onto an airplane bound for Saigon. Vietnam was breaking in half at the seventeenth parallel, and her father chose to stay in the North in defiance of the Viet Minh communist movement. The hatch of the plane shut, and she never saw him again. Chinh continued to walk me through the wild swings of her life that paralleled those of K.C.

Both women built personal empires from nothing in Vietnam, then watched them burn.

Kieu Chinh, circa 1975

After Chinh arrived in Saigon, she was walking down a sidewalk when the feature film impresario Joseph Mankiewicz cast her as an extra in an adaptation of *The Quiet American* (1958). Chinh's uncommon beauty and acting talent quickly launched her to the top of Southeastern Asian fame. In the following years, Chinh traveled across the continent and started a production company, hosted her own talk show, and had starring roles alongside Burt Reynolds and Tippi Hedren. When Saigon began to fall in April of 1975, she returned to her home country to help her family escape. Just as K.C. did.

Chinh converted all her money to Vietnamese dong, right as its value plummeted and Northern Vietnamese Army surrounded Saigon. She boarded a plane headed out of the country right as the airport was bombed. Days later, Chinh arrived in Singapore without a passport, a visa, or a penny to her name, and was immediately jailed. Chinh recalled, "In the morning we line[d] up for the restroom, where in the line, I see a soldier is reading a magazine and *I* am on the cover!

He gave me a dirty look and didn't believe it was me, then opened my centerfold. He let me make one phone call to the South Vietnamese ambassador." A week of flying around the world in search of asylum resulted in Chinh becoming the first Vietnamese refugee in Canada, cleaning chicken coups for a living wage. Between shifts, she called everyone she knew in Hollywood looking for work.

K.C. Koloski also crawled away from the rubble of Saigon, returning to Bangkok in "The Always Goodbye" to find her nightclub and apartment decimated, having to resume prostitution to make ends meet. Both Kieu Chinh and K.C. were cornered into poverty until old friends picked up the phone. Chinh had Tippi Hedren, and K.C. has McMurphy in "Quest."

The twisting paths of Colleen McMurphy and K.C. Koloski reconvene, then separate forever in 1976 on a rainy sidewalk in Santa Cruz, California. Director John Sacret Young paints a depressing, modern post-noir scene in the style of Jack Vettriano, placing a blue umbrella in the hands of K.C. For the first time ever, K.C. looks pedestrian. No make-up, hair pulled back in a ponytail, clothed in baggy thrift store rags. McMurphy stands behind her in a khaki trench coat with a red parasol offering moral support.

The umbrellas illuminate, then accentuate the faces and moods.

A flimsy chain-link fence is all that stands between K.C. and all that really matters. In the distance, Boonie Lanier lumbers on one leg alongside Karen at her school. In another life, K.C. is right there holding hands with them. One cry into the morning air is all it would take for a redemptive reunion between mother and daughter. Instead, K.C.'s tears meet the rain and wash into the gutter. Whatever good thing Karen has going, K.C. can't bring herself to screw it up.

McMurphy and K.C.'s friendship dissolves on that sidewalk without argument or direction. Both are incapable of saving themselves, too exhausted to remember who owes who anymore. If McMurphy and K.C. ever speak to each other again, we'll never know.

Two hours deep into a phone call with John Young, he was describing a mythic, Hollywood party spectacle of Gary Cooper looking glum in a room full of mermaids. He paused, then boiled the four-year mission of *China Beach* down to one rhetorical question. "Maybe this is what we're getting to in this conversation: How do you combine sorrow and joy at once? Or, how do you combine a *gauntness* with a kind of joy?" The methods evolved from music and bombast in the first season to sullen, neighborhood navel-gazing by the series' end.

The sidewalk and chain-link fence in San Jose stretch nine years later and 1,865 miles eastward to Kansas City, Missouri, in "Rewind." After a dozen episodes, Christine Elise reprises her role as Karen Lanier and hits the road to film a documentary about the Vietnam War, twinning as a search for her mother. Director Mimi Leder stalks Karen and her aunt Maria (Amy Steel) from the curb. Steel looks as if she was pulled from the same gene pool as Helgenberger, with a dash of freckles and strawberry-blonde locks. Four years prior, Steel auditioned for the role of Colleen McMurphy, and eventually got her chance to steer the narrative of *China Beach* on a high wire, alone.

Maria stares at a slum through the latticed aluminum, filling her lungs with cigarette smoke. Exhaling Koloski family values. This dilapidated project is where Maria could hear her big sister, K.C., abused through the walls by their alcoholic father. Karen hangs on every word, Leder's camera slow and steady. When K.C. ran away at the age of eighteen, she worked to send Maria away to private school, far from the predatory reach of their alcoholic father.

Intercourse between gauntness and joy resumes, without lubrication or prophylactics.

Every dollar that K.C. Koloski has groveled for must be second-guessed. In the snap of a finger, K.C. is born again—a savior—in the eyes of Karen and the audience. The nail bed of slaughterhouse memories in "Nightfall" and teenage death wishes in "The Unquiet Earth" is torn open once more for another examination. K.C.'s presence hangs in the air, and Karen picks up a cross of gauntness and joy to carry out of Kansas City.

At the beginning of "Rewind," people of all ages and races answer Karen's questions about the Vietnam War for her film. Co-writer Carol Flint recalled going to shopping malls and picking strangers at random to quiz and videotape their answers. Mothers were nurses. Fathers, grandfathers, and uncles never came back. Some have their facts straight, while one kid thinks the Vietnam War happened in "eighteen-something." It's raw, off-the-cuff, and without a filter. Less than twenty years after the war, some believe the USA won.

Elise instills "Rewind" with the tiger blood of a Koloski, tracking down every Five and Dime alumni for her film, except K.C. She finds Beckett teaching at an inner-city school, with Michael Boatman again filling the shoes of a wise old man with ease. The man can tame a classroom full of misled youth with the same levity that brought a room full of the dead to life. Dodger is smiling on a city street in a three-piece suit and an overcoat, more at ease than we've ever seen him. Frankie stands on another block, never looking more glam or indomitable. All of their war stories amass into a documentary, and the conversation drifts from Vietnam to Karen's mother. It's the closest thing to getting everyone from the Five and Dime back together in one room.

Karen ends "Rewind" by doing exactly what many people do in 2018 with excess emotion. She shuts her bedroom door and talks into the lens of a camera. As Karen talks, director Mimi Leder zooms in on the video monitor in the corner of the room, gradually bringing us face to face with Karen. Everyone has shared their feelings about K.C., and now it's her daughter's turn. K.C. can avoid and deny Karen's truth, while Leder's choice of shot gives the viewer no other option. Desperation and determination well up in Karen's eyes, and memories of K.C.'s elegant looks and half-cocked promises are all she has to hold on to.

I ended up retracing many of Karen's steps in "Rewind" while writing this book, asking some of the same questions, sometimes to different incarnations of the same people. Toward the end of her film, Karen finds Trieu Au working in a hair salon. The illusion is lost on me, and I can only see Kieu Chinh. Her voice and her story remain the same—a woman who escaped the wrath of the Vietnam War with only the clothes on her back, and has spent every day since working to reclaim a fraction of her former life. Gauntness and joy meet again, with a story as real as any from "Vets."

THE GREAT PRETENDER

"And every wave is tidal
If you hang around, you're going to get wet."
-Elliott Smith, "King's Crossing"

Long before *China Beach* reaches its gloaming, Dana Delany asserts that she can make it rain as Colleen McMurphy if she pleases. McMurphy ceases to be a role in the fourth season, rather a well-tempered clavier only Delany can play. Her takes on a maverick nurse, a biker, a waif, and a kept woman of the Vietnam War are enthralling, and she saves her most bowel-shaking, ear-piercing chords for the final hours of the show. K.C. Koloski and Dr. Richard have been whittled away from our nurse, and now she must confront what she brought home from the war: survivor's guilt, alcoholism, PTSD. The list goes on. This Vietnam memorabilia curdles into black and white keys, waiting to be hammered by both of the nurse's fists.

McMurphy was just tuning up in "Fever" and "Juice."

It is Christmas of '76 in the opening moments of "Quest." McMurphy wakes up fully clothed, alone in a bedroom, looking disheveled and surprised to be alive. Pill bottles line her nightstand, where the phone is ringing. There is no caption specifying the town she is in, and that's the point. McMurphy later reveals she planned on killing herself until she drank too much and passed out. An opportune time for McMurphy's drinking habit to take control.

Ever since "The Big Bang," *China Beach* has tiptoed toward the grizzled McMurphy of 1985. This revelation is teased in "Rewind" when McMurphy shows up in Karen Lanier's film. Our nurse looks pallid and jaundiced, backed into domestic anonymity with a chopped mane of gray hair. She sits in an empty dining room, accompanied by a still glass of water. She's hardly able to talk about Vietnam, K.C., or any other remnant of the war. At her own table, she looks like a guest. McMurphy reveals little before demanding the camera be turned off. It's an unsettling sight, about to get worse in the next episode.

***Christine Elise:* The thing with Dana is that she's just like a machine when it comes to being able to do emotional work. I swear, her scene when I'm interviewing her in that "Rewind" episode and she's crying—*I* was crying off camera. She was really moving, and she can just turn it on and off like a switch. You would think when it appears to be that simple to do, it would cease to be moving, but it's devastating. If the director said, "I want two tears to come out of your left eye, one out of your right, and then two more out of your left," I swear to God she could do that, because she's fucking amazing.**

Those few minutes with McMurphy in "Rewind" are a dangling carrot leading to the invasion of her home life in "Through and Through." It turns out McMurphy married Joe (Adam Arkin), the wedding drummer from "I Could Have Danced All Night...But Didn't." The couple is living out mid-eighties, urban professional bliss. No kids, no problems, until McMurphy has a public episode while watching Joe play racquetball. The balls smack off the walls, and in McMurphy's head, the arrhythmic clatter turns to gunfire. Visions of explosions and mortars trigger her screams. She beats on the glass, convulsing like a woman possessed.

Brenda Owen Meadows *(USO singer, the Sho-lettes, "Vets")*: **I think Dana Delany played it pretty well when she went back home. You feel like you're away from your family, almost. They say you never live till you almost die, and we were in situations where that was the case. Your senses are heightened, and then when you come back home...It's almost like, "Where is the excitement? How do I get an adrenaline rush? Where is everybody that I need to be around?" I was at home and the lights went out one time and my mom found me under the bed, because I just thought, "incoming," you know? It was an odd transition.**

Dana Delany at the 1992 Prime Time Emmy Awards

On August 30, 1992, almost thirteen months after *China Beach* ended its broadcast run, Dana Delany won her second Prime Time Emmy on the wings of her performance in "Through and Through." Most episodic television is long forgotten within a year, and here was *China Beach* running one last victory lap. When Delany's name was called, shock filled her face. She approached the dais in a magenta, off-the-shoulder gown, and spoke of how proud she was that nurses and veterans, both male and female, got their due attention from the series.

Delany only thanked one person—John Sacret Young.

Young once placed the existence of *China Beach* at stake over the casting of Delany. She was either going to play McMurphy or there was not going to be a series. Young's perpetual stubbornness was only matched by his faith in the people he chose to invest in. Until the very end of *China Beach*, Young had his eyes and ears open for ideal contributors. As he was writing an overlong script for "Juice," he heard his assistant, Angie Ventresca, go off on a tirade about her personal life. Young stopped typing, awed and amused, and listened to her tick off all the annoying uses of the word "sorry." Young adapted the diatribe into a memorable monologue for Colleen Flynn's character, and later drafted Ventresca to co-write "Quest."

Years prior, Young's instincts offered the same latitude and space for Delany, Carol Flint, and Mimi Leder to achieve greatness on their own terms in *China Beach*. "Through and Through" unites the league of Delany, Flint, and Leder and conjures an episode that towers above much of the series. Every bad seed from "The World" and "Fever" puts their root down into the penultimate episode of *China Beach*. The reckoning of Colleen McMurphy.

The inspiration for this episode slithered from a place darker and stranger than fiction. Flint was in the middle of writing her script and went out to lunch to reconnect with a former army nurse, Christine Schneider, who touched every season of *China Beach* with her spirit. She is the woman in "Vets" who really did find her picture on a wounded soldier, and she used to wear Chantilly to make the boys in Vietnam feel more at home—just like McMurphy in "F.N.G." Schneider shared her in-country experiences with the writing staff of *China Beach* for their research over the years, and those memories came back to haunt her in visceral ways.

Angie Ventresca with John Young

Carol Flint *(writer, "Through and Through"):* **Christine was really helping anchor the show and the reality of what that these women had been through, because that had been her own journey during the four years that the show had been on the air. She had been coming to grips and opening up and integrating, and because she was an extraordinary person, she did an extraordinary job of doing that.**

She revealed to me that since the time when I had first come with that pilot script to her office, that she herself had

gone through post-traumatic stress, and a pretty dramatic version of it, and I had not known that. Helping out with some notes and stuff may have been part of the trigger, although I don't really know. She had been home from Vietnam for a number of years and had married a doctor and had two young children and was suddenly secluding herself and unable to go out.

Eventually she went into therapy and talked about all different kinds of things, very much like what McMurphy does in the episode. Never, never did she mention being in Vietnam. She did not think that could possibly have anything to do with what she was feeling, and yet all of a sudden in her therapy session, somehow, very similar to McMurphy, she all of a sudden came out with something that surprised even her. I wouldn't want to quote her because I can't remember what it was.

McMurphy's racquetball outburst sends her to a psychiatrist, and the audience cedes their chair to a professional. A composite sketch of the woman we saw in "The Big Bang" comes into focus. McMurphy is no longer our nurse, or anyone else's nurse: "I wasn't very good at it." She's a hospital administrator, forsaking migrant life and her plight of saving the least, the last, and the lost. She quit drinking five years ago. Nearly killing Dodger, his son, and his father while drunk driving in 1977 during "Quest" wasn't enough to halt her habit, and we'll never know what really did.

The psychiatrist asks her what may have caused her outburst, and McMurphy shrugs. Ma McMurphy passed on a few years ago, but a Freudian slip shows McMurphy's hand. Weeks ago, her dog was hit by a car, and she later tried to dig up the dog from its grave, in the same manner she did after her father's funeral. McMurphy wants antidepressants and is instead directed to group therapy.

Our hospital administrator has her own coping mechanisms in mind.

McMurphy walks into a bar during the lunch hour and orders the usual. The bartender fills a jigger, while Bessie Smith's aptly titled "Tain't Nobody's Business If I Do" skips and hops in the background. Director Mimi Leder offers one of her most iconic shots of the series as McMurphy's face hovers over 1.5 ounces of bourbon. She closes her eyes and breathes in the fumes. The glass may as well be a swimming pool on a summer day. Within the molecules is the addiction she carries from her father, the resentment toward her mom, and the immense loss of blood and innocence in Vietnam. The sum of all experiences in *China Beach* floats within this liquid.

McMurphy can't let go. Can't let it in.

We are back in the Jet Set for a drink to remember, and another to forget. We are kneeling in the deserted church of the Five and Dime, and right back in the credit sequence where McMurphy prays over a bottle. Boonie, Beckett, Richard, K.C.—all those familiar faces that were right there with her are gone. One drink wouldn't hurt. One drink would bring Armageddon. The seconds feel like hours until she dumps the liquor into an empty pitcher. She tips the bartender and walks off. Oxygen rushes back into the room.

> ***Mimi Leder*** *(director, "Through and Through"):* **Dana is an extraordinary, brilliant actress and deep as the ocean. Dana would always come to work completely understanding and knowing who she was and knowing where her character was at that moment. It was interesting to note how the young character became the woman with grey in her hair, and how her voice became a little deeper, how the weight of the war as the young woman just took her to who she was. We modulated the performances as you do as a director and actor, but Dana is an extraordinary actress and it was a beautiful experience working with her, and I've always wanted to work with her again and find something. One day.**

Therapy and group sharing in the episode awaken the trauma McMurphy buried alive in Vietnam. Ned Vaughn has two separate onscreen deaths throughout *China Beach*, and a flashback to 1968 resurrects the agreeable redhead for a third time. The Five and Dime is under attack—and out of boredom and vice—McMurphy and Hyers leave their crowded bunker to get a case of beer. By the time they return, everyone is dead and buried by a mortar, and she attempts to dig them up with her bare hands. Life keeps slipping through McMurphy's fingers, with a drink always in reach.

Discontent spreads to the home, where Joe's bad habits and bad drumming mimic the racquetballs and gunfire that set McMurphy off in the beginning of the episode. She tells Joe what she won't tell her therapist. She can't eat. She can't sleep. She's over forty and worried she will never have children. A note on the fridge lights her short fuse. Dr. Richard called, and Joe actually spoke to him. Delany turns McMurphy up to eleven. She can't destroy the racket in her head, so she annihilates Joe's drum set in a blind rage. Her husband looks on in stunned silence. He doesn't know this woman, and neither do we.

McMurphy heads to the bar to shadowbox with Jim Beam. To claim control of her corner of the world. Nothing is the same; a crowded evening with a different bartender who doesn't know what her "usual" is. For a moment, she sees a wounded soldier behind the bar. "Bourbon," she grumbles. Already defeated. McMurphy repeats her self-flagellation, looking back on her weakness instead of the brick wall fast approaching.

The feedback of Jefferson Airplane's "White Rabbit" squeals in the background, forming a moment of "scorce" with Nero's fiddle. Rome begins to burn. McMurphy's eyes search for strength, faith—anything—right before she pours the contents of the glass down her throat. Delany fills McMurphy's face with regret, shame, gauntness—then nods for a second shot, and slams her glass down to demand a third. She wakes up in her psychiatrist's office, bound for inpatient treatment.

> ***Dana Delany:*** **Most actors will tell you it's so much fun to do therapy sessions because you just get to sit there and talk. [*laughs*] Yeah, I guess alcohol was a big issue, PTSD; I'm really glad we dealt with that, obviously that's a huge issue in our country. The biggest thing for me—God, it kills me talking about this stuff—is that she let somebody love her. That was the hardest thing because she was always giving to everybody else and had her walls up and was terrified to be vulnerable. [McMurphy] finally let this guy in and let him love her, and I think that was the biggest challenge for her.**

Whether Delany is building suspense over a shot glass, getting psychoanalyzed, trashing drum sets, or becoming unhinged while watching a game of racquetball, she takes the character of McMurphy far beyond any expectation or prior performance. Flint's script and Leder's direction metastasize the collective damage of every episode of *China Beach* into "Through and Through," and Delany channels it through the eyes and hands of McMurphy with thunderous, perturbing might.

"Through and Through" is McMurphy's last stand, the realization she can't beat her disease, her demons by herself. The moments where she opens up to others are where her only glimmers of hope lie. Each word said to the psychiatrist, her veterans group, her husband, or World War II vets at the VA is a step toward realizing she doesn't have to wage *this* war by herself. Right before the credits roll, tears stream down McMurphy's cheeks, and Delany adds a subtle human touch by licking a tear from the corner of her mouth. She asks her therapist, "When will this stop?"

There's no reply, no sad harmonica, just that woman from "The Big Bang."

With only two hours left in *China Beach*, "Through and Through" ends inside one of the most disconcerting, dire moments of the show. Delany surmised that the episode is one of her strongest, most rewarding performances, if upstaged by an adjacent series finale full of more uplifting moments and familiar company. "Through and Through" remains one ending of many, placing McMurphy at the bottom of a well, affirming she will always be one drink away from falling down there again.

No final chapter of *China Beach* can erase that.

NAMES WITHOUT FACES

Halfway through the *China Beach* series finale, "Hello, Goodbye," Colleen McMurphy is on a road trip to the Vietnam Veterans Memorial. Karen Lanier is riding shotgun. At a rest stop, they are sitting on a swing set, staring up at the stars, and McMurphy is talking about Vietnam, smiling and laughing. She yells into the night, "I loved it." Our nurse has come a long way in the three years since "Through and Through." She's held on for so long.

Within the coda of *China Beach,* McMurphy lets go.

Any television series finale is in an uphill fight, carrying the burden of an appeasing resolution to all that has preceded. A bunch of acrobatic flips are no good without a clean landing, and the end of *China Beach* gets no reprieve. The double-sized finale episode, "Hello, Goodbye," inherits every awkward and muddied emotion of the fourth season and mashes them together into a misty-eyed farewell.

The finale is guilty of a few false finishes, and that's because *China Beach* answers so many damn questions with *more* questions throughout the final season. It is now or never—and when the final moments come, they feel right. Maybe perfect. *China Beach* has been a story about looking back, and here it empowers everyone to move on with their life, and into the future that awaits them.

> ***Toni Graphia*** *(series writer and researcher):* **What makes me decide whether a show is truly great or just very good, is if when the show ends, you feel like those characters are still out there somewhere. You think about them and it comes to your mind once in a while and you go, "I wonder what McMurphy is doing now?" *China Beach* is one of the few shows where after the show's over, I still feel like that group of people is out there living their life somewhere. I guess the word would be "afterlife."**

***John Wells** (writer, "Hello, Goodbye"):* **I don't know how to begin to even place things in time as far as their value or anything goes. I know it was very gratifying to do the show, to meet the people that we met, and to work with the people that we worked with. I hope in that temporal moment when it was on the air that it had some social value in reminding people that there were all of these heroic, brave men and women (in our case, of course, particularly women) who had served and made a difference and did what they were supposed to do on behalf of everyone.**

"Hello, Goodbye" is one giant pastiche of *China Beach*, reframing many moments from the pilot, running a highlight reel of flashbacks, and time-jumping between the sixties and the eighties. The opening frames are a self-reference to "Vets," with Colleen McMurphy resembling Diane Carlson Evans in a dark room, talking to a camera, trying to remember the name of her last patient in Vietnam. McMurphy has more gray hairs than ever, and some of that sparkle back in her eye.

The *China Beach* finale never sits still, next riffing on the end of *The Best Years of Our Lives* when Dana Andrews' character climbs in to the cockpit of a decommissioned plane, lost in the feedback of war, maybe for forever. Director John Sacret Young reimagines this moment with McMurphy jogging through a park in hot pink leggings. It is 1988, Portland, Oregon. The sight of an old surplus Huey being installed as a playground stops her in her tracks, and she climbs in for a look.

Another decrepit relic of war. What is it good for?

McMurphy's memories fade to 1969, where she is once more counting down her final days left in-country. Our nurse is the lone familiar face left at China Beach, tending to her last remaining patients with Dr. Richard's replacement, another smart-ass surgeon with a double name, Dr. Robert Robert (John Slattery). McMurphy gets a going away party, and what she has had coming to her since the pilot episode—her last chopper out of the Five and Dime.

One wrenching goodbye of many, and somehow, not the last.

"Hello, Goodbye" runs with the reunion theme of countless other television finales, bringing the Five and Dime vets together for the first time in almost twenty years. Everyone makes an entrance in Cooperstown, Ohio, carrying nervous energy and wearing questionable wigs. Wayloo Marie Holmes is now a famous news personality with a bizarre shock of gray hair, and McMurphy enters with her husband, Joe, and a young daughter. The sight is a subtle, happy ending to "Through and Through." The long-awaited eighties reunion between McMurphy and Dr. Richard is made even more awkward by their spouses standing off to the side. Boonie Lanier does the most Boonie thing possible, throwing his arms around all of them, and proclaiming how great this all is.

Karen Lanier's camcorder makes for a fun confessional booth, and director John Young turned many of the actors loose to improvise. Jeff Kober and Brian Wimmer did a number of takes ranging from brotherly love to an all-out brawl, and Robert Picardo returns Dick Richard to vintage form, comically eviscerating his ex-wife, Beth Ann. It's not all fun, and the long claw of the Vietnam War hovers when Lila Garreau reveals her husband, Sarge, has lung cancer.

McMurphy retreats to the bathroom, where Joe finds her hiding from the madness. The screen is divided in half with a toilet stall, redrawing the lines and divisions found in Diane Keaton's episode, "Fever." Husband and wife, sitting on toilets. Together, yet separate. They end up holding each other, looking in the mirror, and we get a glimpse of the support system McMurphy has been leaning on since "Through and Through."

High heels come off and neckties are undone. Boonie is dancing on a table, prosthesis off, and Karen sits side-stage, disappointed, not surprised, K.C. didn't show up. Dodger watches McMurphy from across the room and imagines what could have been between them. He can't go up and talk to her, so he jumps on stage and sings "When a Man Loves a Woman" with Frankie. Rock 'n' roll is therapy, just as it was in the pilot. The Five and Dime reunion is a short and bittersweet spectacle that will only last the night, underlined by the reality of the cast and crew preparing to draw the show to a close and go their separate ways.

John Wells's hour script for the finale doubled in size during production, while Young scrambled between ABC and Warner Bros. to secure financing. Things shifted and morphed, yet were locked on final coordinates that stemmed from so many veteran interviews ending at a certain location. The one place in our country that physically represents the loss incurred by America in the Vietnam War.

The Vietnam Veterans Memorial is a granite wall sunken into the earth of the National Mall in Washington, DC. All the names rising up from below. Reaching. The Wall is surrounded by towering, celebratory, national landmarks: the Lincoln Memorial, the Washington Monument, the White House. The World War II Memorial sits a few hundred yards away on the Mall—a large sphere celebrating the forty-eight states that united to defeat the Axis Powers. Stairways, columns, and fountains propel upward in victory, while the Wall is a gradual descent into a quiet place for contemplation and healing. "The ultimate foxhole," said John Young. Over 58,000 names are etched into the black panels that grow from eight inches high at the edges to over ten feet in the middle. The tallest American still dwarfed by the official record of deceased.

When the Five and Dime reunion runs dry, Boonie Lanier coaxes everyone into a road trip to the capital city to pay their respects at the Wall. *China Beach* mixes fact and fiction one last time, marking an end of its four-year journey bringing the Vietnam War back to life.

> ***William Broyles Jr.:*** **No one could go through that experience and just be the same, and that's the lesson of the pilot and that's the lesson of the very last show—that each of these characters was changed forever. In the last episode, when they go to the Wall, it brought me full circle. When I went to the Wall for the first time, it set off in me this thing that I had to do something about this experience, somehow. Seeing those characters at that Wall in the last episode, I was just overcome with emotion [*pause*] and gratitude to those actors and John, and the studio, and the network for having the courage to put it on the air.**

> ***John Sacret Young:*** **We were so lucky at the Wall. To me, the look is beautiful. The sun disappeared; we shot Dana there first because the other actors were still getting ready and you can see this crease of sun in the distance behind her. What a piece of luck that was. I've been there in the rain, I've been there in the snow, I've been there in the fall. At night, in the morning. It's never *not* moving.**

Jeff Kober: That was the day, probably for me more than any other, where it's like, "Do we have a right to do this?" Even though we had been playing these characters for four years, even though we'd done everything we could to make it real, now we were looking at something that was real, and we were using it for dramatic purposes. It felt almost sacrilegious, but also, I think, necessary. I felt like that scene at the Wall itself probably cost more personally than any of the other work we did. I obviously don't even have words to say what it was like. There was just something awe-inspiring that made my work as an actor seem diminutive in comparison.

Robert Picardo: It was extremely moving to be there. I had not seen the Memorial at that point. It is overpowering in its design; it's absolutely brilliant that you're walking along and the Wall envelops you and rises above you slowly, in the same way that the first small number of people that were sent there as advisors grew into an enormous number of troops there at the peak of the war. Then, in the same way, those fifty-thousand-plus names go from just a few names to a giant wall of names. It's very powerful the way it gradually sneaks up and then overwhelms you.

Concetta Tomei: Along with the torture that actually existed, we were trying to tell their stories. They weren't our stories, and those stories were hard to tell. I remember reading scripts and just weeping in my apartment, and thinking, "How the hell am I going to get up in the morning and not be engaged, but fully engaged to do this and not break down and be truthful and honor the situation and honor the Vietnam veterans?" We all knew that this mattered a lot, that this was a huge responsibility, and I think all of us took it very seriously. To know that you lived at the time that this actually happened in history and that you actually worked with a Vietnam veteran, and that you actually went to the Wall to film that last episode, I mean, you couldn't have asked for any more.

John Wells: We were constantly talking to the park service about how we were actually respecting the work that they had done in putting it up and the experiences that everybody had.

Helgenberger, Giles, and Bill Broyles at the China Beach wrap party

Behind the scenes of "Hello, Goodbye"

Filming at the Wall

They ultimately didn't really want us to do it, but let us get down sort of close to it. They had some camera positions that they allow people to use for news organizations and things. When we got right to the moment and they saw what we were doing, they kind of turned a blind eye for us to actually go down and shoot on the memorial itself, as long as we didn't shut it down in any way or prevent anybody else from coming. It seemed like absolutely the right place to end the series.

John Sacret Young: I was worried. Can they hold the emotion? Because the Wall is so powerful. I went to each one and said, "We're going to have to do it a couple hundred yards away. What do you think? Can you?" and everyone went, "Let's go." To me, they are remarkable. The Washington film commission woman was in a car because it was so cold. We gave her coffee and she wasn't absolutely present when we walked up to Dana with a camera close-up to get those last moments. I feel the ending is, I don't know, beyond good.

Brian Wimmer: Every one of us went in there as a person. I went in there as Brian Wimmer and by that time in the series, pretty much, I am Boonie, Dana was McMurphy. So when you go in there and you take it in and soak it in—what's just happened to us personally and everything—and this is a symbol of that? Oh my God. There was such a reverence amongst all of us throughout the whole thing. There was this hush, this quiet. I remember it being so quiet. There were not the normal sounds you would hear making a movie, shooting television, because the camera was so far away.

They didn't give us any direction, like, "Okay you're going to do this, you're going to have this reaction," none of that. They're like, "Brian, you're up," and you're like, [*sigh*] and you're trying to hold it together. I'm trying not to pay any attention to [the Wall]. You can see it, you can get a glimpse of it, but I'm ignoring it. And then it's like, "Okay, here we go." You walk in and you just lose it. I'm sure they had footage of every single one of us completely losing it. It meant more than any television show or movie or anything I've ever done before.

Nancy Giles: That was another incredible moment of art and life. It was very, very emotional. A friend of my mom's lost her son in Vietnam and one of the things Mom asked me to do was find his name and do an etching of it, so we could bring it home to Mrs. Hawkins. I'd never seen it before. I was absolutely stunned. I'd certainly read about it and seen pictures of it, but when you're there, to see this *slice*, literally a slice in the earth, it's like a cut in your heart. To see all of the memorabilia, the things people left—tokens and gifts and notes to their loved ones—it was absolutely staggering. It was heartbreaking. It was one of the most moving days of my life.

Michael Boatman: There was very little acting going on. There was an awareness, even then for me, that not only was this job coming to an end, this experience was coming to an end. These people I had come to know and love were all going to go off in our different directions. Yeah, we would be friends, and yeah, we would see each other over the years, but it was never going to be *China Beach* again. I think they play a Michael McDonald song (that I later bought and still have on my phone if I need to make myself cry) called "I Can Let Go Now." To this day, decades later, it still sends a shiver up my spine.

Christine Elise: The names seemed to go on infinitely. It is staggering, really, to see them all there—going on forever—but it also made the scale of the disaster so much more real which is—I guess—part of the point.

And then I saw Troy Evans.

He was the only member of the cast that had served in Vietnam. And he was either crouched or kneeling in front of The Wall. And he seemed to be crying. And it was devastating. I walked by him quickly, not wanting to invade his privacy, but seeing him so emotional made me emotional, too. And I cried—more for Troy than the 58,195 names there. He put a face on all those letters carved into the stone. And I felt like there was nothing anyone who had not been there (Vietnam) could learn from The Wall beyond knowing it represented unimaginable suffering and pain and loss by an astonishing number of people. Each name represented not just a dead soldier, but every person brutalized by the loss of that soldier—and the pain of every surviving soldier. It was profoundly humbling.

Troy Evans: First of all, it was the middle of winter in Washington, DC, so it was very, very cold. So that played into everything. I really don't know what it was like for other people, but I was with the Second Battalion of the 22nd Infantry Regiment, and a few years ago I went back with some other guys from the 22nd and we put a regimental flag in front of each guy from our unit that died. 978 flags. 978. [*pause*] That's a lot. The whole experience of being there… there's no way to really articulate that. Anything that needed to be portrayed on camera by the emotional impact of that brilliant piece of architecture didn't require any work on my part, that's all I'm saying.

At the Wall

Dana Delany: We all knew it was over, and when you know the finality of something, sometimes it becomes too precious and you want it to be so good that you're thinking too much about it, and we all had to do this guerrilla-style shooting. We were all exhausted and high and excited and we had to do those close-ups where we're looking at the Wall in the final moments. That's hard as an actor, on top of it knowing, "This is it, the show's done." I think that it came out really well. I'm really proud of that last episode.

> *Marg Helgenberger:* **I was very upset that I didn't get to share in the experience of shooting the final episode at the Vietnam Memorial. I knew that it would be a very emotional and bonding experience for the cast, and I felt left out. Having said that, K.C., unlike me, would have avoided the chance to reunite with everyone. So, from a story-telling point of view, it made sense that K.C. wasn't in that particular sequence. I have visited the Wall several times over the years, and every single time, I'm deeply moved, and overwhelmed by its sheer power and simplicity. Once I get within fifty yards of the Wall, I begin to cry.**

Boonie doesn't let K.C. go quietly into the night of *China Beach.* Ms. Koloski started from the bottom and has surfed to the top of corporate America, where Boonie finds her making international deals in an executive boardroom. A likely destination. Back in the pilot episode, Boonie stood opposite K.C. by a punch bowl and posed the question, "When are you gonna retire?" She fired back with another question, "When are you gonna be rich?" Their exchange echoes until this moment, when a distant mirror is held up to the past.

K.C. and Boonie have another terse conversation, their words augmented by their appearance—what time and circumstance have given and taken from them. Neither have changed; they've endured. Boonie has no idea that K.C.'s greed and work ethic was born within the dregs of life, and it doesn't matter. For all of K.C.'s flaws, he has seen the best in her all along.

Boonie convinced his fellow vets to look at the Wall and pay their respect to the lives lost in Vietnam, and he breaks K.C. down in to considering a life she can reclaim. Her daughter. Instead of one more ending to the series, the reunion between K.C. and Karen tempts a hesitant beginning. K.C. shows up in a limousine, outfitted in a mink coat and her trademark smirk. Shock and awe fills Karen, and Christine Elise is too good to let it reach the surface of her character. There are few words and fewer promises between K.C. and Karen, and they walk away from each other with just enough hope for more.

McMurphy and K.C.'s path broke apart in 1976, and the jam-packed, double-sized finale episode didn't leave a scene big enough for the two of them. Neither character gets the satisfaction of a final word, and they head down separate, parallel paths into the horizon of *China Beach*. Mothers instead of sisters.

China Beach ends as it began, with Colleen McMurphy wearing red. She returns to the Wall in an overcoat, holding her daughter, and dumps out a bag of sand from where she used to dig her toes on China Beach. The vision of this woman in a swimsuit turns one more shade of sepia. McMurphy points out the name of her last patient to her daughter, and Karen's film gives McMurphy the final word of the series: "I couldn't save them all, but I saved some."

Many vets shared moving stories with me about the Vietnam Veterans Memorial and what it means to them. Bill "Ziggy" Siegesmund still hasn't seen the Wall. A friend invited him to come along for a pilgrimage to Washington, and he refused: "I just couldn't see the names, thinking I might recognize a name or two [*pause*] and I'd start thinking, and seeing their faces, so young and everything." The Wall will always be there to remind us what we lost in Vietnam. Time. Life. Trust. Innocence. Precious things we will never replace, emblazoned within the letters of all those names rising up from the earth. When I think of the Wall, I find little solace. Then, I remember something Diane Carlson Evans told me.

"That Wall would be a lot higher and a lot wider without the women who served in Vietnam."

Following pages: (l-r) Nancy Giles, Brian Wimmer, Bill Broyles, Jeff Kober, Dana Delany, John Sacret Young, Robert Picardo, Concetta Tomei, Troy Evans, Michael Boatman, and Christine Elise at the National Mall in Washington, D.C.

REFLECTIONS

China Beach has kept me asking questions from the moment I laid eyes on it. Those questions and their shape-shifting answers have taught me more about myself than anything. I am stunned there is no other book about *China Beach*. I hope this isn't the last one. I hope the show finds a place in the digital streaming realm, with all of its music intact. I also hope that one day, John Sacret Young will share with the world his long-teased novel that continues the story of *China Beach*. The world has more to learn from Colleen McMurphy, her friends, and the Vietnam War.

This, I believe.

At the beginning of this book, I said a voice told me I needed to watch *China Beach*. I now realize that the voice had more in mind than "a book about a TV show about a war." I believe it was the same voice that guided me to my first chance meeting with my wife. I didn't understand any of this until I was in Vietnam, when a three-day cruise in Halong Bay went awry. My wife and I were *not* going to Catba Island, landlocked for a day with no plans. We wandered through the Old Quarter of Hanoi and opted for a quick spa visit before taking a train to Hue.

I was lying on a massage table, unable to relax because I was studying the masseuse's face. Our eyes never met, because she was blind. She was hardly five feet tall and didn't speak above a whisper. I couldn't tell if she was thirty-five or fifty-five, yet her wrinkles implied a life of challenges she had met with Vietnamese grit. I told her not to take it easy on me. I laid face down, and she walked along my spine on her tiptoes, as if I were her tightrope. I almost let out a cry of pain, while my body and spirit reached in opposite directions. I gave her most of the money in my pocket when she finished and told her to do something very nice for herself. She gasped with joy. In the far reaches of my being, I wanted to take her home to America and take care of her.

My wife and I made our way to the sleeper train, and as I laid in the top bunk and went through rough drafts of this manuscript, I couldn't stop thinking about that woman. I prayed and journaled, hoping she had people in her life who loved her and took care of her. I wondered how she lost her eyesight. If she was born that way, or if she was a casualty of the American War. I swore that night to never forget her. I knew she didn't need my pity. I saw it in her smile, and in her eyes that could not see me.

Her iron will made me a believer.

For the past six years, my wife and I have struggled with infertility. I have immense trouble talking about the subject, but two weeks in Vietnam and that hour on the massage table showed me how very lucky I am, and inspired me to do something more than sitting back, watching the world, waiting. The Vietnam War is a ripple in time that is still billowing outward in the pond of life, whether or not anyone else notices. It is a horrible story, both Vietnamese and American that prior generations have handed down.

I can't change any of it, but I will write my own epilogue.

A few weeks after returning home from Vietnam, my wife and I signed the initial paperwork to adopt a child from Vietnam, and soon we will proceed with in-vitro fertilization. I couldn't write a better plot twist for my life than assuming the role of a proud dad to a pair of American and Vietnamese babies, watching and learning from them as they grow up.

The past is right there in the rearview mirror for us to learn from, and just like *China Beach* did, we must make the best of it.

Brad Dukes
January 2018
Nashville, TN

DANKE SCHOEN

Love and gratitude first goes to my wife, Jessica. She kept me well-loved, well-caffeinated, and sane throughout. Peggy London and Vern Boonewell were my warm, furry, constant company, usually pawing at my keyboard.

This book frankly doesn't exist without the words, patience, and time granted to me by John Sacret Young. In person, over the phone, and via email, he fielded hundreds of my questions. His answers and insight never failed to entertain, enlighten, and educate. John, I thank you for every little thing.

William Broyles Jr. was an early supporter of this project and our first conversation was the wind in my sail through the smoothest and roughest of current.

To the brilliant cast of *China Beach*, thank you for your performances and for sharing your craft in conversation, sometimes through multiple interviews. Dana Delany, Marg Helgenberger, Michael Boatman, Kieu Chinh, Christine Elise, Troy Evans, Megan Gallagher, Nancy Giles, Bobby Hosea, Jeff Kober, Ricki Lake, Robert Picardo, Amy Steel, Debra Stricklin, Concetta Tomei, Richard Tyson, Ned Vaughn, Chloe Webb and Brian Wimmer—the pleasure, the privilege was mine.

The writers, directors, editors, and producers of *China Beach* were all forthcoming and generous in conversation and inquiry. Many thanks to Josef Anderson, Alan Brennert, Steve Dubin, Geno Escarrega, Carol Flint, Michael Fresco, Fred Gerber, Toni Graphia, Patricia Green, Rod Holcomb, Georgia Jeffries, Mimi Leder, Christopher Leitch, Cathryn Michon, Randy Morgan, Christopher Nelson, Susan Rhinehart, Michael Rhodes, Angie Ventresca, Chip Vucelich, John Wells, and Lydia Woodward.

Harvey Shephard, Paul Chihara, Chad Hoffman, John Levey, John Rubenstein, and Martin Fisher also offered irreplaceable conversations.

Mad shouts, props, and love to my friends and extended family: LeeAnn Hendrickson Abston, Angela Bunch, Leigh Caudill, Spencer Collantes, Pieter Dom, Bob and Kim Dukes, Peyton Dukes, Richard Gold, Amanda Rowland Hampel, Andrew Hendrickson, Bob Hoag, Brian Kursar, Brittyn Lindsey, Eben Moore, Ann Rowland and family, Daniel and Irina Schaffer, and John Thorne.

Bearhugs and high fives to my designer and buddy, Ross Dudle, and my editor, Paisley Prophet.

Esteemed, distinguished thanks to David Bushman and Scott Ryan for their years of encouragement, support, and feedback for this book.

To the names not mentioned, you were still heard.

I saved the best for last—the vets. William Broyles Jr., Ed Chapin, Tom and Nellie Coakley, Troy Evans, Diane Carlson Evans, Brenda Owen Meadows, Jeanne "Sam" Christie, Noble Craig, Jeff Hiers, Barb Lilly, Linda Pellegrino, Jan Richards, and Bill "Ziggy" Siegesmund—thank you for your service in Vietnam, and for sharing your war stories with me.

You will never be forgotten. You are the heroes.

APPENDIX

I

"Pilot"
Written by John Sacret Young, Directed by Rod Holcomb
Original Airdate: 4/26/1988

"Home"
Written by William Broyles Jr., Directed by Rod Holcomb
Original Airdate: 4/27/1988

"Hot Spell"
Written by Susan Rhinehart, Directed by Beth Hillshafer
Original Airdate: 5/4/1988

"Somewhere Over the Radio"
Written by Ann Donahue, Directed by Rod Holcomb
Original Airdate: 5/11/1988

"Waiting for Beckett"
Written by Terry McDonell, Directed by Kevin Hooks
Original Airdate: 5/18/1988

"Brothers"
Written by Carol Flint and Susan Rhinehart, Directed by John Sacret Young
Original Airdate: 6/1/1988

"Chao Ong"
Story by John Sacret Young, Teleplay by William, Broyles, Jr.,
Directed by Christopher Leitch
Original Airdate: 6/8/1988

II

"Lost and Found, Part 1"
Written by William Broyles Jr. and John Sacret Young, Directed by John Sacret Young
Original Airdate: 11/30/1988

"Lost and Found, Part 2"
Written by William Broyles Jr. and John Sacret Young, Directed by John Sacret Young
Original Airdate: 12/7/1988

"Limbo"
Written by Carol Flint, Directed by Dan Lerner
Original Airdate: 12/14/1988

"X-Mas Chn. Bch. VN, '67"
Written by John Wells, Directed by Mimi Leder
Original Airdate: 12/21/1988

"Women in White"
Written by Patricia Green, Directed by Sharron Miller
Original Airdate: 1/4/1989

"All About E.E.V."
Written by Lydia Woodward, Directed by Peter Medak
Original Airdate: 1/11/1989

"Tet '68"
Written by Susan Rhinehart and John Wells, Directed by Steve Dubin
Original Airdate: 1/25/1989

"Cherry"
Written by Susan Rhinehart, Directed by Mimi Leder
Original Airdate: 2/1/1989

"Crossing the Great Water"
Written by Carol Flint, Directed by Mimi Leder
Original Airdate: 2/8/1989

"Psywars"
Written by Glen Merzer, Directed by Fred Gerber
Original Airdate: 3/1/1989

"Where the Boys Are"
Written by Alan Brennert, Directed by Michael Rhodes
Original Airdate: 3/8/1989

"Vets"
Written by John Wells and John Sacret Young, Directed by John Sacret Young
Original Airdate: 3/15/1989

"Twilight"
Written by Lydia Woodward, Directed by Michael Fresco
Original Airdate: 3/22/1989

"Afterburner"
Written by Carol Flint, Directed by Christopher Leitch
Original Airdate: 4/5/1989

"Promised Land"
Written by Patricia Green, Directed by Michael Rhodes
Original Airdate: 4/12/1989

"The World, Part 1"
Written by John Wells, Directed by John Sacret Young
Original Airdate: 4/26/1989

"The World, Part 2"
Written by John Wells, Directed by John Sacret Young
Original Airdate: 5/3/1989

III

"The Unquiet Earth"
Written by Alan Brennert, Directed by Michael Rhodes
Original Airdate: 9/20/1989

"Skin Deep"
Written by Carol Flint, Directed by Mimi Leder
Original Airdate: 9/27/1989

"Dear China Beach"
Written by John Wells, Directed by Michael Rhodes
Original Airdate: 10/4/1989

"Who's Happy Now?"
Written by Lydia Woodward, Directed by Fred Gerber
Original Airdate: 10/11/1989

"Independence Day"
Written by Susan Rhinehart, Directed by Mimi Leder
Original Airdate: 10/25/1989

"Ghosts"
Written by Toni Graphia, Directed by Michael Fresco
Original Airdate: 11/8/1989

"With a Little Help from My Friends"
Written by Josef Anderson and Carol Flint, Directed by Michael Uno
Original Airdate: 11/15/1989

"China Men"
Written by Josef Anderson, Directed by David Burton Morris
Original Airdate: 11/22/1989

"How to Stay Alive in Vietnam, Part 1"
Written by Georgia Jeffries, Directed by Fred Gerber
Original Airdate: 11/29/1989

"How to Stay Alive in Vietnam, Part 2"
Written by Georgia Jeffries, Directed by Steven Dubin
Original Airdate: 12/6/1989

"Magic"
Written by John Wells, Directed by Mimi Leder
Original Airdate: 1/3/1990

"Nightfall"
Written by Lydia Woodward, Directed by Christopher Leitch
Original Airdate: 1/10/1990

"Souvenirs"
Written and directed by John Sacret Young
Original Airdate: 1/17/1990

"Holly's Choice"
Written by Carol Flint, Directed by Christopher Leitch
Original Airdate: 1/31/1990

"A Rumor of Peace"
Written by Josef Anderson, Directed by Neema Barnette
Original Airdate: 2/7/1990

"Warriors"
Story by Dottie Dartland, Teleplay by Martin M. Goldstein and Neal Baer,
Directed by David Soul
Original Airdate: 2/14/1990

"The Thanks of a Grateful Nation"
Written by John Wells, Directed by Mimi Leder
Original Airdate: 2/28/1990

"Skylark"
Written by Lydia Woodward, Directed by Fred Gerber
Original Airdate: 3/14/1990

"Phoenix"
Written by Toni Graphia, Directed by Mimi Leder
Original Airdate: 3/21/1990

"F.N.G."
Written by Carol Flint, Directed by John Sacret Young
Original Airdate: 4/16/1990

"The Gift"
Written by Josef Anderson, Directed by Michael Katleman
Original Airdate: 4/23/1990

"Strange Brew"
Written by Georgia Jeffries, Directed by Michael Fresco
Original Airdate: 4/30/1990

IV

"The Big Bang"

Story by Carol Flint, John Wells, Lydia Woodward, and John Sacret Young,
Teleplay by John Wells, Directed by John Sacret Young
Original Airdate: 9/29/1990

"She Sells More Than Sea Shells"

Story by Carol Flint, John Wells, Lydia Woodward, and John Sacret Young,
Teleplay by Carol Flint, Directed by Mimi Leder
Original Airdate: 10/6/1990

"You, Babe"

Story by Carol Flint, John Wells, Lydia Woodward, and John Sacret Young,
Teleplay by Cathryn Michon and Susan Rhinehart, Directed by Mimi Leder
Original Airdate: 10/13/1990

"Escape"

Story by Carol Flint, John Wells, Lydia Woodward, and John Sacret Young,
Teleplay by Paris Qualles, Directed by Christopher Leitch
Original Airdate: 10/27/1990

"Fever"

Story by Carol Flint, John Wells, Lydia Woodward, and John Sacret Young,
Teleplay by Lydia Woodward, Directed by Diane Keaton
Original Airdate: 11/3/1990

"Juice"

Story by Carol Flint, John Wells, Lydia Woodward, and John Sacret Young,
Teleplay by John Sacret Young, Directed by John Sacret Young
Original Airdate: 11/10/1990

"One Giant Leap"

Story by Carol Flint, John Wells, Lydia Woodward, and John Sacret Young,
Teleplay by Josef Anderson, Directed by Michael Katleman
Original Airdate: 11/17/1990

"One Small Step"

Written by John Wells, Directed by Steven Dubin
Original Airdate: 12/1/1990

"The Call"

Written by Cathryn Michon and Paris Qualles, Directed by Robert Ginty
Original Airdate: 12/8/1990

"I Could Have Danced All Night... But Didn't"

Story by Carol Flint, Teleplay by Cathryn Michon, Directed by Michael Fresco
Original Airdate: 6/4/1991

"100 Klicks Out"

Written by Susan Rhinehart, Directed by Mimi Leder
Original Airdate: 6/11/1991

"The Always Goodbye"

Written by Lydia Woodward, Directed by Gary Sinise
Original Airdate: 6/18/1991

"Quest"

Written by Angela Ventresca and John Sacret Young, Directed by John Sacret Young
Original Airdate: 6/25/1991

"Rewind"

Written by Carol Flint and John Wells, Directed by Mimi Leder
Original Airdate: 7/9/1991

"Through and Through"

Written by Carol Flint, Directed by Mimi Leder
Original Airdate: 7/16/1991

"Hello, Goodbye"

Story by Carol Flint, John Wells, Lydia Woodward, and John Sacret Young,
Teleplay by John Wells, Directed by John Sacret Young
Original Airdate: 7/22/1991

LINER NOTES

The following literature was of indispensable influence while studying and documenting both *China Beach* and the Vietnam War. I highly recommend and endorse each work for further reading.

Bowden, Mark. *Hue 1968: A Turning Point of the American War in Vietnam.* New York: Grove Press, 2017.

Brokaw, Tom. *Boom!: Voices of the Sixties*. New York: Random House, 2007.

Broyles, William, Jr.. *Brothers in Arms: A Journey from War to Peace.* New York: Alfred A. Knopf, 1986.

Caputo, Philip. *A Rumor of War*. New York: Picador, 1977.

Duiker, William J.. *Ho Chi Minh: A Life*. New York: Hyperion. 2000.

Herr, Michael. *Dispatches.* New York: Alfred A. Knopf, 1977.

Bartimus, Tad, Denby Fawcett, Jurate Kazickas, Edith Lederer, Ann Bryan Mariano, Anne Morrissy Merick, Laura Palmer, Kate Webb, and Tracy Wood. *War Torn: Stories of War from the Women Reporters Who Covered Vietnam.* New York: Random House, 2002.

Marshall, Kathryn. *In the Combat Zone: An Oral History of American Women in Vietnam, 1966-1975.* Boston, MA: Little, Brown and Company, 1987.

Mangold, Tom and Penycate, John. *The Tunnels of CuChi.* New York: Berkley Books, 1986.

Ngor, Haing S.. *A Cambodian Odyssey.* New York: MacMillan, 1987.

Pitlyk, Paul J.. *Blood on China Beach: My Story as a Brain Surgeon in Vietnam.* Bloomington, IN: iUniverse, 2012.

Van Devanter, Lynda. *Home Before Morning.* New York: Beaufort Books, 1983.

Young, John Sacret. *Remains: Non-Viewable.* New York: Farrar, Straus and Giroux, 2005.

———. *Pieces of Glass.* Beverly Hills, CA: TallFellow Press, 2016.

PHOTO CREDITS

p. ix Courtesy of Andrew Hendrickson, Angela Bunch, and Leann Hendrickson Abston

p. x Courtesy of the Rowland family

p. 5 Courtesy of William Broyles Jr.

p. 10 Courtesy of Rod Holcomb

p. 14 Courtesy of Marg Helgenberger

p. 21 Courtesy of ABC, Inc. Copyright 1988. All rights reserved.

p. 25 Source Unknown

p. 30 Courtesy of Chip Vucelich and James Newport

p. 37 Courtesy of William Broyles Jr.

p. 50 photo by Jessica Dukes

p. 54 & 55 Letters Courtesy of John Sacret Young

p. 72 Courtesy of Rod Holcomb

p. 78 Courtesy of Dana Delany

p. 79 Courtesy of Chloe Webb

p. 97 Courtesy of Jeff Kober

p. 98 Courtesy of Jeff Kober

p. 102 Courtesy of Robert Picardo

p. 103 Courtesy of William Siegesmund

p. 117 Courtesy of Robert Picardo

p. 122 Courtesy of Nancy Giles

p. 125 Courtesy of ABC, Inc. Copyright 1989. All rights reserved.

p. 128 & 129 Courtesy of William Siegesmund

p. 130 Courtesy of William Siegesmund

p. 137 Courtesy of Diane Carlson Evans

p. 138 Courtesy of John Sacret Young

p. 154 Courtesy of Alan Light

p. 164 Courtesy of Josef Anderson

p. 166 ABC Inc. Copyright 1989. All rights reserved.

p. 167 Courtesy of Nancy Giles

p. 175 Courtesy of Troy Evans

p. 179 Courtesy of ABC, Inc. Copyright 1989. All rights reserved

p. 189 Courtesy of Jeff Kober

p. 190 Courtesy of Jeff Kober

p. 194 Courtesy of ABC, Inc. Copyright 1988. All rights reserved.

PHOTO CREDITS (cont.)

p. 198 Courtesy of Josef Anderson

p. 202 Courtesy of Nancy Giles

p. 207 Courtesy of Angela Ventresca

p. 216 & 217 Courtesy of Marg Helgenberger

p. 243 Courtesy of Chip Vucelich

p. 247 Courtesy of Warner Bros. Television. Copyright 1990. All rights reserved.

p. 253 Courtesy of Andriete M Karagezyan

p. 255 Courtesy of Tom and Nellie Coakley

p. 272 Courtesy of Kieu Chinh

p. 279 Courtesy of Alan Light

p. 281 Courtesy of Angela Ventresca

p. 292 Courtesy of Nancy Giles

p. 293 Courtesy of Chip Vucelich

p. 296 Courtesy of Nancy Giles

p. 300-301 Courtesy of Chip Vucelich

Author photo by Jessica Dukes

#CHINABEACHBOOK

Made in the USA
Columbia, SC
13 September 2021